FROM POSSESSION TO FREEDOM

FROM POSSESSION TO FREEDOM

The Journey of Nīli-Nīlakeci

R. UMAMAHESHWARI

zubaan

ZUBAAN
128 B Shahpur Jat, 1st floor
NEW DELHI 110 049
EMAIL: contact@zubaanbooks.com
WEBSITE: www.zubaanbooks.com

First published by Zubaan Publishers Pvt. Ltd 2018

10 9 8 7 6 5 4 3 2 1

ISBN 978 93 85932 28 1

Zubaan is an independent feminist publishing house based in New Delhi with a strong academic and general list. It was set up as an imprint of India's first feminist publishing house, Kali for Women, and carries forward Kali's tradition of publishing world quality books to high editorial and production standards. *Zubaan* means tongue, voice, language, speech in Hindustani. Zubaan publishes in the areas of the humanities, social sciences, as well as in fiction, general non-fiction, and books for children and young adults under its Young Zubaan imprint.

Typeset in Gentium 11/14 by Jojy Philip, New Delhi 110 015
Printed at Raj Press, R-3 Inderpuri, New Delhi 110 012

In Memory, Ramani Rajamani...

Did she come by as one of those parakeets on a fine winter morning
in the hills?
Or did she pour out her love as snowflakes the other afternoon?
Was she that dove who sat, miraculously, on my notebook
the other day?
Or the butterfly—that brown one with yellow spots—round the corner
in the garden?
Does she watch me now, nights and days?
Does she now affirm the soul of the Jaina-Jina
Or the non-soul, yet Bodhisattva Selves, of the Buddha?

Wherever she may be, or not-not *not be*, this Becoming of Nīlakeci
from Nīli, through the Cerebral Discourses of an ancient time,
is owed to her, who,
was, otherwise, my mother.

CONTENTS

Schemata for Transliteration and Diacritical Marks for Tamil and Sanskrit Vowels & Consonants Used

Tamil

அ	ஆ	இ	ஈ	உ	ஊ	எ	ஏ	ஐ	ஒ	ஓ	ஔ
a	ā	i	ī	u	ū	e	ē	ai	o	ō	au

க	ங	ச	ஞ	ட	ண	த	ந	ப	ம	ய	ர
ka	ṅa	ca	ña	ṭa	ṇa	ta	na	pa	ma	ya	ra

ல	வ	ழ	ள	ற	ன
la	va	ḻa	ḷa	ṟa	ṉa

Sanskrit Consonants

ஜ	ஷ	ஸ	ஹ	க்ஷ	ஶ
ja	ṣa	sa	ha	kṣa	śa

Soft Equivalents of four hard consonants

க	ட	த	ப
ga	ḍa	da	ba

Examples of usage: Mahāvīra; Nīlakēci; Paḻayaṉūr Nīli; Kuṇtalakēci; Caṅkam; mūkkaḻaku; piḻai; viṉai; kṣanika; nallaṟivu, naṟkāṭci, naññānam, naloḻukkam; pōṟṟi...

ACKNOWLEDGING AND A FEW WORDS

I dedicate this book to my amma, Ramani. It is only because of her enthusiasm and help for an errant daughter and our hours of reading together that a small chapter in my doctoral thesis happened. My insistence that she simply 'read, and not interpret' must have been extremely difficult for her. It was only later that I realised how much her comments and insights had helped me. The hours my mother spent with me as we travelled with Nīli on her painful journey and later Nīlakeci's scholarly journey, also reflected her own enthusiasm of spirit and her immense inner strength (especially in the years after my father passed away). In her death, back in September 2004, even before my thesis had taken final shape, I lost that joy that I would have seen on her face, holding a book that is for most part filled with her memory. What I do have, though, are the printed Nīli tales and the book, *Nīlakeci*, filled with the smell of her touch in each of its pages. Her new-found enthusiasm for Jaina history and literature – reading just about everything she could get her hands on, even before I had begun to read the first page—and, in particular, the texts the Tamil Jainas donated to me, but also archival material, such as inscriptions, was amazing. Like an enthusiastic child, she would tell people in our neighbourhood, even those who were quite uninterested, the Tamil Jaina story of persecution by the brahmins and by the bhakti tradition. Coming from the context that they did, my amma and appaji were rare people and they had a firm belief in their daughter's dreams. I dedicate this work to amma and her total trust in, and respect for, her daughter through most trying times.

This book owes itself to those moments spent with my mother.

After amma's demise in 2004, I continued on a long and lonely journey with the Tamil language, reading over longer hours; it took me many painful years to understand because I had been brought up in Delhi and Hyderabad. I learnt the Tamil script very late in life. So, with a slow pace of learning picked up late in life, the task of reading *Nīlakeci* (and other books that the Tamil Jainas gave me) fell upon my mother, who took it up ever so gladly (being a voracious reader by habit, anyway) and it is for the relationship between my mother and me that the text *Nīlakeci* assumes a deep significance in my life. Thanks to my mother I got my womb connection with Tamil back again. I continue to learn—each day, alone, mostly and do regret having lost out on a great mass of literary gems during my growing years. Yet, I am realising the beauty of this language by the day and its many intricacies. Thanks to this process, the sheer pain of love for a text/language, as well as non-access to a script/literacy, has become clearer to me. At the same time, the intensity of the reading experience of *Nīlakeci* with my mother, for me, foregrounds this book.

I must acknowledge a few people who were instrumental in getting me to do this book, and in giving this book the final shape. First and foremost, I thank Professor Padmanabh Jaini (Professor Emeritus, Buddhist Studies, Centre for South and Southeast Asian Studies, University of California-Berkeley) who was the first to see a book in a mere chapter of my doctoral dissertation, and whose suggestion inspired me to think of a book. I also thank Dr Peter Flugel (at SOAS, Centre of Jaina Studies) whose constant encouragement has been most crucial in making me see the worth of my research on the Tamil Jaina community. I also thank Prof. Kunal Chakrabarty (who supervised my doctoral dissertation at JNU) who, in his own way, encouraged me, with ample freedom to work on my ideas, and was always an excited listener whenever the topic veered towards the characters, Nīli and Nīlakeci.

Prof. Uma Chakravarti was willing and generous in giving the earlier draft of the manuscript a thorough reading, and her feedback helped immensely in enriching this work in more ways than I had earlier envisaged. I thank her from my heart. I hope she will find out for herself where her inputs have lent substance to parts of this book.

I am truly grateful to the Prakriti Foundation (of a different time), Chennai and to Ranvir Shah and V.R. Devika, for an invitation (back in year 2003) to present my paper ('*Retrieving, Seeking, (An) other Woman, (An) other Goddess*') on Nīlakeci at a seminar titled 'Women and Goddesses: Reimagining the Feminine in Tamil Cinema'. In fact, the entire 'movement'—the seminar; meeting Dr. Venkatesh Chakravarty there, who I am indebted to, as well for his suggestion to explore the Roja Muthiah Library for the folklore on Nīli, the pēy—happened as if in a pre-destined fashion. I thank profusely the entire staff at the RMRL, which was then located in a quiet, unconscious corner of Chennai, called Mogappair (and happened then to be closer home when I was there!) for patiently bringing out the Nīli stories, Paḻayanūr Nīli (two of these) and *Nīli Nāṭakam,* and allowing me to photocopy these for my reference. I thank Theodore Bhaskaran, then Director of RMRL, for giving me the initial permission for access to these invaluable sources.

To Golu (Sai Shashank), one of my nephews, I owe a special 'thank-you' as ever for constant joy and words of encouragement both at, and from, Chennai, over the phone, at crucial moments in life and during the making of this particular manuscript. A lot of practical help was at hand from my other two nephews, Siddharth (Mrithyunjaya) and Karthik (Dhananjaya) during the completion of my PhD and writing up my original Nilákeci chapter. I thank them, too. And I indebted to my sister, Viji (and

Bala athimber), for constant encouragement from afar and near, helping me stay afloat, through regular rough patches.

I thank R. Sivapriya, formerly at Penguin, for putting me in touch with Urvashi, and finding my idea interesting in the first place. I thank Urvashi Butalia and her team at Zubaan Books for giving space to my idea of Nīli-Nīlakeci and agreeing to see it in book form and most important of all, for having waited so very patiently for it.

I wish to particularly thank two anonymous reviewers of an earlier version of the manuscript who understood the meaning of my work and words and saw me in this work (and my mother's labour) in a way very few can and gave extremely valuable insights which have helped me bring out facets that this book may have otherwise missed. I hope they will see the difference.

In the process of giving the book its final shape, I thank the entire staff and workforce of the Indian Institute of Advanced Study, Simla (a quaint space that, I hope, will continue to allow the mind to grow without surveillance of the intellect) for allowing space for a special, absolute solitude-filled beautiful winter in the last months of giving final touches to this book; a few local neighbours (for their generosity in feeding a woman they think is alone and needs to be fed); a few Fellow colleagues and the surrounding innumerable species of flora and fauna which lent support, in their own nature, of their own kind. Towards the final editing phase of this book, new friends came into Malli's, and my life, at the Institut d'études avancées de Nantes (France) and I owe '*merci beaucoup*' to all of them (Daniela-Gri Gri, Griselda, Gerardo, Celine, Philippe, Parfait, Antonio, Deresse-Moulu, especially), for all their love and caring from near and far, and for their respect for all my work,and organising a seminar around my other book on the Tamil Jainas. I am truly grateful to the IEA-Nantes team (including Dr. Samuel Jubé) for the fellowship, which gave me space for valuable additions to the earlier draft of this book while simultaneously aiding in other research interests of mine amidst camaraderie and idea-sharing, across cultures and continents.

Malli spent hours of days and nights beside me as my silent, caring, canine-companion, always seeing to it that my pen and heart are in good condition. And through her, other same-species friends in Simla, especially Bruny and Munni, gave welcome appearances and disturbances in the course of writing. Acknowledging Malli's contribution is to acknowledge the beauty of someone's unconditional love and acceptance of me, as well as every situation, geographical location (including France and our sojourn by the IEA) and extremity of weather I put her through. I am indebted to this love.

1

INTRODUCING...

I. Jaina Literature in Tamil

It is important to know the trajectory of Tamil Jaina literary history in order to understand their ideas of the self vis-à-vis Tamil language and literature. For the Tamil Jaina community, Tamil has always been an intrinsic part of their identity. Though this book does not engage with this particular aspect; rather, it is about the text and characters, Nīli and Nīlakeci. Yet, if one were to remove the Tamil-ness from the Tamil Jaina construction of the self, an entire history of this minority, marginalized social/religious group, would be deleted from the larger history of the Tamil country. It is in this sense that I locate the work called *Nīlakeci,* which, being an ancient classic of Tamil literary tradition, has remained mostly unexplored, much like the history of Tamil vis-à-vis the Tamil Jaina community. So, in a sense, one is looking at a rare classic in Tamil, written by the ancestors of the Tamil-Jainas. And this at a time when debates and public discourses on 'religion'—(in a narrow sense) abound, without basic acceptance of even a possibility that the nature of reality could well be explained differently by different religious systems. At the same time, historically speaking, there wasn't always a romantic sense of camaraderie (peaceful co-existence') and 'democratic' (not in the political, but a philosophical sense) acceptance of others' points of view. There were also clashes and sheer animosity, at times. But still, the discourses happened, and some were long-drawn out (some, until date), such as the debate between the Buddhists and Jainas and even among or within the different sub-sects of the Jaina (Śvetāmbara-Digambara; northern-southern, and so on) communities. Thus it may appear that one is picking up a chapter from those episodes of the larger discourse on whether there is a god, or whether there is a soul or on what today seems more relevant, on the perceptions of nature and consumption, vectored as these debates were through ideas of ritual abstinence versus ritual excess or excess consumption and dominance of a tradition over the others. In this, the Buddhists and Jainas seem to have fought a losing battle which got confirmed by their becoming marginal over time while thought-systems such as those of the materialists or the determinists have as good as disappeared.

Let me begin with a brief introduction of the Tamil Jaina community, whose predecessors have left us a veritable treasure-trove of Tamil literature, some lost, some languishing without sufficient interest shown in bringing these out for public consumption in a manner where anyone at all (not just ones steeped in academic life) can access them. When the Tamil Jaina community members chose to take their last official census in the year 2001, their numbers were a mere 30,000 and may have risen marginally in subsequent years. In effect, the numbers are absolutely microscopic. The Tamil Jainas have had a long journey from having flourished as a major religious-social group—from the earliest centuries BCE—to relative obscurity and near-unknown existence today. The earliest Jaina vestiges include around 26 rock-cut caves and natural caverns with Tamil Brāhmi inscriptions (2nd-1st centuries BCE), around 140 stone beds for monks and nuns at places in Madurai-Ramanathapuram, Erode, the former North and South Arcot districts, paintings of Pudukkottai-Sittanavasal and so on. Today we can find Tamil Jaina villages mostly in Tiruvannamalai, Chengleput, Kanchipuram and very marginally in Tanjavur districts. Most of the Tamil Jainas have been agriculturists (few of them were later employed in government and private sectors) and have been predominantly agrarian throughout Tamil history. The Tamil Jainas have contributed phenomenally to the Tamil classical literary corpus (including to the Caṅkam literary corpus commonly dated from 3rd century BCE to 5th century CE), with works such as *Cilappatikāram*, *Cīvakacintāmaṇi*, Tamil grammar *Naṉṉūl*, *Tirukkuṟaḷ*, *Valaiyāpati* and *Nālaṭiyār*, among many others. The Jaina Tamil literature includes secular literature—major and minor *kāvyas* (talking of Jaina ideals, etc); didactic works; the Purāṇas (which talk of the 'universal' Jaina history and norms for lay followers) and; grammatical treatises. So far as I am concerned, so striking was the Tamil Jainas' hidden-ness as a community in mainstream history writing (in spite of mention of these works, authored by the Jainas, at different periods in Tamil history in most writings) that it led me to explore their community history, in the course of which I discovered Nīlakeci.

Winternitz had noted that there existed, a 'Sramaṇa literature' (samaṇa), not Jaina or Buḍdhist, as such...along Brahminical literature; and this samaṇa literature treats of kings, merchants as its heroes, and not gods; and of popular tales, themes...'[1] According to Caldwell, 'the largest portion of Sanskrit derivatives found in Tamil language was introduced by the Jainas. They altered the Sanskrit words which they followed in order to bring it in accordance with Tamil euphonic rules.'[2]

Among the major *kāvyas* (poetry) are *Cilappatikāram* (the famous story of the lay anklet), *Valaiyāpati* and *Cīvakacintāmaṇi*. The *Cilappatikāram* (3 cantos of 30 stories—*katai*), was written by Iḷanko Aṭikaḷ, a Jaina monk, who was the brother of the Cera king Ceṅkuttuvaṉ; this is the story of Kaṇṇaki and Kovalaṉ, hailing from two prominent merchant families and their tryst with an unfortunate set of events which led ultimately to Kovalaṉ's execution at the royal court of Madurai and Kaṇṇaki's famous anger, her hurling her breast at the city of Madurai, which got burnt to ashes. This work has been dated by some to the 2nd century CE (some say it was part of the earlier Caṅkam works), but the generally accepted date is 5th century CE.[3] There is a connection of *Cilappatikāram* with Nīli, too, which will be discussed in later sections of this book. *Valaiyāpati* is no longer available in its entirety. Around 50 verses of this work were published in *Sen Tamil* (a Tamil journal) in an early issue prior to 1920. This work deals with the Jaina ideals.[4] *Cīvakacintāmaṇi*, said to have been composed between 8th and 13th centuries CE, is based on the Sanskrit treatises, *Kṣatra Cūṭāmaṇi* and *Gadyacintāmaṇi*. According to tradition, it was authored by one Tirutakkattevar of the Chōḷa country. He is believed to have studied all the early Caṅkam works and gone to Madurai to attend one of the Caṅkams. There he was challenged by non-Jaina writers and poets to compose an erotic work, which according to them, would be impossible for the Jaina monks. He first composed a short quatrain, called *Nariviruttam* to secure his teacher's approval, based on the story of the jackal from the Hitopadeśa. When the teacher was convinced of his literary prowess, he gave Tiruttakkattevar permission to compose *Cīvakacintāmaṇi*, which is believed to have won great praise from non-Jainas, as well.

Among the minor *kāvyas, Nīlakeci* is the most important. It was composed around the 5th century CE (though the date is still a matter of debate). Vanamamalai dates the composition of *Nīlakeci* between 5th and 9th centuries CE. He also points out that the materialist school in the Tamil region has a history from the early centuries BCE.[5] We know only of the commentator of this work, Samayadivākara Vāmana Muṇi. *Nīlakeci* is styled after the Buddhist text *Kuṇṭalakeci*. The other minor *kāvya* is *Peruṅkatai* (after the Sanskrit *Bṛhatkathā* of Guṇāditya) of 5th-6th century CE written in the Paiśāci language by a certain Koñguvel, a petty chieftain of Koñgunāṭu. This work deals with the life of Udayanakumāra, king of Vatsadeśa. Then there is the *Yasodarakāvyam*, dealing with morals, written by an unknown Jaina teacher/monk. There are also two didactic works, called *Nāgakumārakāvyam* and *Cūlāmaṇi*.

Among the didactic works are *Nālaṭiyār* and *Paḻamoḻinānūru*.

Nālaṭiyār, a work of 400 quatrains in 40 chapters, has an interesting anecdote regarding its genesis. Around 8,000 Jaina monks had once visited the Pandyan kingdom when famine had struck in their former place of residence. The allusion is to the famine in Magadha; or could also be a metaphor justifying the Jaina migration. After the famine ended, they wished to go back to the place they came from. But the king would not give them permission to do so since he did not want to lose people of such eminence. The monks suddenly left in the middle of the night, leaving one quatrain each for the king. The next morning, when the king learnt of this, he threw each of these quatrains into the Vaikai river in anger, and four hundred of these swam back against the current. These were collected around 470 CE. These quatrains mention the Kālapra Muttaṟaiyars. The Christian missionary G.U. Pope referred to these quatrains as '*veḷḷāḷar vedam*' (the Vedas of the veḷḷāḷa community). One of the quatrains (quatrain 243) refers to the Jaina-Brāhmiṇ conflict.[6]

Paḻamoḻinānūru (400 proverbs) was written by a Jaina king of Muṉṟurai who was perhaps a feudatory of the Pandya kings. P.B. Desai alludes to a tradition from Mahabalipuram, which shows that members of the Kurumbar community (shepherds and hunters, some of whom were smaller chiefs) from an early period of the region Muṉṟurai, were followers of Buddhism and Jainism.

Kaliñkaṭṭupparaṇi is seen as a unique and exemplary Jaina work on war. It is a long verse on the battle of Chola Kulōttuṅka with the Kalinga king of the north. Among the grammatical texts are *Naṉṉūl*, written by the Jaina teacher-monk, Pavananti (12th century CE); a lexicon called *Cūṭāmaṇi-nikaṇṭu* by Viramantala Purusa, who was a disciple of Gunabhadra ācārya of (Tirunaṟunkuṉṟam, also referred to as Tirunarungondai[7]—an important early Tamil Jaina settlement) who lived in the time of the king Kriṣṇadevarāya of Vijayanagara. It is interesting to note that between the 11th and 12th century CE, there was profuse output in grammatical Tamil (Jaina) texts. In the larger context of the hegemony of Sanskritic brāhmiṇism, on the one hand, and the bhakti tradition in Tamil, with its own gradual hold over the temple and ritual paradigm, these Jaina grammatical texts signify an interesting secular tradition. In this connection, it should be mentioned that a 10th century CE Jaina text, Prabhacandra's *Nyāyakumāracarita,*[8] rejects the 'absolute authority of Sanskrit in an obvious effort to bolster the position of a community whose scriptural texts and liturgy were composed in dialect... Prabhacandra says, "contrary to brāhmaṇ supposition, dialect is based on an ordered system of grammar and does not reflect a state of linguistic anarchy".'[9]

A point of importance related to a regional linguistic tradition is that the region around Madurai (and Madurai itself) has been a most common site of reference for all ideologies and polity that prevailed. The Jainas themselves talk of the mūlasaṅgha (the first Tamil literary convention), which was established around 5th century CE. There seems to have been a long-drawn and persistent contestation for Madurai and its tradition of Tamil literary corpus between the Jainas, Buddhists, Śaivas and Vaiṣṇavas in Tamil history.

The significant components of Jaina literature, the *Purāṇas*, were composed between the 8th and 10th centuries CE. The more important among these for the Digambara tradition in the early Tamil country were the *Ādipurāṇa* of Jinasenā (about 8th century CE) and Mallisena's *Merumantarapurāṇam*. The Jaina purāṇas, unlike their brāhmiṇical counterparts, do not speak of sacred spaces, *tīrthas* as being associated with divine visitations; in other words, the supernatural has no role to play in creating that sacred space. The place becomes sacred/revered only in terms of its association with an extraordinary individual, the ford-maker, or *tīrthankara,* who successfully 'crossed over the ocean of this world', with its many temptations. A powerful *tīrthankara* controls, by virtue of his supreme knowledge, and in turn, is also presided over by, a yakṣi, and sometimes a yakṣa, as well. The Jaina *Purāṇas* have also re-interpreted, in terms of their own cosmogony, the epics and the epic heroes, the *Rāmāyaṇa* and the figure of Kṛṣṇa. In the Jaina story of Rāma (who is called Padma)—the *Padmapurāṇa*—it is Lakṣmaṇa who slays Rāvaṇa (the latter being one of the minor deities, the Prativāsudeva of Jaina cosmogony) and suffers in hellish misery, having to undergo a period of repentance for the killing. Lakṣmaṇa, like Kṛṣṇa, is among the Vāsudevas, a group that has to undergo some pain before redemption, to finally gain liberation from the cycle of births and rebirths. Sītā, interestingly, is depicted as the daughter of Mandodari and Rāvaṇa. The Jainas carefully adopted Rāma's figure to spread the basic tenets of Jainism, like ahimsā and *aparigraha* (non-possession/non-aggrandisement), by making him a Jaina adherent. On the other hand, Kṛṣṇa—with an ambivalent status even in the brāhmiṇical system[10]—has to purge himself of his sins. It is probable that the sensuality associated with this figure and his many associations with women as part of his overall persona may have been one reason for the Jaina reticence towards him; and instead, his brother Balarāma gets a superior status as a Baladeva. Thus, re-interpretation seemed to be a common practice in order to get the Jaina point across to the common people.

An important aspect of a textual tradition is the audience it addressed. Given the Jaina storytelling tradition and that the Jaina textual tradition precluded a receptive audience (in this sense, the Jaina texts could not have existed *a priori*, impervious to a social context), there are not too many studies on the 'dialogue' of these texts with the laity, at least in the Tamil context.

According to William Graham, 'A text becomes 'scripture' in active subjective relationship to persons, and as part of a cumulative communal tradition.'[11] Text, therefore, cannot be seen in isolation from the context. And, scripture is a 'relational phenomenon'[12] and the response to it must be an important concern. In a similar vein, though in the context of the ritual reading of the *Kalpasūtra* among the Śvetāmbara mūrtipūjak

Jainas of Gujarat, John Cort places the Jaina text within two categories—'canon near' and 'canon far'. In the canon near concept, 'The primacy and authority of the text is defined by praxis and resultant contextualised understanding.'[13] Further, a canon near 'changes with time and place, and authority flows from the accumulated tradition into the texts.'[14]

In the canon far text, on the other hand, 'primacy and authority (are) located in some intrinsic ontological value of the text themselves...'[15] and these texts convey 'fixed and closed authority, vectored via the texts'. However, these two categories are not mutually exclusive and one text can exhibit both these characters. In our case, then, perhaps, the minor kāvyas are 'canon near', and the Purāṇas the 'canon far'. But *Cīvakacintāmaṇi* also displays the 'canon near' qualities, when one looks at its intrinsic relationship with the Tamil Jainas.

In this larger context of Jaina literature, and Jaina literature in Tamil, *Nīlakeci* exists in an interesting location, neither as a 'canon near' nor as a 'canon far'. It is not a purāṇa, with its hold of authority over the Tamil Jaina community. It holds a sort of 'ambivalent' position in this context—much like its protagonist, in her former identity as the dreaded Nīli. It does not claim the same place or space as *Cīvakacintāmaṇi*. But written in Tamil, for a Tamil audience, with the intention of highlighting the Jaina-non Jaina debate and discourse, it stands its own ground in a larger (more than the necessarily 'purely' Jaina) context in the history of Tamil literature and the Jaina community's response to historical, social contexts.

Nīlakeci, the text, highlights Jaina philosophy and its author is unknown (as yet), an important minor *kāvya* ('*ciṟukāppiyam*') of the Tamil literary tradition. The text, dated anywhere between 1st and 5th century CE, is definitely acknowledged in most treatises on Tamil literature, especially those with the 'Jaina' connection. What one does not find in adequate measure about *Nīlakeci*, however, is the contextual locating of it, or analysis of the text and its significance in the context of the polemical discourse within the history of Tamil literary traditions, especially the Buddhist and Jaina.[16] In a sense, the *bhakti* tradition and the Śaiva and Vaiṣṇava literary tradition and scholarly works on these have been rather overwhelming. Mine is a small attempt at *locating Nīlakeci* as an amazing literary intervention in Tamil to make a *Jaina* sense of things, as they are: the world, existence, matter, soul, non-killing, among other things, expressed through a female, scholarly voice. It was not merely any other *pēy* that the author picked up for his female protagonist; for, there was an entire cult of Nīli worship in some areas, mainly in Tiruvalangadu in North Arcot, which was also the region of Jaina settlements; this was also the area that came into the sphere of influence of the Śaivite bhakti and temple pilgrimage circuit. The *isakki-ammaṉ* temple in this place becomes a space for performing the *villuppāṭṭu* dedicated to Nīli. There is also the legend, or myth-making, involving Kāraikkal Ammaiyār, who, popular legend says, witnessed the dance competition between Śiva and Pārvati in Tiruvalangadu; the legend/myth is of course of a later period than the composition of *Nīlakeci*, even as the story of Kāraikkal Ammaiyār has very striking resemblances to the Jaina story of the yakṣi Ambicā. So, in the process of selecting *pēy* Nīli, the Jaina author also selectively picks on a predominant village deity of the region—deified and worshipped precisely for being a *pēy* who must be propitiated to keep her 'calm' and 'within bounds'. Her anger has to be appeased at all times, lest she start off on her round of revenge and bloodied murders, even if, within her story, her revenge was purely meant for Nambi, her husband/lover from a former life and for the village Palayanur, where her brother, Nīlan, was killed. Interestingly, there is one Nīli temple in another Palayanur, which is in Sivaganga (near Madurai), and this is the only temple dedicated to her (as Nīli, and not *isakki* (or yakṣi) *ammaṉ*, and not in the place where the Nīli story actually occurs, which is in North Arcot.

II. A Character from the Fringes and Spaces In-Between

Sometimes texts, or stories, or characters, come to you; they almost reach out to you in the strangest of ways, through peculiar spaces and corners; they seem to *want you* to seek them out, when you never went in search of them, in the first place. They seek you out, too, and urge you to read and re-read them or represent them, if need be, and pull them out of their relative obscurity, claustrophobic existence (as books on a library shelf, perhaps, or as a manuscript in someone's home or as characters within these, or other, spaces) and oblivion. That is just how Nīli-Nīlakeci came to me: years ago, on an autumn afternoon, in the quaint corner of the Sahitya Akademi library in Delhi—in the midst of my other readings on Jaina and other philosophy—in the form of a book that seemed to virtually protrude from a shelf I was allowed access to at that time. Initially, it was the name that attracted my attention, for it seemed beautiful: *Neelakesi*. This was a book that claimed to be an English translation by one A. Chakravarti of the original Tamil text.[17] It was, then, from an initial curiosity, pleasure and the thrill of 'finding a text' (which anyone who enters the world of research would understand) that I read this work. I did not know then, that it would ultimately become a longer relationship with the characters Nīli-Nīlakeci (and a deeper bond with my mother) and a hitherto unchartered realm within Tamil Jainism. But there is yet another story here. I had come across reference to the Nīli (*pēy*) story in an article many years ago, in a totally different context—of looking at myth and folklore in Tamilnadu. The folk story itself (now one can say, one version of it) was narrated by K.P.S. Hameed[18] in an article on two traditional Tamil narratives (using Vladimir Propp and the question of 'structure' in folk narratives), but what was interesting (and intriguing in being a mere small, off-hand mention) was an end-note reference to the Jaina work, *Nīlakeci* in the article. An urge to learn more of that story, mentioned in the note, finally led me to the text in Delhi; as also some other references to *Nīlakeci*.

So, a very long engagement precedes this book, which commenced with a very humble attempt to share the excitement of discovering an ancient Tamil text. I was using a summarised translation in English initially, and found one Tamil edition in a tiny shop in Chennai, subsequently.[19] In year 2003, even as I was in the midst of my doctoral research, a chance invitation arrived for me to participate in a seminar organised by the Prakriti Foundation, Chennai, where I presented, for the first time, my interpretation of the *re-imaging* (as I called it then) of Nīli the *pēy* (possession spirit) in the Tamil Jaina tradition.[20]

The story of the *pēy,* Nīli, though, had been recounted in few of the older scholarly works, some of which I shall mention in due course in the pages of this book. Mostly, these refer to the story as it appears in the Śaivite tradition (in the Tevāram hymns, for instance) and one or two mention the fact that Nīli appears in the Jaina text, *Cilappatikāram* and also in *Nīlakeci*, besides narrating the popular lore of Nīli of Pa<u>l</u>aya<u>n</u>ūr. These works do not dwell on the context of the creation of *Nīlakeci* or on the post-*pēy* transformation of Nīli and her debates with other traditions/schools of thought prevalent in the period of *Nīlakeci*'s composition, which to me are extremely significant from the point of view of the historical trajectory of the debating tradition, in general, and Jaina contestations with other prominent thought systems, in particular. The most important aspect is that these are debates in the female voice, and in each of these debates the woman wins over her opponents. Even if it is the regular method employed by the Buddhists and Jainas in that time, to have propaganda material for their systems (in literary tradition), yet it is a unique text written around one single woman character called Nīlakeci. So, from the point of view of the female voice of a female philosopher, I deal with a few of the most prominent debates recorded in the text. Another significant fact that there is not a single translation (into English or other languages) of the entire text of *Nīlakeci.* Other Buddhist and Jaina Tamil works have been translated—

such as *Cilappatikāram, Maṇimēkalai* and *Cīvakacintāmaṇi*—but this poetic treatise has seen only two editions so far. One of these, Chakravarti's, has only an English summary (sort of inadequate, for this isn't a literal, or poetic, translation), but it is still the only work we have for a quick and easy access to the main discussions in *Nīlakeci*. I wonder if this is because the work is in long verse, is Jaina, and relatively inaccessible? My book here is also not a literal translation and does not analyse the entire *Nīlakeci*, which comprises of 894 verses in all, which means that there will need to be a separate work totally dedicated to *Nīlakeci* (and all the debates therein), which may perhaps happen in a future time. Yet I have tried to stay true to the verses wherever the verses are translated. I have tried also to give the translation a poetic slant to the extent possible; it was indeed challenging, because the poetry of *Nīlakeci* is actually deep philosophy. You could either approach it as a philosophical treatise or as poetry alone (in a critically literary sense) and one would have to make a personal choice there. My only idea was to bring to notice this work more in terms of the context of its creation, its spectacularly vast content in relation to some of the significant debates it addressed in ancient times between religious—atheist and theist—schools through a female voice, something that will be a difficult terrain today, too, if a woman were to start such a debate with all the major philosophical schools, many of which have now become dogmatic organised religions, with no room for alteration or change, even from within.

Scholars such as Hameed, Zvelebil, Indira Peterson, David Shulman,[21] and Vijaya Ramaswamy, have referred to the legend of *pēy* Nīli in their works, all of which I refer to as I go along. But between the years 2007 and 2010 a few more articles seem to have appeared on the *pēy* Nīli, and the idea of 'recasting', as well, within the Tamil historical context (not necessarily keeping the Jaina context as their central core).[22]

So, in the long gestation period between the research on Nīli and *Nīlakeci*, and its book form now, some light seems to have shone on *pēy* Nīli again. Yet, I proceed with my own further exploration, in the spirit of the initial moment of the discovery, not merely of a book called *Neelakesi* on a shelf in a library, but also the initial moments of joy experienced on discovering, similarly, the manuscripts (that were until that moment of my discovering them, unseen) of the *villuppāṭṭu* (bow-song) of Pal̲ayan̲ūr Nīli and the drama called *Nīli Nāṭakam* at another library, locating which, in a quaint corner of Chennai, called Mogappair, was an equally exciting journey.[23] And an exploration here is not merely of Nīli and her claustrophobic existence within a tradition that restrains her there, but of Nīlakeci and her travels across cities/towns of ancient times, in a kind of intellectual 'travel' allowed for her within a tradition that believed more in her 'coming out', accompanied by her internal progress, from *pēy* to someone with a mind to debate/discourse.

Reverting to the moment when I first held that English book in Delhi, as I read through the summarised translated version (with its focus, of course, on the Jaina philosophy in contradistinction to other systems of thought), an element that most fascinated me was the context of the creation of the text itself and the story of a fringe-'being' transforming into/'becoming' a central character. To me, the *pre-text* seemed more intriguing than the text itself and urged me to place the text in a different context than one of a simplistic Jaina poetic device manufactured as propaganda literature of the early centuries CE of the Tamil country. But at that point, I only had this translated version—borrowed from the library—which I read with great interest. Later, I would possess a copy myself. Yet I had not seen the original Tamil version, which also happened a year or two later. *Nīlakeci* is an unusual Jaina literary-folk/popular interface with an equally unusual use of a popular tradition or even subversion of it, in some senses. That we do not know the name of the poet/author only renders a sense of drama to this work. He/she(?) used a brilliant device of retrieving a *pēy* from the village tradition, and altering it in a radical and affirmative form, which is redemptive. So the idea of 'being' (what you are born into, or condemned into being) and 'becoming' (what you could, by your own efforts and action) which the Jaina religion–ideally–allows for, is beautifully brought forth in this work. Thus, if someone as dreadful as a possessing spirit can become a philosopher, it is possible for anyone to transform into redeemed selves, following the Jaina tenets. Apart from this, what seemed to me to be of prime importance was the idea of using a female voice, a female *persona* to debate with the most prominent teachers of various schools of thought prevalent in that time. And strangely enough, with one exception, the debates are all with male teachers. The one exception is yet another unusual one: a female Buddhist nun, Kuṇṭalakeci, with her own tale of transformation and redemption.

What began with finding a woman philosopher in a library in Delhi, ended up with my seeking, and finding, her original self, the ('untransformed') *pēy*, who may have (in those early centuries CE) urged a certain poet/author to give her a new meaning and a new life, as it were. So, I look at the tales of the much-feared *pēy* of Pa̱layaṉūr, named Nīli. This is the first time that these versions of a popular story – as found in a performative context—are placed alongside the Tamil Jaina version. I was led, through these diverse traditions, to understand the context of all the texts and their audience. So there were, the bow-song version (*villuppāṭṭu*); the elaborate dance drama (*Nīli Nāṭakam*) version and instances from the Nīli stories referred to in the *Tevāram* hymns of the Śaiva tradition and; the Jaina work was a counter-rendering of these stories. Speaking of Nīli and her ambivalence in the Śaiva tradition, I recount the point made by Kunal Chakrabarti on the Bengal *Purāṇas*:

> Since the adoption of a tāntric ritual form was practically unavoidable the Bengal Purāṇas employed the familiar technique of being openly inconsistent, thus creating space for dissent either from the adherents of the Vedas or from the

> practitioners of the Tantras... A rigid frame of reference is not amenable to that variety of manipulative jugglery with which Brāhmiṇism has always maintained a certain distance from Tāntrism, granting it the status of a parallel tradition.[24]

But this did not happen in the case of Nīli in the Śaivite tradition, or the brāhmiṇical. And that makes her inclusion as central figure in the Jaina text important. Yet, interestingly, Nīlakeci never became a deified figure within the Jaina tradition at any point in time. As one moves into the stories of the *pēy* Nīli, one comes across a *veḷḷāḷar* motif[25] which seems to reveal a deeper level of mistrust and friction at some point that developed between the social groups that worshipped (either out of fear or other reasons) the Nīli figure, and the *veḷḷāḷars,* at some point.

Zvelebil notes that, 'Kambar (10th century AD?) mentions Paḻaiyaṉūr Nīli as a deity of the vēḷāḷar community.'[26] Hence, while in the *villuppāṭṭu* (bow-song) version of the Nīli story the 70 *veḷḷāḷars* (*eḻupatiṉmar*) jumping into fire is mentioned as just the most appropriate action, without much literary flourish, in a sense, the Śaivite texts (Cēkkiḻār's *Periyapurāṇam* and the *Nīli Nāṭakam* versions) give the event a high sense of drama, on the lines of the Greek tragedy. That the Śaivite bhakti movement had as its adherents the *veḷḷāḷars,* then, becomes a point of historical and social significance in these stories. The *veḷḷāḷars'* self-immolation motif inserted in the Nīli story is by itself intriguing. In one of the versions, the 'group of 70' *veḷḷāḷars* are identified by their villages as well, such as '60 from the village Ālankāṭu, 10 from Moṭṭūr'/'10 from Paḻayanūr', etc. And it may not be a coincidence that these villages have had their Tamil Jaina settlements in the past. Mottur, today, near Arani, still has a handful of Tamil Jaina families residing there. The text, *Nīlakeci*, along with the original versions of the Nīli story, thus make for a very complex multi-layered contextual social canvas, which the stories reveal, with the Jaina re-interpretation adding one more layer to it. It must be noted that the Tamil Jaina version seems to be the last of the re-interpretations of the Nīli legend in any literary text in Tamil.

Stuart Blackburn writes:

> To the well-known Hindu perspectives on death, the cults of the deified dead add something new. In the Purāṇas (and in ancient Tamil poetry) death is deified, but in these cults, it is the dead themselves who are deified. If elsewhere in Hinduism death separates humans from gods, in these folk cults it joins them together. However, not just any death has this effect; only a special kind makes the dead hero an object of worship. First, the death must be premature, an end that cuts short a person's normal life span. Second, and more important, the death must be violent, an act of aggression or a sudden blow from nature. Many deified heroes are killed in battle, some in less glorious conflicts; others (especially women) commit suicide. Lastly, the death that deifies is undeserved; the person killed is an innocent (if often fated) victim. However, unlike the problem of theodicy, this deification does not depend on the innocence of the victim. Indeed—and this cannot be overemphasised—it is not moral considerations but violence that transforms humans into deities.[27]

The context of creation of this book's Nīli-Nīlakeci

Most works so far that have at least 'touched' the Nīli pēy stories or even mentioned Nīlakeci for that matter have stopped at a mention of 'recasting' Nīli, the pēy, as Nīlakeci, the Jaina philosopher. They have focussed on the Nīli pēy stories in the Śaivite tradition (usually) and worked on the question of the woman in that form of a *pēy*. I am taking Nīli throughout her journey as a character, in the Tamil country, from the *pēy* to the philosopher where (in the latter character) I would like her to stay, really, being a woman myself, because she is here, as a philosopher, travelling, on her own, a cerebral being (even a cursory glance at the nature of the debates with different schools of thought will prove that amply), a female-embodied one, dreaded not for her violent retribution of wrongs, but for her intellect, just as her predecessor (in terms of time and history of the character) Kuṇṭalakeci (who also happened to be a historical person, unlike the Nīlakeci character, who may have been modelled after a historical Jaina nun, one would not know, until further research is done on that) was dreaded by all her opponents in cerebral duels. The other difference in the works on *Nīlakeci*, the Jaina text, is that there is pure focus only on the debates and not on the Nīli aspect of this Nīlakeci. I am connecting the two streams—Nīli and Nīlakeci—and going further, where not much scholarship, especially by a woman, has gone before.

I am interested in what I would like to call *alter-texting* of the *pēy* stories that *Nīlakeci* does; or its author/poet does. It goes beyond any simplistic 're-casting' (a term I would not use anymore) idea, for here the folk-lore is taken up, its original structural form (as a text and characterisation of its protagonist) and ritual context is completely overturned and in fact subverted to make for an entirely new form (unfamiliar to the audience until that point of its creation) where the original then becomes a mere footnote in the new scheme, just as the *pēy* Nīli story does. You meet this Nīli at the beginning of *Nīlakeci* playing the role she is condemned to play forever in one particular tradition, and then that is it; the transformative meeting with a Digambara Jaina monk happens, and the entire person of Nīli gets a makeover, of a radical kind. This *alter-texting* is about creating a text with an alternative paradigm and dramatic overturning of a simple folktale into a deeply intellectual discourse of the contemporary time, which addresses not just one woman who was wronged and what she is capable of doing (when wronged), unless appeased, but an entire way of looking at *reality*, *existence* and *ethics*, subjects that apply to a general way of life and Nīlakeci wishes to prove that there is a better way of life, which she proves logically and without recourse to emotional haranguing. So there is an entire politics to her discourse. This is the *alter-texting* I am interested in, which I hope will get reflected in the pages of this book. But for that *alter-texting* to happen, which will reduce the original 'imprisoned' (as) *pēy*-woman to a footnote, one has to go back to Nīli's having become the kind of Nīli she became and the why of it. The presence of a cheat of a man—as in other folktales, reflecting the reality most women generally had to contend with—is the basic reason. Yet, even in the tradition that keeps her that way, her becoming the dreadful blood-thirsty possession spirit is hardly seen with an amount of compassion or sadness but always as something that needs to be controlled or destroyed. Only in one of the bow-song versions do we see some semblance of empathy for the wronged woman. Otherwise, the person who made her the *pēy* she became (the man) is usually never criticised, even by the way, in any of the versions. Nīli, for that matter, would not get the kind of empathy that Kaṇṇaki (of the epic, *Cilappatikāram*, who later got deified as a chaste, wronged woman, whose husband was executed, on a wrong premise, by the orders of a Pandyan ruler of Madurai) got. One does not know the answer to this question, as this is the case with most possession-spirit stories, which always have a sad antecedent where the woman is usually killed or betrayed. Hence, the alter-texting of Nīlakeci is to me significant, both in literary and cultural terms. The hegemony of one tradition is totally rejected and a new form is created out of it.

It is a story from three sources, each unconnected to the other, but about the same character. It is a story that needs to be told; the first and second stories (in the sequence that I use in this book) end at a point where the third picks up, from where it all ended, in a way, for the central character, and began, for the same person. The characterisation ended at one point in one tradition, but only just began in the other. The first two stories, from which the third one is picked up, have obviously been floating around for a while, mostly in the northern Tamil country. The third story picks up the character and twists her fate about, to give an elaborate flourish to her; as to what is possible with a character confined within spaces, if the spaces and opportunities are provided for her. What might this character possibly become, in fiction, as in real life? The methods adopted to redefine that character are possible in real life situations, but unless the character is a grand persona, whose very name causes fear and trepidation everywhere, the redefining or 'fixing' will not seem too grandiose or dramatic. And dramatic it has to be; a simple, simplistic transformation in the central character will not suffice, for then we would not have been so delighted to read these stories: Angulimāla in the Buddhist tradition, for instance; or in real life, Aśoka, from being the cold-blooded 'murderer' in the Kalinga battlefield, to a king who apologised, and became Buddhist in word and deed. In the Jaina case, here, we have a story of a similar dramatic transformation, which is dramatic not merely because of the level of transformation, but because of the subject chosen for that transformation, who is not a full-bodied woman of this world, but a *pēy*. She has that female voice (following the tradition of the Therigāthās of the Buddhist canon) which can assume, at will, a female body in the ontological sense, but essentially she is a *pēy* who can only make people 'real'-ise her when she possesses them or seeks them out for her revenge. Strangely, though Nīli's revenge was only meant for her former lover/husband who murdered her in the previous birth, yet people unconnected with her story continue to be afraid of her and worship her only to appease her anger. Perhaps they do so from guilt of other betrayals, of acts that actually turned Nīli into the *pēy* she is, from having been a trusting, gullible woman or a simple 'wife'. An entire tradition of ballads surrounds the sad Nīli, the character. Hence you have a voluminous poetic treatise (no less), heavy on philosophy and polemic, created around the central character, Nīli-Nīlakeci. The literary device used to convey this transformation couldn't have been any less, for the transformation is that much more dramatic/fantastic.

At this point, I refer to a unique aspect to this work which connects to me on a personal plane: numerous hours spent with my mother (who may not be called by others a 'Tamil *pulavar*'/ scholar in the literal, literate mainstream sense) reading the Tamil *Nīlakeci* and the Pa<u>l</u>aiya<u>n</u>ūr Nīli *katais,* which made us both discover that inner dynamic and structural contours of the text by way of continued reading over a period of time, although with long circumstantially imposed intervals. I vouch for the integrity and truth of those readings and decided to use those for the book, as I did, initially, for a small section of my doctoral dissertation long ago. But like the years gone by, and the circumstances mid-way, the nature of my reading this text has changed; I now do it alone, in solitude, with each word throwing a challenge, wondering if I will understand it at all. When I discovered the meaning of each such word, the joy was out of this world. While I have retained many of the original readings and interpretations that happened in my mother's company, a whole lot of reading has happened subsequently, in the last few years, so I have been able to understand—of course, not without much head-banging—and translate many of the verses on my own. But there is a way to read *Nīlakeci*: which is to read the Jaina epistemology, cosmogony, or idea of reality, as well as those of the systems she contests, without which, purely as a literary exercise, this work can never really 'come' to you. That bit, I realised later. And that way, improving upon the earlier drafts of my manuscripts, have involved unlearning and learning afresh. It thus led me to the Buddhist philosophy after many years, all over again, and other scholarship on related matters and that has made a great difference to the way I read it and write about it. This is regarding *Nīlakeci*. But there was also a lot of re-reading the Pa<u>l</u>aya<u>n</u>ūr Nīli stories (all the versions I have referred to); the bow-song version is fascinating in the use of metaphors and popular Tamil idioms (which anyone familiar with everyday Tamil and the use of these therein, would relate to); the *Nīli Nāṭakam* version, again, is a long poem, and each of these versions could be taken up for separate detailed study. But what really touched my heart with deep sadness in the Nīli stories is the abject cruelty meted out to her, which is an emotion that the popular stories (especially the bow-song version, not so much the *Nīli Nāṭakam*) bring out in you; I am sure hearing the *villuppāṭṭu* live, would create a similar feeling; unfortunately, the only time I heard a *villuppāṭṭu* was at a general musical fete (with different kinds of music and dance) held in Chennai at the Adyar Kalaksheta auditorium,[28] but the *villukkārars* who performed there, chose a different story and not the Nīli *pēy* stories. And even otherwise, the bow-song tradition itself requires a serious study.

I would also like to make a point here—in connection with the readings with my mother—that scholarship is not always present in titles (honorary or earned)[29] constituted by social and economic systems but is inherent in people's sense of eagerness to grasp whatever little they can of knowledge that happened to pass their way (as it did in my mother's case, through my research on the Tamil Jainas) that would otherwise not be known to them (as it happens in the case of many people) and such knowledge, earned through that sense of eagerness to know, and to read on and on, forever, voraciously, like there was no tomorrow,[30] needn't be debased and dishonoured. Even with this possibility, so far as this book goes, I consciously retain the translations based on the readings of a mother-daughter duo, which I have also substantiated with translations in the edited versions of the text, besides of course my own translations using the lexicon and dictionaries. In most cases the translations, unless otherwise mentioned, are mine, so I take the responsibility for those. At the same time, I gained immense help from the editorial notes of the two editions of *Nîlakeci* I utilised throughout.

This book does not claim to be simply a literal English translation of a Tamil text.[31] Originally, Professor Chakravarti brought out his bi-lingual book, with the original Tamil text and a summarised English (not verbatim) translation in 1936, but copies of that original work were hard to find.[32] Chakravarti's son, whom I had the occasion to meet in Chennai, did not have a copy with him either, since his copy, which he lent out to someone, never came back to him. Long after, the Prakrit Bharti Academy only printed the English version of Chakravarti's book in 1994. However, I had the happy chance of revisiting the Tamil Jaina villages and people (whom I had earlier met during the course of my research many years ago) and, amidst the celebration of the ritual of *pañcakalyāṇaka* (the ritual enactment of the five significant events in the life of a tīrthankara, which the Tamil Jainas celebrate once in many years their villages) at the village Vembakkam, near Kanchipuram, I re-connected with S. Bahubali Jain, who gave me the reprint of the original *Nīlakeci* (Tamil-English bilingual), edited by Chakravarti, finally.[33]

I have used both editions of *Nīlakeci*. One of these is edited by Professor A. Chakravarti, the Tamil section of which has another Jaina work, *Aṣṭapatārtham* appended to it, which I am yet to read. The original edition is available in one of the libraries in Chennai, while the Tamil University in Thanjavur brought out a reprint of the original in the 1980s. The other is a Saiva Siddhanta Publications edition by P. V. Somasundaranar[34] (who will be referred to as Po.Ve.So, in this work, in the Tamil manner).

Chakravarti's work has the advantage of his knowledge of the Jaina tradition as an insider (a Tamil Jaina, to be precise), with an equal command over Buddhism and other schools of thought, since he was a lecturer in philosophy and later Principal, at the Government College, Kumbakonam.[35] He was equally well-versed in Western traditions of Philosophy, as is reflected in his other writings on Jaina religion and Indian philosophy. In bringing out the first ever scholarly edition on *Nīlakeci*, he made use of manuscripts available then with the chief pontiff (Bhattaraka, maṭhātipati) of the Melcittamur Jaina matham near Cenji, Tamil Nadu; Mr. Samantabhadra Nainar of Perumandur village; Dr. U. V. Swaminatha Iyer and; Mr C. S. Mallinath[36], who was the editor of the Jaina Gazette. But the first two of these had the original manuscripts. U. V. Swaminatha Iyer, in fact, transcribed several palm-leaf manuscripts of other Tamil classics, including *Nīlakeci,* and brought out several edited volumes of works in Tamil. Chakravarti had an objective (not entirely in the context of Jainism, merely) in bringing out this book in the late 1930s, prior to India's independence, as he says in the *Preface* to his book:

> The work that is now offered to the public is a well-known Tamil classic. Why I have undertaken to edit this, instead of leaving it to more competent Tamil scholars, is due to two facts. One, scholars who have had the manuscript with them for several decades have not made up their minds to publish the work for some reason or other; and secondly the knowledge that there were only three or four manuscripts extant, naturally implied that if these few manuscripts were lost or destroyed, the work itself would be lost to the world like the celebrated classics, *Kundalakesi* and *Valayapathi.* Hence I have ventured to publish this work so that it might be available to the Tamil public...It is hoped that this work will be of great use in Modern India in as much as it emphasises the doctrine of Non-violence in general and its corollary in special that the social organisation is to be based upon character and merit and not upon birth. Such an appeal to Modern India is certainly of great importance to leaders of thought in their attempt to reorganise the Indian society and rebuild the Indian nation.'[37]

Though one has begun to wonder if a book of this nature would ever have seen light of the day in the present context, considering the scathing critique it presents of different schools of thought. Prior to this was the Buddhist *Kuṇṭalakeci,* which was also a text in the same tradition of debate and discourse.

I referred to both these editions for purposes of comparison and to eliminate any possibility of a mistaken reading. I have read and re-read the Tamil verses, taking help from the Tamil-Tamil-English and Tamil-English dictionaries and the elaborate commentary within the text, as well as the editorial comments of Chakravarti and Po.Ve.So. These intense multiple and simultaneous readings have been of great help in giving the final shape to this book.

In matters of authorship, the text *Nīlakeci* presents an array of interpretations. There is a moment in the course of this book that I find the very question of authorship intriguing. Was Nīlakeci written by a woman, for instance? Could we possibly conjecture that a Jaina nun wrote *Nīlakeci*, sitting in the calm and beautiful precincts (overlooking green fields of millets and pulses and some paddy) of the Jaina temple at Pundi (which, according to local legends in the place, was the site of its composition)? Or at some other place in the region of Tiruvalangadu, perturbed by the nature of demonisation and imprisoning fear that the legendary Nīli pēy was subject of? Was she thinking of an alternate text that might redeem not just Nīli, but also women, through the tenets of the Jaina faith? And hence composed the long poem? Why doesn't anyone speak of the possibility of a female authorship for *Nīlakeci*?

So far as the debates in *Nīlakeci* are concerned, the largest number of verses is dedicated to the Jaina-Buddhist contests, which happen with four people representing Buddhism, namely, Kuṇṭalakeci, Arukaccantiran, Mokkala (or Mokkalana), the prime disciple of the Buddha) and the very Buddha. The verses numbered 150-231 comprise Nīlakeci's debate with Kuṇṭalakeci; verses 232-462 are with Arukaccantiran, introduced as one of the Buddhist monks; verses 267-462 are with Mokkala, one of the prime disciples of Gotama, the Buddha, and verses 463-658 are with the great Buddha. Verses 824-853 are dedicated to Nīlakeci's debate with Pūtikaṉ, of the Vedic school and verses 854-894 are dedicated to the debate with the Bhūtavādin (materialist), Picācakaṉ. These are verses that I am concerned with for the present book, so if you add the debates with all the other schools of thought that Nīlakeci engages with, you can imagine the sheer volume of this minor *kavya*. Each debate can be a book in itself - which is a possibility for a future time—so I do not, for this book, concern myself with a literal translation of all the verses. I have taken the most important verses, that present the dominant streak of the difference between the Jaina and the respective schools of thought; hence, for example, the authority of the Vedas, caste and question of authorship, in that section.

What is Nīlakeci saying to me?

How does one approach Nīlakeci, the person? What is Nīli saying? What is Nīlakeci saying? The usual route taken so far has been that of the Śaivite/Vaiṣṇavite bhakti tradition; eulogising the 'mad-woman' or the kind of woman who has been radicalised by feminist scholarship within the bhakti paradigm. Should only a 'mad-woman', or 'pēy'-like, Kāraikkāl Ammaiyār be the epitome of the 'liberated' woman (who she may not really have been)? And there has been a lot written and said about bhakti being a redeeming, liberating tradition, being anti-caste, giving space to a woman (that three of the saints were women). But you already had (before bhakti) the *Therigāthā* (Psalms of the Buddhist nuns) and works such as *Kuṇṭalakesi* (the Tamil poetic treatise) with the protagonist being the Buddhist nun, Bhadda Kuṇṭalakesa, where women were writing, as well as debating. I have given a brief story of Kuṇṭalakesa/Kuṇṭalakesi and also a mere glimpse into what she was saying as a nun, based on a book that compiles the only few remaining verses of this great Tamil work, now lost to the world (that being the general opinion, but perhaps someone someday will search for it, seek it out and thence find it—surely all the history of this world has not all been written down forever?), in the section where Nīlakeci debates with her. The author of *Nīlakeci* has also given a Jaina rendition and answer to the unending cycle of murder, revenge, birth and re-birth, due to karmic influx which is exemplified in Nīli's story. Instead of accepting the ritual acceptance of Nīli's painful death and the solution of revenge by an equally bloodied killing (in all the folk versions, Nīli bites into the throat of her former life's lover/husband and sucks his blood out, which is a revenge for the manner of her death, again in all versions, her husband/ lover crushing her head with a stone), *Nīlakeci*'s author seeks for her the Jaina path of salvation. Interestingly, the *villuppāṭṭu* Nīli story refers to this (also a very crucial Jaina) idea of *karma* thus—

> *kuṟattimoḻi keḷāmal koṭumpōkkāyp pōkaluṟṟāṉ*
> *jeṉmaviṉai taṭaiyāmal tiruppiviṭa voṭṭāmal*
> *karmaviṉai piṭariyilē kaikoṭuttut taḷḷiṭumām*
> *taḷḷiṭave kāṉakattil taṉivaḻiyē vārapōtu (lines.275-8)*[38]

> [Disregarding the soothsayer's warning, he started off
> unhindered by the defect of his birth (stars), which will not touch him
> bad karma caught him behind his neck[39]
> taking him on a lone route through the forest[40]]

Nīlakeci wants to be seen as a philosopher and to be taken seriously. Her having 'become', is the part of the story that should not be underplayed in the iteration of her pēy self or the self of an avenging woman/spirit. She seems to tell me, as if she would be debating about her own identity, as well (or so I hear, in my head and heart, that if she did speak to me, this is what she would have said):

> Here I am, doing hardcore philosophy as a woman, defeating the men in debate just as there was Kuṇṭalakeci before me. You better get used to this self of mine, which in fact still falls behind in scholarly discourse on Kāraikkāl Ammaiyār, who was rendered a *pēy* and not even allowed to be a woman—a full-bodied woman, who wrote or composed. She had to be *pēy* because they could not digest a poet being a woman. In fact, it was simpler for her to be canonised, because she spoke of the love for god. Now, god does not exist in our system; hence my discourse has been purely on philosophical merit, or otherwise, of systems and schools, around issues of existence, or otherwise, of soul; existence, or otherwise, of the authorial voice; discussion of atom, matter and principles of life. Once, when I was stressing on authorship

and its validity, I was conferring the practical and this-worldly aspect to any tradition which, for me, has an authorial voice and that, the Vedic teacher found hard to digest. He in fact made me conscious of a caste—he called me a śūdra; nobody I debated with throughout my journey ever identified me with a caste status. But, even if he did, let me tell you this–people who worshipped me were mostly communities who have been looked down upon by the brahmins, of course. If because of that my status becomes that of a śūdra, even then, my story as a philosopher is what I would like to be remembered by, rather than as one stuck in an avenging demon form[41]. My own tradition—which is, for all purposes, Jaina, which I became—does not concern itself with caste. I am in the tradition where you are free to become your best through your own individual action. You are free to become what you chose to become through acting on your own thoughts and deeds; why, even so-called 'infernal beings' (that was who I was, a *vyantara devata*) in the Jaina tradition, in spite of all the hell they suffer due to their bad *karmas,* have the possibility to redeem themselves by their actions. So, pray don't let me remain the *pēy* Nīli, yet again; that part of my life you have known; you followed my story right through that life. Now let us accept that I am Nīlakeci, who I have become. That is the part I want to be spoken about, remembered about me, because I stand right next to—as an equal—all those men, including the Buddha, in matters of philosophical discourse. As a woman, my intervention in philosophy is important. Hence, do not rush through my debates as incidental to the story of a 'fringe' or 'mad-woman'. I do not dance with any god anywhere on a fringe land; I stand and make my point in an open debate with men, and on one occasion, with a woman, who stands, also, as an equal.[42]

So, I decided to take Nīlakeci's idea (which was ringing in my head) and focus on the debates that give her the status she remains in, in the Tamil Jaina tradition. Significantly, she is not deified, nor are there any iconographic representations of Nīlakeci in any of the Tamil Jaina temples or villages. I say this to contrast this with what happens in the case of Kāraikkāl Ammaiyār,[43] who becomes deified, as a 'bag of bones' or 'ghoul', and is represented, as such, in iconography. And that iconography seems to remain undisturbed, even in scholarly treatises on the woman poet/'saint'. Not being deified—in the case of Nīlakeci—re-affirms the idea that Nīlakeci must be treated as a philosopher even if she is fictitious (as a character), though the debates are not fictitious in terms of the content of the debates with various schools of thought, and the content of these debates actually reflects the genuine and historical points of difference between Jaina and other systems. Perhaps Nīlakeci was even styled after one of the nuns (and there are several instances of nuns occurring in Jaina donative inscriptions found in Tamilnadu, where they are referred to as '*aṭikaḷ*') of the Jaina order as in the Buddhist order, and the *Therigāthā* as a compilation of nuns' sayings in verses predated the composition of *Nīlakeci*, as did the major poetic treatise, *Kuṇṭalakec*i. So a model already existed for the author of *Nīlakeci* to style his radical woman on. Focussing on Nīlakeci, the debator, would also assert the fact that one has to alter the prevalent and mainstream discourse on questions of gender that almost always pick up from the Śaivite or Vaiṣṇavite bhakti tradition for their role-models.

So I assume the role of a chronicler of Nīli-Nīlakeci and set out on her journey, with a focus on five major philosophical debates that came her way or rather, debates that she took on, with a resolve. I focus only on five of her debates keeping in mind the significance of the content and depth of those particular debates. Otherwise, *Nilakeci* has debates also with Ājīvika, Sāṁkhya and Vaiseṣika schools. If we could locate *Kuṇṭalakeci*, we could have understood the structure and composition of *Nīlakeci* better, and also as to whether or not it was a direct counter to *Kuṇṭalakeci*.

So I will begin the journey from where it all began for Nīli and proceed as her life proceeded, until that fateful night when she had an unusual encounter and through all her subsequent travels in the sequence as she undertook them, skipping a few of her halts, mid-way. Though all of her life's journey should make for a very interesting revisit, should someone be able to retrace it someday.

In all the Nīli stories, the endings are usually violent; even the 'end' visited upon Nīli is violent, and not just the kind of violence Nīli unleashes on her victims. In an old Malayalam movie (in black-and-white) titled *Kalliyankaattu Nīli*, they show an elaborate ritual being performed to bring an end to Nīli, who has taken her revenge on the husband of her former life who killed her by smashing her head with a stone and ran away with all her jewellery. The obviously tantric priest actually nails Nīli's head on to a tree in a scrub jungle in the midst of *kaḷḷi* (prickly pear/spurge) plants. In this movie (as in the villuppāṭṭu tradition) the *kaḷḷi* plants are supposed to have been witness to the brutal murder of Nīli and she urges them to be the witness when she dies of her wounds. She is shown as resident among the *kaḷḷi* plants once she becomes the *pēy*. The brutality shown on Nīli by her husband is not given so much thought in these folk tales, but the larger message is to bring an end to the possession spirit who avenged her death and the death of her brother. The pain of her past life inflicts further pain in her present life, equally bound, through a ritual enactment of brutal killing. So the life of violence remains a fixation in all these Nīli stories. But in the Jaina version, there is an end to the cycle of violence and victimisation; besides bringing to an end the violent trajectory, a new path is created which is of an intellectual pursuit with the final goal of liberation from all bondage to Self and the persecuted body of Nīli, in the form of Nīlakeci. Kuṇṭalakesa's was also a story of putting an end to the violent tale, she having killed her husband in self-defence. She becomes a Jaina nun, too, initially, and then a Buddhist nun, ordained by the Buddha. In both these cases, the women are not judged by their violent acts, nor are they persecuted, nor worshipped, in their violent form. The element of fear and guilt is removed from their stories once and for all, through the opening up of a deeper, intellectual means—which could be either Buddhist (Kuṇṭalakesa) or Jaina (Nīlakeci).

The phenomenal/radical change in the nature and form of Nīli can only be understood by comparing the 'text' of the folklore and that of the Jaina poetic composition. What I engage in, in the following sections, is a journey with Nīli followed by a journey with Nīlakeci and I end with Nīlakeci, as she desires, to leave her as an image of a free intellect. Though Nīlakeci insists I focus more on the debates and thereby celebrate this form of hers, I would like to say that without understanding the form she so desires to break free from, we can not appreciate the forward movement. Yet, a close reading of the text would reveal, as it did to me, that Nīlakeci's confidence and brashness from her former *pēy* Self does not really seem to go away, in the sense that she does not become a totally submissive, subdued spirit, especially in the manner of her handling the debates with her opponents. Whether for the purposes of the Jaina 'victory' necessary for the text, or for her own self, she ultimately gives people what she does, as she used to, when she was a *pēy*. People have to listen to her. There is a particular structure to the debates in the *Nīlakeci* text. Most times, you find verses elaborating upon the school of thought Nīlakeci would challenge, followed by her detailed 'fault-finding' or critique. But there are also times, for instance, in the Buddha's case, or relatively fewer times in Kuṇṭalakeci's case, that either Buddha or Kuṇṭalakeci would engage in a point-to-point discussion with her. However, the largest part consists in Nīlakeci asking the opponent to explain his or her philosophy, following which she will critique, logically, the inconsistencies or inadequacies of each of the ideas presented before her.

I will translate the *villuppāṭṭu* version as it occurs in the printed text, keeping the structure as it is and then proceed to the *Nīli nātakam* (again, staying true to its structure). However, I do not give both these texts in their entirety, since these two versions can themselves be separate books. This will be followed by *Nīlakeci*. I am not citing all the original Tamil verses in this book. In some cases, I have written parts of them in footnotes if I have some point to make by citing them, while in others, where I find it very important to begin with the Tamil verses, I include them in the main text. I have found it useful to refer to what is being conveyed rather than a poetic translation of the original. Where it seemed interesting, or significant, I have attempted to translate in verse form. All the translations of verses, unless otherwise mentioned, are mine.

The best way to approach this book, as with Nīlakeci, is to be aware of some of the basic points of the schools of thought that are being debated. It may, of course, be possible to approach the Tamil *Nīlakeci* as a purely literary output, or purely philosophical ramblings, and in each of these cases, the slant of this book would also significantly change. I have tried to be true to the philosophical underpinnings, as well as to the importance of those for a 'transgressive' persona and the history of that persona.

The format of this book and other matters

The sequence of my book is a journey through the Nīli stories. The chapters are sequenced accordingly. So I start with the Nīli stories, with two versions, one a traditional bow-song and another an extended dance drama text. This is the section that is called *Being Nīli* and looks at her *Possession* paradigm: possession can be seen as both possessing (others to avenge them) and being possessed (the latter by the tradition). The next section is *Becoming Nilakeci*, and her *Freedom* (from the former life). There is, following that, placing the texts in perspective. The titles are self-explanatory so I will not dwell on them too much here.

It must be noted that all the Nīli stories have a violent ending. Apparently, there is a Nīli story even in Kerala where the tradition locates Palakanallur in Kerala in the southern part of Trivandrum and Nīli in her former birth is called Aḷḷi. In the Nīli stories, the brother of Nīli, Nīlan, is burnt, through the burning of the *neem* tree he resides in. Violence is writ large in all these tales, from start to finish. Nīli is crushed with a big stone by her husband/lover of the former birth. The brother either jumps into the well or hits his head against the stone, committing suicide when he sees his sister's crushed face. But in the Jaina story, there seems to be a Jaina means to an end to the cycle of violence; there is a new path available, were Nīli to choose it on her own, for a kind of intellectual journey that also happens to be a spiritual journey. But, like the Jaina scheme of things, the embodied soul has to take that first step towards ending the influx of bad karmas. The choice remains with that embodied soul alone. Where would Nīli belong in the Jaina schemata?

> In accordance with the difference in the Becoming or status (*gati*) the souls are divided into four classes, viz.:- 1) the celestial (Deva); 2) the infernal (Naraka); 3) the Human (Manuṣya) and; 4) the sub-human (Tiryak). According to the Jainas the Devas are either a) Bhavana vāsi or home-living or b) Vyantara, beings living various places or c) Jyotiṣka, luminaries or d) Vaimānika, ie., living in high heavens. The Bhavana-vāsi deities are of 10 kinds, viz:- Nāgakumāra, Asura-kumāra, Suparna-kumāra, Agni-kumāra, Dik-kumāra...[etc.]... The Vyantara Devas are of eight modes, viz:-Kinnara, Kiṁpuruṣa, Gandharva, Mahoraga, Yakṣa, Rākṣasa, Bhūta and Piśāca. The jyotiṣka are of five kinds, viz:- Sūrya, Candra...[etc.]... The Infernal beings live in various hells. They are endowed with the power of assuming any shape or form, but this power is only a source of trouble and pain to them... On account of vicious acts, done in their previous incarnations, they become denizens of the hells and suffer untold and unbearable pains for a long time.'[44]

Nīli thus would be one of these infernal beings, one of the *vyantara devas* (a piśāca) who would have to work hard to get rid of the past life karmas. Being a 'soul', Nīli is however, capable of positive progress, since,

'...For a Jaina the knowledge, bliss and energy of the soul can never be totally extinguished, whereas karmic influence is subject to complete elimination. Hence the soul possesses a sort of in-built advantage, an ever present tendency to develop its qualities and temporarily reduce the influx of the karmas. When the Jainas say that a soul is free to work for its own salvation, it is this inherent tendency towards self-improvement that it is referred to...Jainas have given us a detailed picture of the ladder one must climb as he progresses from the depths of delusion and entrapment to the pinnacle of omniscience and freedom. This ladder has fourteen rungs, called guṇasthānas, stages of perfection. The state of mithyādṛṣṭi (the incorrect view of reality) is designated as the first of these rungs; it is here that every embodied soul must dwell until it undergoes the momentous shift described above. This event is followed very quickly by the experience called samyak-darśana having the correct view, in which the soul for the first time glimpses its true nature. Such an experience is compared to that of a blind man who is suddenly able to see; although the event is momentary, it involves less than absolutely undistorted view of reality.' [45]

Meanwhile, in the other tradition, Nīli remains (to this day) an important part of some Tamil communities and in some villages. There is a Nīli temple in a village called Palayanur near Sivaganga (Madurai) but this is different from the Palayanur of the Nīli stories, which is in North Arcot, near Tiruvalangadu, where it is called the Isakkiamman temple within which the *villupāṭṭu* singing happens on certain occasions. There is an entire audio recording of one such Nīli villuppāṭṭu of the Isakki-amman temple available on the internet.[46]

There are three versions of Nīli story that this book is concerned with—one is a folk theatre performance in the bow-song tradition of Tamilnadu; the second is a classical dance drama performance within temple precincts (mentioned in the text of the performance) and the third is a philosophical treatise in Tamil verse. The former two are restricted to the Nīli form while the last one is the story of Nīlakeci. In her context, one also came across the other radical (historical) transformation story of Kuṇṭalakesa, the Buddhist *theri*/nun. It is important that Nīlakeci starts her debate with Kuṇṭalakeci, as both women who have undergone pain, of different kinds and, after one meeting with an ascetic (in both cases, a male monk), redefine their life-story.

It is important to note that *Nīlakeci*, the text, is a signifier of two crucial aspects: it is steeped in the Jaina tradition, in terms of the nature of the character chosen for the radical redefinition, which falls within the Jaina cosmogony, even though the author of the composition (as I later note) confessed about charting a radical course by creating this work, for which she/he sought 'concession' from the purists of tradition. Interestingly, the exact context of the creation of this work is given. This is a dream that the poet has seen, with the character Nīli in it and that he or she decides to build upon. Perhaps what she/he seeks the indulgence of contemporaries on, is making Nīli a central character, although the form of Nīli is not impossible within Jaina cosmogony. Secondly, it is an exemplar of the debating tradition prevalent in what we have now begun to call (for want of a better term), 'Indian' histories. That philosophical debates were rather commonplace, is by now well-known and many scholars have also pointed this out. The text therefore is a work of intellectual debate, and it takes up for discussion, as a sub-text, the Jaina idea of what constitutes reality; Nīli, being a *pēy* from the hellish realms, really needs to come out of that existence forever through her own volition and action to attain liberation at the end of her life cycle. The text offers scathing criticisms of other schools of thought by highlighting the logical (and it is important for the author that there be a logical explanation to both, the points that other schools make, and the Jaina critique of it) inconsistencies of each system.

However, that there was never a non-problematic, all-encompassing 'Indian' universal thinking of reality or the unreal, is clear from texts such as *Nīlakeci*. N.N. Bhattacharya had also remarked that it is a fallacy to think of the Indian (again, for want of a better category) philosophy as syncretic, even though there may be aspects that seem common to all.

> The law of karma is accepted by the six orthodox schools and also by the Buddhists and Jainas. Some systems like the Nyāya-Vaiśeṣika believe that the law of karma is under the guidance and control of god. In the Sāmkhya, Mīmāmsa, Buddhist and Jain, the law of karma is autonomous. Another common view is that ignorance is the cause of bondage, and liberation is the state of perfectness which can be achieved through knowledge, self-control and meditation. The Sāmkhya, Advaita-Vedānta, Buddhism and Jainism hold that liberation can be attained in this life. All Indian systems, except Cāravākas, hold that liberation is a total destruction of sufferings which life in this world brings about. On the basis of such common characteristics writers on Indian philosophy want to lay emphasis on the synthetic[47] outlook of our ancient philosophers. But this is evidently an exaggerated notion. Rather it will be logical to say that it was the *contradictions* that constituted the moving force of development in the field of Indian philosophy. The very manner of our philosophical writings is to expound one's own views by way of a critical rejection of the ideas opposed to it... The clash of ideas was not confined to philosophical writings alone. It frequently found expression in open or public debates. Such debates were often arranged with great pomp in the presence of the king or any high rank person, and the defeated or discredited philosophers had to face a miserable lot. [48]

The last point rings true when one reads *Nīlakeci* and the manner in which she defeats Kuṇṭalakeci in debate, which is organized by the king of Cāmpili, who sends the latter away in disgrace. Further,

> 'The basis of the so-called synthetic outlook was formulated as early as the late medieval period with the purpose of giving Vedānta a lead. Thus Vijñavikṣu and others fabricated the

> Sāmkhya in the light of Vedānta and following this tradition, great scholars like M.M. Jogendranath Tarka-Sāmkhya-Vedānta-tīrtha or Candrakānta tarkālankara did not hesitate to say that "the different philosophical streams got mingled in a perfect homogeneity after reaching the great ocean of one nun-dual *Brahman*." Similar view is shared by Radhakrishnan [Sarvepalli]... Notwithstanding all the twists of textual interpretation, displayed by the champions of the synthetic theory, it is impossible to conceal the real clash of ideas.'[49]

And that is the point that Nīlakeci too makes, just as perhaps the Buddhist text *Kuṇṭalakeci* (which is no longer available to us) did in its time. Anyway, the Jaina-Buddhist debate has been of long-standing and so also the Jaina-Cāravāka and Jaina-Ājivika. Not to mention the Jaina points of contestation with the Vedic schools, the last one, especially on the question of the creator and supreme authority of the Vedas. Within the atheistic schools, the Jainas, Buddhists, Ājivikists (as long as they held sway in some parts of the subcontinent, before disappearing into oblivion) and the materialists had several occasions to debate and call each other names, too, if needed.

So far as *Nīlakeci* is concerned, I have taken up for this book, the debates that are important from the Jaina point of view and the history of epistemological differences between some of the more significant schools of thought of the time when this poetic treatise was composed. The debate with the Buddhists is part of the long-drawn battle between the two religions on the question of soul and non-soul and the nature of ahimsā (non-killing/ *koḷḷāmai/ūṉ-uṉṉāmai*) in both the religions, and the question of suffering and self-inflicted pain in the context of Bodhisattvas' life-experiences elucidated in the Jātaka stories to extol the greatness of the present Buddha. This last point also comes in the context of the Buddhist criticism of Jaina (Digambara) kind of extreme asceticism which, according to the Buddhists, was not really required to gain self-realisation and final release. But the Bodhisattvas also inflicted pain upon their own bodies and to their person, in the pursuit of righteousness. With the Bhūtavāda (*pūtavātam*-materialist school) the debate is around, again, the idea of soul, and presence of a consciousness. Though Jainism was equally atheistic, within *Nīlakeci*, this section starts to look more theist, vis-à-vis the Bhūtavadin's ideas. As far as the Vedic school is concerned, the debating point is both the authority and assumed primordiality of the Vedas and, very importantly, the question of caste. The last one is important because this seems to come from a particularly Tamil context of Jainism in the early centuries, considering that there is an elaborate discourse that Nīlakeci gives, rubbishing the very notion of caste and high and low birth. And for the first time in the text, her caste (i.e., her presumed caste) is brought forth in clear terms.

Finally, I say this before the journey begins. In between the past and the present, the pain and the joy, parting and reunion, is a space—of movement, if one chose it; or stillness, if one chose that, too. An idea, or a person, or even a moment in nature's time can lead one to that movement, or that stillness. Nīli's was the story of that movement. Of her becoming Nīlakeci. Hers is a story of that space between Nīli and Nīlakeci—a *pēy* and a Jaina philosopher. And an intervening space between her Candana Naṅkai-self and the Nīli pēy-self, even as there is that space between Candana Naṅkai and Nambi, who she once showered her love on. Hers is a story of the space between bondage and release, imprisonment and freedom; it is the space to her redemption from a long history of violence and vengeance. This is the story of that open space between Kancipuram and Palayanur, a space that allows Nīli a last and final embrace that she had once lost her human form to: an innocent embrace that had led to her doom. In this open space—of shrubland merging into wooded forests—lies a liberal space for her to be what she wants to be, to complete an unfinished embrace, an unfinished story. At the same time, the spaces between every new root of the banyan tree, that essentially came from its branches, drooping downwards, meant more and more spaces for more possibilities, of relationships yet undefined, unformed. Had they been allowed that space, of course. But the space that did come about, was beyond these corners and from an idea that took her on an uncharted path, that this book seeks to trace.

Even in that ancient time, Nîli ('of the south') broke from the tradition she was born into, to enter a world of such a possibility: of debate on inconsistencies and limitations of traditions. And one is reminded of all the others who did the same (break away), across historical times and spaces. Being 'within', for many, never worked. But they could 'opt out'. Today, we have reached a stage where even 'opting out' leads to violence and censure, what to speak of critiquing from 'within'! So here is a text that lives (so far, thankfully), in another realm altogether, even if imagined (where even the author broke from conventions); and what a moment for its debating voice to be female!

May then, the onward journey of these stories and their characters, commencing from ancient Toṇṭaimaṇṭalam, in Tiruvālaṅkâṭu (Tiruvalangadu), in the ancient Tamil country, begin!

Notes

1. M. Winternitz, 1946, pp. 7-8.
2. Caldwell, 1974, p. 85.
3. R. Parthasarathy, 1993.
4. A recent publication was Srichandran, ed. *Manimekalai, Valayapati, Kuntalakeci: Mulamum, Telivuraiyum*, Tamil Nilayam, Chennai, 1996.
5. N. Vanamamalai, 1997, p. 26.
6. M.S. Ramaswami Ayyangar, 1982, p. 57.
7. I do not use transliteration marks for modern place-names or ancient place names (of places) that have continued till date. I use them when referring to them within texts or ancient tradition. Going against convention, when referring to the Cho<u>l</u>a (king/rule/dynasty, etc), I retain the spelling Cho<u>l</u>a (with a 'ch') and not Cola/Co<u>l</u>a.

8. An edited volume of the same exists: edited by Mahendrakumar, Manikchandra Jain Granthamala, vols. XXXVIII, XXXIX, Bombay, 1938.
9. Paul Dundas, 1991, p. 171.
10. The allusion is to the episode in the *Mahābhārata*, regarding the curse on Kṛṣṇa, for having destroyed the entire Kaurava clan, which consumes the whole Yadu clan.
11. William Graham, 1987, p. 5.
12. Ibid, p. 7.
13. John Cort, 1992, p. 175.
14. Ibid, p. 175.
15. Ibid. p. 175.
16. I would mark the difference between the two terms, Tamil Jainism and Jainism in Tamilnadu. I believe that the former refers to the Tamil, localised, context of the Jaina doctrine, of people who accepted the Jaina faith in the early centuries BCE in Tamilnadu; and the latter to Jainism and the changes it witnessed in the course of history of Tamilnadu. I posit that there *is* such a concept as 'Tamil Jainism', in the manner of a Tamil culture, Tamil idioms, and so forth.
17. A. Chakravarti, *Neelakesi,* 2nd edition, Prakrit Bharati Academy, Jaipur, 1994.
18. K.P.S. Hameed, 1968, pp. 196-204.
19. I shared that excitement in a section of my doctoral thesis which was titled, *Identities in Conflict: Jainism in Early Tamiḻakam*, Jawaharlal Nehru University, New Delhi, 2009.
20. My paper was titled, 'Retrieving, Seeking, (An)other Woman, (An) other Goddess'. The seminar was titled, 'Women and Goddesses: Reimagining the Feminine in Tamil Cinema'.
21. 'The Structural Pattern of Two Traditional Narratives in Tamil'; 'Some Tamil Folklore Texts: Muttuppaṭṭan Katai, Kāttavarāyaṉ Kataippāṭal, Paḻayaṉūr Nīli'; *Poems to Siva; Tamil Temple Myths*; 'The Metamorphosis of Aḷḷi and Neeli: Folktales and Mythic Images of Tamil Women' (complete citations given elsewhere), are some of the works of these scholars, which I have referred to.
22. For instance, Vijaya Ramaswamy, 2009, pp. 57–61, 64–67; 2010, pp. 129–157.
23. In the years 2002-03, when I chanced upon this unique repository which was then headed by the Director, S. Theodore Bhaskaran. In

later years, the RMRL library moved into its own new building at a place called Tharamani in Chennai.

24. Kunal Chakrabarti, 2001, pp. 192-193.
25. A term used for a caste group in Tamilnadu, usually landholding or peasant-based social group with various caste titles. The Tamil Jainas since early times have belonged to this category largely. There are also the Śaiva veḷḷāḷas who have been adherents of the Śaiva tradition. The Tamil Jaina community's collective memory refers to the period between the 7th and 9th centuries CE (when the Tamil country saw the rise of what has generally been referred to as 'bhakti' tradition) as being responsible for the conversion of many Jainas (as an outcome of persecution) into Śaivas and the Śaiva veḷḷāḷas having once been Jainas. Incidentally, the Śaiva veḷḷāḷas (whom the Tamil Jainas refer to as *nīr pūci nayiṉārs*—ones who smeared the sacred ash over their foreheads, fearing persecution) also eat their last meal before dark and are confirmed vegetarians. One can also find architectural similarities in the homes of these two communities in the rural areas; but no generalised conclusions can be drawn without probing deeper into the other side of the same story from the perspective of the Śaiva veḷḷāḷa community in a historical context. For a detailed discussion and analysis of various versions of this community narrative (regarding persecution and conversion), see Umamaheshwari, 2017.
26. Zvelebil, 1989, pp. 298-299.
27. Blackburn, 1985, p. 260.
28. This was an event called Svanubhava, organised by the musician T.M. Krishna (in year 2011) where the bow-song performers had presented their ballad. Hope someday I will get to see a live performance of the Nīli story at the Isakki-amman koil, too.
29. In my mother's case, she was forced to discontinue studies after 'matriculation' in her times. But she learnt to type, and cleared a level of Hindi exams enrolling into a course, on her own (thanks to a temporary job as a telephone operator before her marriage while at Coimbatore) thereafter. She could not converse perfectly in English or Hindi, but read every book, magazine and newspaper she could lay her hands on; she made notes from many of my library books from college (as did my father, later, in my university times, with the Fort St George ASI library staff finding only one

father-daughter team, with a lunch box in hand, working their heads off through the day, pouring through inscriptional records; a fist-time experience for my father) and she loved smelling books, something I have inherited.

30. In her case, it actually became so—she did not get to see the fruition of the thesis, nor the chapter, to which she gave so much of her time and intellect.
31. In case of the folk versions, there wasn't much problem in literally translating from the original work. In case of the Jaina text, however, there were places where verbatim translation was not possible, in the beginning, until one got the sense of the text and its own structural contours, where even inferences could be made.
32. It must be mentioned that the U.V. Swaminatha Aiyer Library in Chennai has the only (by all probability) copy of the 1936 original bi-lingual *Nilakeci* of A. Chakravarti. Incidentally, there is not yet a complete translation of Nilakeci into English or any other language, which seems quite a strange thing to happen to a Tamil literary classic. Hope someday this work will be translated in its entirety for non-Tamil readers.
33. I am truly grateful to Mr. Bahubali of Tiruppanamur-Karandai (now resident at Kanchipuram) for this latter version whose reaching me meant a lot especially after years of searching and letting go of the search.
34. A copy of which I had purchased way back in the year 1997.
35. Though there are a few instances within his book where his Jaina self becomes more than obvious and sometimes also looms large, even if it is not in any way reflected in elaborating on the philosophies of various schools. The Jaina self becomes evident in his interpretation of why Kuṇṭalakeci left the Jaina order of nuns to become a Buddhist nun, may be a case in point (pp. 81-84 of the English summary section in his *Nilakeci*).
36. What a marvellous coincidence that I met the descendants of both these Tamil Jainas—Mallinath (out of the blue, at a temple in one of the Tamil Jaina villages) and Samantabhadra Nayinar (in the village Peramandur) in the course of my research.
37. A. Chakravarti, 1984, Preface, p. v.
38. S. Shanmugasundaram, 1978, p. 15.
39. Folding hands behind one's neck is considered inauspicious.
40. Where Nīli awaits him.

41. In the chapter, *Being...*, in this book, the social context of the *villupāṭṭu* tradition is referred to. And by the way, this Nilakeci is talking to me, if she is, when the Constitution did not exist. Hence I refrain from using the word 'dalit' or Scheduled Caste. Another point: the nature of sharp critique found in *Nīlakeci* on caste is located in an earlier time. As I imagined Nīlakeci to be saying to me. But by the later periods, the Jaina community too, seems to have become susceptible to the idea of caste though the original Jainism does not have a place in the doctrine for birth-based status. But the sharpness and tone of the critique we see of the caste system in *Nīlakeci* does not seem to appear in too many texts of later periods that one has come across, but it would be important to dig some more to find out any similar (Jaina text) with similar views on caste as in the Tamil *Nīlakeci*. But some more research will need to be undertaken to give a clearer picture as to the status (existence or otherwise) of caste in the Jaina tradition over time.
42. As I imagined Nīlakeci to be saying to me.
43. There is some discussion on Kāraikkāl Ammaiyār later in the book.
44. Hari Satya Bhattacharya, 1966, pp.316-317.
45. Padmanabh Jaini, 1998, pp. 141-142.
46. Simply typing 'Nīli villuppāṭṭu', on a search engine on internet, took me to the relevant pages; some are live performances recorded, some are just audio records, on www.youtube.com.
47. Perhaps the author means, 'syncretic' or 'composite' here?
48. Bhattacharya, 1976, pp. 204-205.
49. Ibid., p. 205.

2

BEING, OR THE PAIN OF POSSESSING

Nīli, the Pēy Stories

Scenario 1—Villuppāṭṭu version of the Nīli Story (Genre and the Background)

> *'paṇṭu toṭṭu iṉṟu varai-intap poruḷḷōr payamāykkūṟum*
> *caṇṭāḷa nīliyeṉṉum cāmuṇṭi isakkiyaruḷ*
> *koṇṭu aṭiyēṉ avaḷ kataiyai kutūkalamāypāṭumentaṉ*
> *aṇṭaiyile niṉṟavarum veku āṉantamāyk keṭkaccolvēṉ'*[1]
>
> [I beseech all those gathered, here to enjoy
> the story of Caṇṭāla Nīli, Cāmuṇṭa isakki (yakṣi)
> who filled people with fear, since time immemorial
> which I sing with pleasure
> seeking her grace]

This may be called a wandering tale since the author is not known and also because it is open to interpretations, additions and deletions, but with a firm base on which these changes can be made. The *villuppāṭṭu* comes in the genre of a performative ballad and in that sense, an audience, a performative context and space are important elements for this genre, as also, the *villuppāṭṭukkārar* (the performer/storyteller). In the case of the Paḻayaṉūr Nīli story, it is supposed to have been performed in the Isakkiyamman temple of Palayanur village during a summer festival (*kōṭai viḻā*) sometime in the months of March-April.[2]

Speaking of how this version came to light, Shanmugasundaram says that he procured the Nīli story in the form of a handwritten manuscript from the *Villukkārar* (bow singers) of Kanyakumari district, Ishak and Kannanceri Shankaranarayanan. In the edited version which I have referred to here, the author compares the handwritten manuscript and a 1934 published version called *Muppandal Isakkiyammaṉ Katai* (story), highlighting similarities and differences. It may be mentioned in this connection that the village Muppandal (which has a temple apparently dedicated to this Isakkiyammaṉ, where they also have a tradition of singing this story) had Jaina settlements since the early centuries CE.

The villuppāṭṭu performers' group comprises of a lead singer, *pulavar* or *aṉṉāvi*, a second singer and instrumentalists, who play the *kudam* (shaped like a pot), *jaalra* (like a cymbal) and *uduku* (a small hand-held drum). The *pulavar* is central and plays the *villu* (bow); he is expected to be an expert with a sense of humour and timing, to keep the audience hooked for hours. The performance begins with a prayer and invocation.

About the tradition of the bow-song, Stuart Blackburn writes:

> The most traditional form of the bow song exists in Kanya Kumari District (approximately 600 square miles and one million people) which surrounds the tip of India This narrative and musical tradition takes its name from the bow (six to twelve feet long) around which the performers sit as they sing. The Tamil bow-song group has a minimum of five performers, each of whom both sings and plays an instrument. The lead singer plays the bow by striking its cattle-hide string with a pair of thin sticks that shakes both the variously pitched bells hanging from the bow's wooden frame and the tiny bells attached to the sticks. The four other performers each play one of the following instruments: a small hourglass-shaped drum, a large, earthen pot (played by slapping its open mouth with a paddle made from a sheath of the areca nut tree), a pair of slim wooden blocks, and a pair of brass (or bronze) hand cymbals. To this basic set of five performers, one or two more with hand cymbals or wooden blocks

may be added. The lead singer may be either male or female; if the singer is female, another woman accompanies her as an assistant. All other performers are male. The performers come from the low and middle-level castes in the area (Natar, Tevar, Konar) and from low-status segments of higher castes (Pillai). The tradition is not supported by the numerically insignificant Brāhmiṇ castes in the area, nor by those segments of high-status castes that emulate them for reasons of social prestige. It is also rarely found among Untouchable castes because they lack the financial resources to patronise their own singing groups. It is a strongly oral tradition, though many of the narratives, which number at least a hundred in the local area alone, are also inscribed on palm leaf...The only performance context for the tradition is a festival (kotai) held at local temples in villages and the few towns in the area; it is not performed in temples dedicated to pan-Indian deities (Siva, Vishnu, Ganesha, or local forms of Parvati, wife of Siva)... In fact, a bow-song performance is itself an act of worship; a correct recitation of a deity's history is an extended invocation. The primary purpose of a performance is thus to summon a deity to manifest its presence and display its power by possessing its medium... Divine-descent deities and their birth stories will be referred to as Type A; cut-up spirits and their death stories as Type B...In Type A stories, the action is set in Kailasa, the heavenly mountain where Siva rules among various gods, goddesses, and other celestials. Such a setting immediately throws the story into the distant and otherworldly realm of pan-Indian mythology. Following a description of fantastic Kailasa, Type A narratives move to the birth of the main character. More important deities are born directly from Siva or Parvati (from their sweat, blood, eye, or throat); lesser ones emerge from a sacrificial fire. Other motifs are also used but the common feature among them all is that birth is supernatural and therefore painless. By contrast, Type B narratives are set in the human world and pinpointed in local geography. After a brief description of the fertility and beauty of the land, the action is quickly centered in a named (and usually known) village and in a particular caste. Sometimes, in the case of a story supported by a small kin group, even the names of specific ancestors are used. Within this historical setting, the birth of the protagonist is presented in social and physiological detail. A barren woman, ridden by guilt and ridiculed by family and friends, undertakes a difficult pilgrimage to several temples where she endures long hours of deprivations during worship for a child. Then follow her months of pregnancy, her intense labour, fears, screams, and finally the excruciating pain of birth.[3] In short, in these Type B narratives, birth is human and it is painful.[4]

The story of Nīli, the *pēy of Paḻayaṉūr,* is one of an uncontrollable, vengeful possession-woman (spirit). Before moving ahead, it would be worthwhile to note that wherever there are shrines to Nīli, the iconography shows a goddess with blood-stained teeth, holding a child at her waist, though not all versions of the story have a child character, even if in some there is no real child, a 'fake' child is created by Nīli, as will be seen, later.

Blackburn refers to stories in the bow-song tradition of the 'cut-up spirits', within which would figure the Nīli *pēy* stories. In his study, of course, there is no reference to the Nīli stories; he had recorded some of the other popular bow-song stories based on which he analysed this popular tradition within Tamil religiosity. He says

> These stories tell how humans (like Nātaṉ Cāmi) are born on earth, are treacherously killed or forced to commit suicide, and then are 'taken' by Śiva to Kailāsa where they are given new names. Now deified, the heroes/gods return to earth (like the birth deities) to avenge their murders and to win worship. Significantly, this last segment is extremely short in texts; instead, the death and ascent to Kailāsa is the focus in both narrative and performance. Yet, the actual act of deification itself in the narrative is uneventful, usually on the order of, "They went to Kailāsa to receive boons from Śiva." ...But one should not expect that the deification process would be any more important in these narratives. For Śiva, in granting new

> names and boons, is only rubber-stamping what already has been conferred on the dead by their worshipers on earth. When fortune or misfortune is attributed to the spirit of a dead person, and when formal rituals are performed to him, that person is deified.[5]

What follows here is the narration of the story in the *villuppāṭṭu* structure, in the sequence as it is sung. It begins with invocation, with which I began this section, followed by a description, right at the beginning, of the beauty of Candana Naṅkai, the female protagonist and the priest falling in love with her. The *villuppāṭṭu* narrates the story in small sections/divisions devoted to each character of the story. The characters are introduced to the audience, as it were, with brief descriptions of each, the story flows through each of these characters. This version begins with the character description of the courtesan Candana Naṅkai who is the most important character in this Nīli story. And this is the way the singer describes Nambi's love.[6]

> In the beautiful Pa̱lakanallūr temple
> She works, lighting the lamps, the vēcai, Canta̱na Naṅkai
> A young unblemished woman with eyes shaped like two spears
> Which ensnare... daughter of the dāsi[7]
> ...One day...[8]

In the temple, their eyes met and he was besotted with her (*vaciyamāṉāṉ*, lit. came under her spell), and finishing his worship rituals quickly, followed her as she went out. And thus commenced the love story between the brāhmin priest and the *dāsi's* daughter; she would take Nambi home, indulging in sweet talk and establishing a bond with him at once, in spite of her mother's (who is referred to as 'old woman') counsel (*kiḻaviyin pōtanaikaḷ*); a mother, who depended on her daughter for livelihood reasons, tells her, 'money does not come freely to us' and that only a resourceful man who can pay should be brought home and not just everybody. The words do not affect Candana Naṅkai, who gradually falls in love with Nambi. The 'old woman', or the mother, plays a crucial role in this story; in fact, she becomes the reason for the tragic story, in many senses.

The details of the story in the sequence of its events as sung by the *villukkārar* (in the version I have referred) are as follows:

The brāhmin Nambi[9], the priest of the Po<u>nn</u>ūr[10] temple and the *dāsi* (temple dancer), Candana Naṅkai have entered into a relationship. The old woman, her mother, also prepares a potion which is administered to the priest on the sly (through her daughter), which manipulates his mind[11] and he begins to shower all the wealth of the temple on the daughter. Over time, he evades his duties as temple priest and and what is more, splurges the temple wealth on her. In due course, the wealth has dwindled, and the priest (who is referred to in this version as *vedi*), comes home to Candana Naṅkai filled with love, but without any money. He is told that Candana Naṅkai is lying ill with fever. But finding her in her mother's house, sewing, he entreats her to say if she desires him, he would at once call for the *pandits* (to marry her). Hearing this, the mother charges him of being crafty enough to wean her daughter away. She then tells him if he still wants her daughter, he has to do certain things for two months with diligence: he must take care of the daughter on a fine bed, administer medicines, spoon-feed her large measures of horsegram pudding and eggs and chicken wih rice, topped with clarified butter and goat curry. And she blames him for bringing her daughter to this state, with her body all dried up and wasted and that they have been fooled by him, not knowing he has no money. Hearing that, he quickly rushes to get all the things demanded of him, and waits, "like a scabied-dog, that *brāhmiṇ*", that the old woman would give him his lover.

But when he does return with the things demanded of him, he overhears the old woman commanding her daughter not to entertain Nambi anymore, as he is a pauper. Angry and dejected, Nambi leaves the place in a huff and is wondering where he would go, for there is no point returning to the temple anymore, after all this has happened and he decides to leave for another town. In the meantime, Candana Naṅkai, who is in love with him and can see all the things that he did for her, follows after him and entreats him to return to her, and give a damn to her vicious mother's words. She pleads with him to stay with her as she cannot think of another man in his place. While she pleads with him thus, what is Nambi thinking and what happens next?

> Banished from my house and the temple, now comes she,
> Shouldn't I kill her now,
> here, amidst the *kaḷḷi*'s shadows?
> While they ate betel and nuts,
> she sought him to braid her hair
> and that vicious man, while braiding her hair,
> strangled her.

Relieving her body of ornaments, which he surmised, would amount to 'six lakhs', he thought, 'with this treasure, I can stay home and not work at all' and so piled up all the ornaments. Leaving her there, he started off, but then, in a while, on second thoughts, he returned to the spot where he left her, and picking up a huge stone, crushed her face with it, watching her writhe in pain and die.

> Curse of the prostitute:
> I came here, with a pure heart, to make up (with you)
> alas, dear man, you reduced me to a corpse!
> Not a thought you spared, thinking of your own future in a
> foreign land
> with this *kaḷḷi* tree as witness
> oh god, this deed I shall avenge!

Over there, Candana Naṅkai's mother ordered her son to bring back his sister, who, she knew must have followed after the temple priest. Finding his sister's smashed skull in the forest, the brother wailed:

> Aah, that evil brāhmiṇ, the demon!
> mercilessly killed my sister

like a demon, he destroyed the guileless woman
without gratitude; that cruel man, with a heart of stone
has dug the earth and disappeared
but will the brāhmiṇ escape the revenge of Palakanallur?
oh god, I seek the boon to avenge the misdeed;
On that very stone that crushed his sister
he slammed his head, the brother,
and reached the abode of lord Śiva

What did Nambi do? Having committed the murder, he walked away, and after a while, thought at some leisure, 'after killing a prostitute, there is no more obstacle left for me now; I can go to Kashi now and start a pawn business'. And he walked with a song in his heart, thinking he will find out the cost of the jewels he was carrying. But as he carried on, looking for water to drink at the well, a poisonous snake bit him and he died on the spot.

The story of rebirth ('*maṟupiṟavi vaṟalāṟu*')[12]

The three of them are reborn. Their second births are described in this section. Candana Naṅkai and her brother are born to the wife of a Chōḻa chieftain/king (*Chōḻamaṇṇan*) as twins, Nīlaṉ and Nīli, while Nambi is reborn as Āṉaṉtan, the son of a Chettiar[13] pawn broker in Kaveripumpattinam. Nīlaṉ and Nīli, however, are not 'normal' children and actually retain an element of the '*pēy*' in them as they have both died unnatural deaths in the previous birth. They act as normal children during the day but assume the *pēy* form by night, with an insatiable urge to eat flesh. They finish off almost all the cattle and livestock of the village in this manner. Naturally, there is chaos and the people seek their father, the chieftain's, intervention. The father gets to know, in the course of time, that his two little children are the culprits and, sad though he is, orders them to be banished to a forest. Nīlaṉ and Nīli are left by the trunk of a Neem tree in a forest. On a certain day, the people of Palakanallūr (the place name alternates in different versions as Pa<u>l</u>aya<u>n</u>ūr and Palakanallūr) fetch the Neem tree for constructing a temple at their village. They are unaware of the presence of Nīla<u>n</u> in the tree's hollow and they realise this only after the tree has been brought to the temple site. Out of fear, the priest of the temple conducts a *hōmam* (ritual fire) and burns Nīla<u>n</u> (or the Neem tree where he resides). Nīli, who gets to know of this, is seething with anger and promises to avenge the death of her brother in due course—since her first 'victim' would be Nambi of the past birth.

In the meantime, the Ceṭṭi's son, Āna<u>n</u>tan has grown up. One day, he decides to leave for Palakanallūr to sell gold and precious stones and help his father in his business. His father dissuades him from going there as soothsayers had foretold that this place is the nemesis for Āna<u>n</u>tan, but he, of course, allays their fears and proceeds. He is given a special dagger to carry with him for his safety. The *villuppāṭṭu* version describes ominous signs (that would forewarn audiences of what was coming next)—for instance, new pots breaking to pieces, a blind man crossing Āna<u>n</u>tan's path, and so forth. As he walks past all these and into the forest stretch between Kaveripumpattinam and Palakanallūr, Nīli catches up with him, as was destined. She is a beautiful maiden, and seems to be lying in wait for him:

> *'kaḷḷiyanta nīli kaṭuñci<u>n</u>amāy va<u>n</u>amalaiyāy*
> *oḷipi<u>r</u>anta cevvāyum uyarnta kumi<u>l</u>mūkka<u>l</u>akum*
> *telintoru ku<u>l</u>aia<u>l</u>akum cī<u>r</u>pu<u>n</u>ainta nakaia<u>l</u>akum*
> *kuḷirnta mukaccuntariyāy koḷainīli tō<u>n</u><u>r</u>uvaḷām'* [14]
>
> [The vengeful Nīli (*koḷainīli*) appears,
> bitter with pain and anger,
> bright as the vermilion-hued sun rising over forests and
> mountains,
> one with aquiline nose, soft, tender neck,
> bedecked with ornaments,
> with a pleasing beauty]

In the forest, Nīli addresses Āna͟ntan as '*atta͟n*'[15]. She gives him the feeling that she has been waiting for him since long:

> Oh handsome one, dear one, oh, have you come, my *atta͟n!*

Hearing him being invoked by that suffix, Ceṭṭi asks her:

> Oh beautiful one, who are you? What are you doing here
> in this forest alone, addressing me thus, waiting for me
> pray do not stay,
> what do you want? See, you are a young woman, too

Nīli replies:

> Does it suffice for you to realise I am a young woman, oh *atta͟n*!
> do you not realise you have forgotten me?
> didn't you come to see me and marry me the same day?
> and then she said, please give me some lime-paste for my betel leaves[16]

There are two versions of the conversation in *Pal͟ayan͟ūr Nīli,* one of which is poetic and filled with sarcasm:

> *'cuṇṇāmpu tārīrō ceṭṭiyāre cuṇṇāmpu...*
> *cūṭum maṇalum poṭiyum karukutu...*
> *paṇṇik koṭukkum paricappaṇam pōla'*

> Give me the lime-paste, Oh Ceṭṭiyār, the lime-paste
> give me the lime-paste,
> in this moment, under this scorching sun[17]
> the soil burns, and the betel-nuts melt!
> the wound festers and thirsts for water
> the eyes and the mouth bleed for the taste of
> the delicate blend of betel-leaf with nuts and lime-paste
> just as young men eagerly wait for the wedding gift [or to get married][18]

Though Āna͟ntan refutes her charge that he is married to her, he gives her a close look and is reminded of the soothsayer's prediction; he is trembling in fear as he understands this to be his nemesis—death at the hands of a *pēy*-Nīli. There is an extended conversation between the two in the *villuppāṭṭu*, where she charges him with adultery, saying he had left her and his child for the 'other woman'. Scolding her, and fearing for his life, Ānaṉtan walks quickly ahead, in an effort to reach Palakanallur before dark. Nīli follows relentlessly. But she reaches the place, assuming the form of a woman with a child, ahead of him. There she pleads with the village *veḷḷāḷa* elders to reunite her with her husband. She weaves a story of the courtesan for whom he left her and their child to their fate. She pleads with them to make him see sense. When confronted, Ānaṉtan tries hard to convince the *veḷḷāḷas* that she is a *pēy* and not his wedded wife. The *veḷḷāḷas* ask him to spend the night at the village temple with her and the child, assuring him nothing untoward will happen. They also give a word to him that should something happen to him, as he feared, all of them would give up their lives by jumping into a burning pyre. They also take away his sword from him as a means to protect the woman they feel responsible towards. They tell Ānaṉtan that they would return the sword to him the next day if he spent the night with this wife. Now the Ceṭṭiyār is without the protective sword and totally vulnerable.

Nīli and Ānaṉtan are made to spend the night in a room (*maṇṭapam*) within the village temple. Nīli kills him and drinks his blood. And to ward off the *veḷḷāḷas* who are lying in wait outside trying to be protective, Nīli sings a lullaby to the (non-existent) child. Interestingly, the lullaby is full of hidden meanings and metaphors that reveal what she is up to:

> *'paccai paccai niṟattōṉē*
> *pāl vaṭiyum mēṇiyōṉē*
> *ucciyile pūttōṉē uṭampeḷḷām pāmalāṉē*
> *....mulniṟainta mēṇiyōṉē...*
> *nīlaṉ maṟumāṉē....*
> *cittiraiyil piṟantavaṉē ceṭṭiyineṉcil pōykiṭṭāḷ*
> *pōtumaṭā oṉ ācai—eṉ puṇakkam tīrntataṭā...'*[19]

Addressing her (imaginary) child, she sings:

[You (my child) of green colour, with body oozing milk[20]
full of thorns (*mulniṟainta mēṇiyōṉē*)...
(you who are the) nephew of Nīlaṉ (Nīli's brother)[21]
...one born in the month of *cittirai*[22],
it is enough to reach[23] the ceṭṭi's heart,
to fulfill your desire and mine (for) revenge...]

It is interesting that Nīli refers to the splurge plant as her child—considering she is a *pēy*. In normal connotation, '*pālvaṭiyum mēṇi*' as a term is used to refer to a fair and soft skinned body, but here, since Nīli describes the child, to begin with, strangely, as one of green colour—'*paccai paccai niṟattōṉē*' she essentially compares the child with the poisonous green plant with milk like substance oozing from its body/leaves.

After having killed Āṉaṉtan, Nīli is ready for her second revenge, avenging the killing of her brother Nīlan. She assumes the form of an old woman, this time as the mother of Āṉaṉtan, who comes to the village looking for her son. By this time, the veḷḷāḷas have learnt of the murder of Āṉaṉtan. The 'mother' breaks into a long *oppāri* (a dirge sung at the death of a person, a practice still followed by some communities). The 70 veḷḷāḷas, true to their word, jump into the fire and give up their lives. But Nīli's fury does not end there. She now proceeds to destroy the whole village, assuming different forms. Thus:

'*kiḻavi kumari āṉāḷ...kumari tayirkāri āṉāḷ ...*'[24]

[The old woman became a young woman, the young woman turned into a curd seller...]

As a curd-seller, she sells poisoned curd to the village womenfolk and kills them all. In this version, unlike in other versions, the revenge of Nīli assumes dramatic proportions, with her ending up killing everyone—remotely, indirectly, and directly—connected to her past and her immediate life story. The womenfolk, for instance, have no role to play in the death of Nīlaṉ, her brother, yet they are killed. The idea is to portray the unbridled and uncontrollable anger of Nīli, which is capable of consuming all that comes in her way. Nīli is the pēy to be dreaded by all. This kind of revenge, it may be noted, is also present in the Kaṇṇaki story (in that famous tale of the lay anklet, *Cilappatikāram*) where she burns down a whole city of Madurai in rage over the wrongful judgment meted out to her husband, Kōvalaṉ, who was ordered to be executed, by the Pandyan king on charges of stealing his queen's anklet. In the case of Nīli, though, she is constructed as a dreaded *pēy*, so as to be remembered for generations after her story has been 'played' out. Nīli must be a larger than life figure. A wronged woman forced to become a *pēy*, seeking revenge for the wrong done to her. So, finally, "*Nīli naṉaittatē muṭittāḷ*"[25]—Nīli accomplished what she set out to do.

The *villuppāṭṭu* does not end with the revenge of Nīli. After completing her task, Nīli prays to Śiva *(īcaṉ)* and he commands her to be a 'good' woman, henceforth, and return to the village/ *nāṭu* and help people:

> *nāṭṭiṉilē iṉi ceṉṟu nalla kuṇacīliyeṉa*
> *tēṭṭamuḷḷa uṉ aṭimai tesattār taṉaiyaṭuttu*
> *vāṭṭamiṉṟi avarkuṟaiya tīrttāḷvāy pōveṉṟār...*[26]

Śiva tells Nīli,

> Go back to your country (*nāṭu*) as a virtuous woman,
> help those who seek your blessings
> and relieve their suffering...

The bow-song thus ends with an everlasting dimension to the story:–

> *'aṉṟu mutal iṉṟuvaṟai ammaiyavaḷ*
> *paḻavūril niṉṟu nammai kāttuvarum nilamaiccolla veṉṟālē*
> *oṉṟāḷum muṭivatalla uttamarē ulakōrē*
> *naṉṟāka yivaḷkkataiyai nāḷtōṟum pāṭuvīrē.'*[27]

> And hence, since then, we pray to the
> mother (ammai) residing in Paḻavūr, that

she may be our protector
good people of this world never stop
singing well, her story

So, her story does not die.
Blackburn writes:

> 'In the bow song tradition, and in other local cults, the deified dead are the most powerful gods and goddesses; they may lack the status and authority of the other deities with divine origins, but they have a more immediate power. They are as powerful as death itself, perhaps because they met it in its rawest form; in other words, the deified dead have become the violence they experienced. That force, driven inside them at death, then becomes a source that worshippers can call on to counteract other elemental forces of disease, disaster, and even death.'[28]

There are some noticeable changes between the printed version (published in 1934) and the handwritten manuscript (which was narrated earlier). I highlight some of these here.[29] The printed version does not give the name of the temple dancer (Candana Nañkai). She is referred to as '*vilaikkeṭukkum mu̱raikkāri vēcai*' (meaning prostitution as her vocation) in the handwritten manuscript and as '*kūttāṭum mu̱raikkāri*' (dancer) in the printed version. The lullaby she sings for her (non-existent) child is also different in each. In the handwritten manuscript it starts as '*paccai paccai ni̱rattō̱ṉē pāl vaṭiyum mēṇiyō̱ṉē...*' whereas, in the printed version it begins with '*vīṭṭilē pi̱rakkāmal veṭṭavaḻiyilē pi̱rantā̱ṉē*' (my child, not born in a home, but out in the open/by the wayside). After taking her revenge on her lover of a previous birth, Nīli's inclination towards god (Śiva) and the latter sending her back to the earth to protect the righteous is specific to the oral and handwritten manuscript version alone and not found in the printed version used by the editor Shanmugasundaram. Importantly, in the printed version, Nīli asks people of the village (after her vengeance) to build a temple for her at Muppandal. She protects Palakanallur. This is not mentioned in the handwritten manuscript. Both the versions, however, are in compliance with the fact that the 'deity' Nīli protects Palakanallur.

An interesting element in the performative tradition is a prose rendition after the song is sung, by some of the balladeers. According to Shanmugasundaram, only a few *villukkārars* (bow-songsters) add this to their performance at the end. What is important for us, though, is the implied meaning in this prose version of Nīli—which obviously, gives a brāhmiṇical rendering to her story and is a later interpretation to the oral narrative (and thereby added to the performances) by a few singers, not all. This prose text[30] is as follows:

> Today Nīli resides in Pa<u>l</u>aya<u>n</u>ūr, but at a certain time in the past, she saw a temple priest diligently offering prayers everyday. Nīli accosted him and asked him to offer prayers to her. The priest knew of her prowess. So he placed the thorn of the strychnine tree (*kaḷḷi*) on her hair to control her power and her arrogance. Though Nīli tried a lot, she could not remove these from her hair. So she transformed herself into a maiden and began to work in the priest's house as an obedient house help. The timing was just right, as the priest's daughter, Cūli, had just arrived home to deliver her first baby, as was the practice. Nīli befriended the daughter and looked for an opportune moment. One day, she requested Cūli to remove lice from her hair. Cūli, on seeing the thorns in her hair, asked Nīli what to do with those. Nīli requested her to remove them. Cūli did as she was told. Since these were hard to remove, she removed them with her teeth. Soon as this was done, Nīli became a demon again and killed Cūli and her child in the womb and ate it. The priest returned to see this horrible sight and decided right then to build a temple for Nīli, humbly accepting her power, and also in order to protect others from her anger. Nīli has been propitiated in Pa<u>l</u>aya<u>n</u>ūr since that time.

According to the author, the Isakki amman temple at Muppandal is in front of the temple dedicated to Nīli as the goddess here has bloodied teeth and is shown with a child at her waist, perhaps symbolising Nīli.[31] He believes that the Nīli worship here could have changed in later periods to Isakki worship.

Nīli's 'Site'/Space

The 'site' of the Nīli (the possession woman/spirit and her story at the same time) is Pa̲layan̲ūr, near Ālankāṭu. Now this is also the Ālankāṭu (Tiruvalangadu) of the Tevāram (Śaivite) hymns. It is surrounded by *brahmadeya* and *agrahāra* (brāhmin land grants) settlements (as evidenced from a few inscriptions found in connection with a Śiva temple in the area). By extension, a brāhmiṇical context surrounds the site. It may be important to analyse this site a little. It is virtually a 'no-man's land'—as almost all other versions that are concerned with the Nīli story (the bow song, the Tevāram version and the Jaina *Nīlakeci* text) mention the area as such. It is perhaps a tract of scrubland or a patch of forest between two places—two villages or a village and a town. That is the site where the spirit (Nīli) dwells. It is intriguing that in almost all Tamil folklore, or tales of possession sprits, the *pēy*, the spirit (almost always a woman) dwells in this kind of site, an in-between land. Why is this site always connected to something dark, sinister or pathos-filled and evil? Is alienation built into this kind of a construct? To 'keep-out-of-bounds'? But looking at it from another perspective, it is also a place for 'transcendence'—from one form to the other. Kāraikkāl Ammaiyār transforms (in the same kind of site) into a saint from a ('chaste') housewife;[32] Kaṇṇaki goes through a similar 'transcendence' (though not in this above manner) in this kind of site—in fact her separation from Kōvala̲n has a lot to do with this kind of a site. Kuṇṭalakeci, the wronged princess, too, goes through a transformation from a murderer (of a cheat-husband) to a Buddhist nun in a place such as this—a mid-way land. In fact, the site itself can be seen to have an equivalent of '*pālai*' ecotype (*tiṇai*) of early Tamil Caṅkam poetry: a place that does not have as specific a characteristic as the other ecotypes, such as *mullai* (pastureland), or *marutam* (agrarian tract). It is a place that travellers pass through, and metaphorically, a 'movement from, or towards'.

The importance of this site also lies in the fact that precisely for this reason it becomes a place that gives itself readily to the notion of getting *control of.* The oral performers who keep the stories of these sites (and hence the site itself) alive also, perhaps not incidentally, belong to a certain rung of the social order, mostly the last rung. The site of the folklore, then, interestingly becomes 'their' site, the one they relate to, which is the periphery—of land tenure, ownership, resources, temple, brāhmiṇical religiosity, too. Much of the ambivalence of the site, and the darkness of the tales, come from this connection, as well. Hence, in an obviously brāhmiṇical version of the Nīli story, as written about in the Tēvāram hymns, 'control' of Nīli becomes a crucial element. Metaphors of control abound. And not incidentally, a temple to the consort of Śiva is also built in this site and the priest finally controls Nīli, the *pēy*. It is also the site where Śiva dances his 'cosmic' dance to defeat (in an assumed obvious male gesture) Kāli, and thus 'humbles' her (characteristically by raising his legs in the course of the wild dancing in a way that Kāli is unable to repeat after him). Control of the mythic folkloric element is perhaps just the subtext. In the Nīli case, it is not merely suppression of a wandering tale, a wandering woman/possession woman, but also a form (the *villuppāṭṭu* genre and its social base) in some sense, which both the Tēvāram hymns and the Jaina text *Nīlakeci* do, although in different ways. In the Jaina text, a possession spirit of a popular folklore is given an affirmative voice and a character of a philosopher, while in the Tēvāram works, she is ultimately brought under control by a priest and remains, yet, an ambivalent figure, not completely suppressed, but not as dominant as she was supposed to have been in the Nīli story.

For me this story suggests conflict between a certain kind of organised religion–temple worship and a priest refusing to propitiate a local goddess and a folk cult. The motif of putting thorns on the head of a woman deity/or *pēy* shows an obvious attempt at controlling: either the sexuality and prowess of a powerful local, fearsome, vindictive goddess, or, the powers of the local cult itself. There is also implied prejudice about who is to be propitiated and who should not be. Nīli's ambivalent nature is obviously not welcome in a religion that the priest belongs to. Interestingly, his daughter is named Cūli (another name for the mother goddess in the Tamil country). However, it is clear that the popularity and local acceptance/acknowledgement of Nīli have far overpowered that of any goddess in that particular region to be 'controlled' for long. The story's end—which is at once cruel and fearsome—speaks of what ensues for those who do not recognise her powers. And what is feared is to be worshipped, as the priest realises. And this Nīli becomes a deity—one of the many village deities—of Pal̠ayan̠ūr worshipped and feared (or worshipped because she is feared). The relationship between Cūli and Nīli and the removing of the thorns from her hair with her teeth also signify elements of the sexual and intimate, falling in line with a series of stories of folk goddesses and their women devotees in Tamilnadu, where the relationship between the woman (devotee?) and the goddess are intimate and very often even a male companion (perhaps husband) is not given/allowed space in the relationship and, in fact, often causes a certain kind of discontent and tension between the husband and the wife (or lovers). [33] Though an analysis of this phenomenon is out of the purview of this book, it does call for further exploration.

Scenario 2—Nīli Nāṭakam

> *'pal̠utilāvaṇikan̠uyir par̠ittavan̠āḷvēḷāḷar*
> *el̠upatin̠marerimul̠ki yir̠akkacceyta ā ā*
> *pal̠ayan̠ūrnīlikatai pāramītinānpāṭa*
> *al̠akumayilēr̠ivarum ār̠umukavan̠ tuṇaiyē-jeyajeyā'*
>
> (lines 1-8)[34]

[As I sing, with a heavy burden
the story of that Pal̲ayan̲ūr Nīli
who took the life of the innocent merchant
causing the seventy veḷḷāḷas to to jump into the burning pyre
I seek the protection of the six-faced one, with the spear,[35]
astride the beautiful peacock.]

This version comes from a printed copy—the author, date, place of publication, etc. are missing.[36] This version and the *Pal̲ayan̲ūr Nīli* (*PN*), incidentally, are the only two copies of the Nīli story available today in printed versions. *Nīli Nāṭakam* (*NN*), as the title suggests, is meant for a performance. It is structured as a full-length dance drama with each character and scene described in extraordinary detail, something missing in the bow-song version, which is based on an oral narrative and perhaps meant as a shorter ritual performance. *NN* is also about a woman turning into a *pēy*, as being born as Nīli in her second birth and avenging her murder by killing the man in question. Only, unlike in the previous version, Nīli here is not a temple dancer in her previous birth, but the wife of a brāhmiṇ priest. *NN*, right at the beginning, sets a context, which may be its performative context, or the context/site/setting of the story itself: the Ekambaranathar temple in Kanchipuram. The entry of the characters, one following the other, happens only after the *kaṭṭiyakāran̲* (the panegyrist; herald), along with the priest of the temple has arrived, to an announcement in a *pallavi* (starting lines) set to *raga* Mohana:

'kaṭṭiyakāran̲ vantān̲, ciñkāramāka kaṭṭiyakāran̲ vantān̲.'

NN begins with invocatory verses to all the major gods and goddesses: *ār̲umukan̲* (Subrahmaṇya), Tirumāl (Viṣṇu), Pārvati, Mahālakṣmi, Śiva, Saraswati and the 'great people'/ great 'souls'. Very interestingly, it also offers salutations to Subramanya Bharati, the Tamil revolutionary poet.[37] Perhaps as a performative genre, these were included as a ritual. Inclusion of Subramanya Bharati means little else than the fact that this particular version may have once been performed either during, or after the colonial times. Adding Bharati's name would give the performance a nationalist/contemporary edge, as well. And perhaps the play/drama used the concept of invoking prominent people of the times. Interestingly, it does not begin with the invocation to Ganeśa, who is invoked later, with an entire śloka devoted to him. After the invocatory verses is the *maṅkalam* section, where again gods and goddesses (including Nīli) are offered prayers. The invocation to Nīli is as follows:

> *'muntiya pi̱rappi̱nil nintaiyāykolaiceyta*
> *añtaṇan̲ceykaiyai cintaikoṇṭē*
> *pintiyapi̱rappi̱nil antapa̱laiyan̲ūril*
> *vantupa̱livāṅkuñ cuntarikkum (maṅkalam)*'[38]
>
> [Invocations to the beautiful woman who,
> thinking of her disgraceful murder at the hands of the priest in a former birth,
> returned in the next birth to Pa̱layan̲ūr, seeking revenge]

The entire *NN* is set to Carnatic ragas and *tālas*, each character's entry and each part of the story is set to and sung in a particular raga also mentioned in the text. In the verses, the singer seeks blessings from gods and goddesses to sing the story of Pa̱layan̲ūr Nīli, who is described variously: as one responsible for the death of the '70 *veḷḷāḷars*' and her vengeance on the merchant, as one whose fame has spread far and wide and continues to do so apart from every other characteristic feature of her story.

The story in *NN* goes as follows:-

The priest of a temple, a married man, squanders all his wealth on a courtesan (here neither the courtesan's, nor his wife's names are mentioned). Fellow priests complain to the *dharmakartā* (benefactor/caretaker) of the temple, asking that the priest be thrown out as he is failing in his duties to the temple. The priest, meanwhile, sends his wife away to her mother's place in Mayilapur (in present-day Chennai) and continues his 'wayward' ways. In this version, the courtesan pleads with him to spend time with his wife and asks him not to send her away. But he does not heed her advice. Meanwhile, the temple *dharmakartā* asks him to leave his job, unless he leaves the courtesan and brings back his wife and stays with her. The priest has no other way but to bring back his wife to retain his job. He goes to Mayilapur, tells his wife he plans to begin a new life with her and asks her to return. Her parents do not trust him and hence send her brother along on their return journey to Kanchipuram. His wife, meanwhile, is pregnant with the priest's child. On the way back towards Kanchipuram, in the forest, the priest sends his brother-in-law to fetch some water to drink. And in this time, with the sole objective of taking all of his wife's jewellery, he starts an argument. He questions her about her pregnancy and accuses her of un-chaste behaviour. In a fit of anger he strangles her and pushes her into a well, after snatching her jewels. He then goes to meet the courtesan with these jewels. But she throws him out. Dejected, he walks away, only to be bitten by a snake and die. Meanwhile, the wife's brother, seeing the plight of his sister, takes his own life, as well. The siblings are re-born as Nīli and Nīlaṉ to a couple called Sabhapati Mudaliyar and Paccaiammāḷ of Paḻayaṉūr, who are blessed with children after several prayers and offerings to various gods. The brāhmiṇ priest, meanwhile, is re-born in the house of Nagendra Chetti in Kanchipuram. Their birth is made out to be an extraordinary event in *NN*, with both the women bearing these children (the siblings and the brāhmiṇ priest, to their respective mothers) after long hours of labour. In the case of Nīli and Nīlaṉ (the twins) the midwife actually praises her prowess to their mother. She says she had helped with the birth of many great children, such as Indrajit (son of the epic *Rāmāyaṇa*'s characters, Manṭōṭari and Rāvaṇa), Śakuni and Duryōdhana (from the epic, *Mahābhārata*) and she encourages the mother that more labour pain indicates the birth of more illustrious children:

kēḷum paccaiammā inta kaṟpanōyikku nī payappaṭa vēṇṭām
nāṉeṉṉa lēcāṉavaḷā anta rāvaṇaṉ peṉṭāṇṭi maṇṭōtari
intiracittaṉaipperṟakālattilum cakuṉi māmaṉpiṟantakālattilum
anta kāntāri turiyōtaṉaṉ mutalāṉa nūṟṟuvarai ppeṟṟa kālattilum
nāntān maruttuvam
pārttēṉ. atanālētāṉ avvaḷavu yōkiya piḷḷaikaḷeḷḷām
piṟantārkaḷ nalla vegumatikaḷum peṟṟēṉ[39]

Paccaimmā, do not fear this pain
do you think I am a simpleton? I have handled the deliveries
of Indirajit, son of Maṇṭōtari, Rāvaṇa's wife, and was there
during Cakuni uncle's times, when Gāndhāri bore hundred
children, beginning with Duryōdhanaṉ
isn't that why they all turned out to be such illustrious men!
I also delivered many illustrious women...

In a sense, the storyteller, or playwright, uses some satire here: all the characters mentioned here happen to be ones associated with negative qualities more than positive ones in the mainstream tradition. All of them turned out to be infamous. This lays the ground for the audience to presume what kind of offspring would the twins turn out to be, whom the midwife helps Paccaiammāḷ with. Until this time, the description had centered on Paccaiammāḷ and her husband offering several prayers, conducting yajñas (sacrificial rituals) for being blessed with an offspring. Finally, Paccaiammāḷ gives birth to Nīli and Nīlan. At the other end, the priest is born as Dinakara Cheṭṭi. Again, after many prayers and ritual offerings to brāhmiṇs, etc. When the brāhmiṇs cast his horoscope, they predict his death at the hands of a *pēy* of Paḻayaṉūr. But of course they find a solution too: a *yajña* (ritual sacrifice) to procure a special dagger that would protect the boy. But they warn that were he to place the dagger facing north (where Paḻayaṉūr is located) at any point of time, the *pēy* would consume him.

Years pass. Nīlaṉ and Nīli are growing up. Even in their child form, the siblings are creating havoc in the village, as every night they kill the livestock of their village out of hunger for flesh. The villagers find out and complain to their father. The father asks the children to be left in a forest and, just as in the *villuppāṭṭu* version, here too, after being thus left, Nīlaṉ gets killed and Nīli takes revenge on the villagers. Meanwhile, Dinakara Cheṭṭi (the priest of the former birth) gets married and has a child. One day, he decides to go to Paḻayaṉūr for business purposes. His wife—with their child—accompanies him till some distance, but he leaves her by the side of a lake in the forest while she is asleep as he does not wish to cause her inconvenience of a long journey. Nīli, who has been wandering about, waiting to get her revenge, accosts this woman and her child abandoned in the forest thus and questions her. She realises that the woman's husband is the one she is seeking to kill. She thus takes Dinakara Cheṭṭi's wife and child back to their home in Kancipuram, and on the way back to Paḻayaṉūr, assumes the form of his wife, produces a child by her powers, and rushes towards Paḻayaṉūr to get her revenge. Within no time she has caught up with Dinakara Cheṭṭi in the midst of the forest. She chides him for having left his wife and child alone in the forest. Cheṭṭi finds it unbelievable that his wife should catch up with him so soon. He is suddenly reminded of the prophecy of the brāhmiṇs about his death at the hands of the *pēy*, and he is scared. He is in a tearing hurry to reach Paḻayaṉūr. Nīli chases him, and on reaching Paḻayaṉūr, her entreaties to the village elders (the 70 *veḷḷāḷars)* follows—as in the other version, though here she has assumed the name and form of Cheṭṭi's spouse. The elders (from the Mudaliyar community here, specifically mentioned in the text) direct Chetti to stay with his wife and promise him that if something untoward happens, the 70 of them would jump into a burning pyre. Importantly, here the village to which the '*mudaliyars*' belong is given—adding to the number '70'. So, there were '60 from the village Ālankāṭu, 10 from Moṭṭūr'.[40]

However, in the same text it says, '10 from Paḻayaṉūr':

> *'...ivvitam pulampukinṟa ceṭṭiyārai*
> *ālañkāṭu mutaliyār aṟupatupērum mōṭūr mutaliyār p*
> *pattupērum āka eḻupatupēr mutalimārumtēṟṟi anta nīliyuṭanē*
> *aḻaittukkoṇṭupōy avvūrkāḷi koyilukkuḷḷē viṭṭuk*
> *katavai veḷippūṟṟum mūṭikoṇṭu ivaṟkaḷ ullai eṉṉa pēsu*
> *kiṉṟārkaḷō ataiyaṟiyavēṇṭumaṉṟu ūrkārkkum talaiyārikaḷ*
> *pattupēraiyaḻaittu avvālayattai cuṟṟikkāval vaittu ik*
> *kōvilukkuḷ ētāvatoru cukkural naṭakumāṉāl uṭaṉē van*
> *tu colluñkaleṉṟu uttiravuceytu taṅkaḷ taṅkaḷiruppiṭampōy*
> *cērntārkaḷ...'*[41]
>
> [In this manner, the sixty Mutaliyār of Ālankāṭu and ten of Mottūr, comprising seventy, took Nīli (and the Ceṭṭi) to the Kāḷi temple in that village and, locking them from outside, in order to hear their conversation,called ten village officials (*talaiyārikaḷ*) to stay guard outside against any untoward incident, they left for their respective homes.]

Nīli, meanwhile, continued to live up her role as Ceṭṭi's wife, knowing fairly well the there were people outside. While in the *villuppāṭṭu* version, she sang a meaningful lullaby to an imaginary child, here she calls out to the Mutaliyārs, saying all is well now and that the Ceṭṭi is about to go to sleep. The Mutaliyārs, happy with the state of events, retire to their homes. Soon thereafter, Nīli assumes the demon form and with her sharp teeth, bites into the Ceṭṭi's throat. Later, she assumes the form of the Ceṭṭi's mother and 'arrives' in the village, and blames the Mutaliyārs of the village for her son's death. True to their word, the seventy of them light a pyre and jump into the flames.

It is interesting to note that there are quite a few places where the *Mahābhārata* epic is invoked, directly or indirectly. For instance, when the mid-wife tells the pregnant wife of the Chōḻa king/feudatory that she had helped deliver the hundred sons of Kunti, and again there is an assembly where the veḷḷāḷars are gathered to give judgment about a case of adultery involving a washerman and his wife. At one point, the washerwoman (*vaṇṇātti*) tells the veḷḷāḷars (and this situation is created in order to focus on the veḷḷāḷars' 'famed' penchant for justice, and is running parallel, in the *NN*, to Nīli and Ceṭṭi's attempts to convince the veḷḷāḷars of the veracity, or otherwise, of the former's claim that she is his wife) that in Paḻayaṉūr, if her husband was having affairs simultaneously with women (she says, five in number) on the sly, least bothered about his own wife back home, what is the harm if the wife had relationships with those five men whose wives he was running after? So she asks them to give a decision accordingly.[42] It is an interesting point. And there seems to be a hint (with some element of sarcasm) here, at Draupadi's five husbands in the *Mahābhārata*.

Nīli in Popular Perceptions and Tamil Literature

Meanwhile, the story of Nīli found its way into idioms and proverbs in the Tamil country. And nearly all of them treat her persona with some amount of denigration.

"*Nīli kaṇṇīr nettiyile*"[43]—implies shedding crocodile tears.

"*Nīlikku kaṇṇīr nimaiyilē*"[44]—*signifies how Nīli's beauty is a cover-up act filled with falsehood.*

"*Nīlitanam*"; "*ivaḷ Paḻayaṉūr Nīliyammā!*"[45]—Both the phrases signify a crafty woman, or one causing pain to others.

> *vayyakattil palavuruvam pūntu naṅkai*
> *vayiṟuṇṭu vāyuṇṭṭu pēcamāṭṭāḷ*
> *kāciṉiyil vekupērai keṭutta nīli*
> *aiyamiṉṟi vāritanil vicayañ ceytu*
> *akilam ellāṅ tericanañ ceytāṉantippāḷ*
> *mey vēntar vīṇarukkum viruntuk kēṟpāḷ*
> *mētiṉiyi-livaḷāreṉ-ṟiyapuvīrē*[46]

This is a Tamil riddle: Tell me what on earth is this (creature), which has a stomach, but no feet; is small, with matted locks, and a mouth, but cannot speak and has no hands? It is (like) Nīli, who destroyed (the lives of) many on this earth, and it calls up for a feast, without reason...? The answer to this is apparently a kind of fish, according to Shanmugasundaram (Ibid. p. 39).

But there are also some other perceptions. For instance, in one of the Tamil dictionaries,[47] Nīli is shown as equivalent of Durga, Parvati. And Winslow's dictionary cites these meanings for Nīli: "Kali, the goddess; Durga, Parvati; a cruel, vindictive woman...; *nīlittaṉañceyya*: to act impudently—said of women; *nīliāṭṭamāṭā*—to recite the drama of Nīli, to behave without shame."[48]

In the *Cilappatikāram*, Nīli is equated with goddess Koṟṟavai by the author Iḷañko (in chapter 12, '*Vēṭṭuvavarī*': v. 67 to 90). "*...kumāri kavuri cāmari cūḷi nīli malavaṟku iḷankiḷai...*"[49] These are various names of goddess Koṟṟavai; Nīli is one.

"In the Kaṇṇaki legend...the tutelary deity of Madurai tells Kaṇṇaki that in her previous birth she was Nīli, wife of the merchant Cañgkaman of Siṅgapuram..."[50]

A popular song dedicated to goddess Māriammaṉ goes thus:

> *'āyiram kaṇṇuṭaiya aḻakil ciṟantakaṇṇu*
> *patināyiram kaṇṇuṭaiya*
> *pātakatti nīliyava'*[51]
>
> [She is the beautiful one, Nīli, she is, of a thousand eyes, who inflicts pain.]

Māriyammaṉ is also called Nīli, since she too wreaks vengeance, when displeased, and hence she is propitiated to keep her happy and pacified. She is another of the Tamil folk deities with a potent anger and stories abound of her turning into a vengeful foe if things go amiss in propitiating her, or if vows made are not fulfilled, or forgotten. The *villuppāṭṭu* version of Paḻayaṉūr Nīli story ends with the construction of a temple/ shrine for her and propitiating her as a goddess. Her *pēy* form, at times, then, could in fact merge with that of a goddess. In Tamil textual tradition Nīli's story found place in different periods. The *Tēvāram* hymns, too, mention the '*pēy Nīli*' or make reference to the '*one of Paḻayaṉūr*' whose story evokes terror in people's minds. In one of his *patikams*, Jñānacampantar says of her: "*mun̲ai naṭpāy vañcap paṭutorutti vāṇāl koḷḷum vakai kēṭṭu añcum paḻayan̲ūr*"[52]

'Paḻayan̲ūr is terrified of her, whose love transformed into cruel vengeance and a killing spree.'

The story of Nīli also appears in Cēkkiḻār's *Periya Purāṇam*. The story is of the brāhmiṇ, his wife and his affair with the courtesan. This is the same story as in the *NN*. The wife goes away to her parents' place. He brings her back, and on the way, kills her and pushes her into a well (with her child). In the second birth, he is born as a *veḷḷāḷa* merchant. His father gives him a sword to protect him from harm (as foretold by a soothsayer). As in the other versions, Nīli accosts him on his way to Paḻayan̲ūr. Then follows the sequence of her plea to the *veḷḷāḷas* of Paḻayan̲ūr; her seeking revenge by killing the merchant (her husband in the previous birth) after cleverly taking away the protective sword from him and the death of the *veḷḷāḷas* by jumping into a flaming pyre.[53]

Umāpati Civācāriyar's *Tirutōṇṭarpurāṇam*, Cēkkiḻār *Periyapurāṇam* has the following verses about Nīli:

> *'mār̲ukoṭu paḻayan̲ūr Nīli ceytava*
> *ñcan̲aiyāl vaṇikan̲ uyir iḻappa tāṅkaḷ*
> *kūr̲a uyacol piḻaiyātu tuṇintu*
> *centik kuḻiyileḻu patupērum muḻkik kañkai*
> *āraṇiceñ caṭaitiruvā laṅkāṭappar*
> *aṇṭamur̲a nimintāṭumaṭa aṭiyin̲min̲kīḻmeyp*
> *pēr̲upēr̲um vēḷāḷar perumai emmāl*
> *pirintaḷavit ṭivaḷaven̲ap pēcalāmo*[54]
>
> [Should we speak of Paḻayan̲ūr Nīli, whose vicious deed claimed the life of the merchant, or the greatness of the veḷḷāḷars of Tirvālankāṭu (of Śiva-Pārvati)[55] who, for their word of honour, prepared the fire pit and jumped in.]

Indira Peterson also refers to the Śaivite tradition and the importance of Paḻayan̲ūr, the veḷḷāḷas' honour-suicide therein, though Nīli is not referred to by name:

> 'Our Lord in Paḻaiyaṉūr in Ālankāṭu,
> home of men who feared for their honour
> when they heard of the woman
> who took her lover's life by foul means,
> is the god who comes to me in my dreams
> and makes me praise him.
> He is the one who enters my heart
> to awaken his remembrance
> when I have been unaware.'[56]

Zvelebil points out that

> 'The first occurrence of Nīli as attested in ancient Tamil literary texts is...much older: *Cilappatikāram* (c. AD 450) 12.21.3 mentions her as a manifestation of the mother goddess Koṟṟavai...'[57]

> *vaṃpalar palki vaḻiyum vaḷampaṭa*
> *amputai valvi leyiṉkaṭa ṉūṇkuvāy*
> *cañkari yantari nīli caṭāmuṭic*
> *ceñka ṇaravu piṟaiyuṭaṉ cērttuvāy*
> (*Cilappatikāram, Vēṭṭuvavarī: 12.21*)[58]

Zvelebil translates the above verses (not in its entirety) as 'O Sankari, Antāri, Nīli, who wear in your hair the red-eyed serpent along with the crescent! Accept this sacrifice.'[59]

And, he writes:

> 'We cannot say whether this Nīli is identical with the gruesome heroine of the Tamil folktale. She probably is, since the Nīli of the quoted stanza is a rather ferocious female deity. *Cilappatikāram*, though, offers us much more interesting material: it gives us, in 23.138-69, a brief story of Nīli, the wife of Cañkamaṉ and since this story occurs in the integral text of *Cilappatikāram*, it must have been well-known, and is at least 1800-1600 years old in the indigenous Tamil tradition. In fact, this story may have provided the original underlying motif of the "laws of preordained fate" in the Tamil oral tradition, as well as the motivation for the fate of Kōvalaṉ and Kaṇṇaki, the protagonist and heroine of *Cilappatikāram*.'[60]

In *Cilappatikāram* 23.138 *ff*, writes Zvelebil:

> 'The presiding deity of Madurai, while explaining to the heroine of the epic, Kaṇṇaki, her fate, tells her that there raged a war between two kings of Kaliñkam, and while they were fighting, "none could penetrate that region." A merchant by name of Cañkamaṉ, "anxious to increase his wealth, came with his wife, like people escaping unnoticed, carrying a large bale on his head, and began to sell his precious wares in a bazaar of the famous Ciñkapuram... Your husband Kōvalaṉ, in his previous birth known by the name Parataṉ, being in the service of the valorous king, had given up the vow (of non-injury) and was hated. His mistook Cañkamaṉ for a spy, had him caught, brought him before the king of the conquering spear and beheaded him. Nīli, the wife of the murdered Cañkamaṉ, found herself without rest, wandered through the streets and squares, creating a great commotion and shouting: 'King, is that your justice? Merchants, is this justice? Citizens, is this justice? Workmen, is this justice? She raved thus for fourteen days, without rest; inspired by the thought that the day was auspicious, she climbed a cliff in order to join her husband in heaven, and threw herself down shouting a curse: 'He who had inflicted this injury upon us shall suffer the same injury upon him'. That unerring curse (*vaḻuvilcāpam*) you have therefore suffered now!'[61]

According to Chakravarti,

> 'The object of this story evidently is to praise the nobility and honour of the veḷḷāḷas who forfeited their lives in order to keep the honour of their word. It is quite evident that this Nīli, though an evil spirit, has nothing to do with the Kāli-Neelakesi.'[62]

He also says, "the title of the work Neelakesi according to the author is borrowed from the Kali—Neelakesi of Pazhayanur...It no doubt refers to the Pazhayanur adjacent to Tiruvālangādu of Thevaram fame (that all) Thevaram singers have referred to...a village in North Arcot district. This Pazhayanur...had a famous Kāli temple (which) is evident from the book called Tiruvālangādu Sthalamāhātmyam..."[63]

According to this *māhātmyam* the gods, in order to crush the arrogance (and control) of Kāḷi of this place appealed to Viṣṇu who directed them to Śiva in turn. Śiva invited Kāḷi to a dancing challenge with him. And in his *tāṇdava* dance, he defeated her.

> "The author of this sthalamāhātmyam, in his introduction, calls this Kāḷi as Neeli...'[64]

The Nīli story can also be found in other texts such as *Tiruttōnṭarpurāṇam*, *Āḷañkāṭṭu-ttalapurāṇam*, *Mūvartevāram*, *Rattinakanṭakam*, *Tiruppukaḻ*, and so on. Kamil Zvelebil, in his analysis of the Dravidian elements in Tamil Hinduism (as he calls it) speaks of the concept of '*ūrammā*', the village deity/goddess/mother.

> 'Ūrammā was most probably the Neolithic prototype of the ubiquitous goddess, of Devi, in her many various multi forms: above all of korṟavai, the ferocious female deity of war; of all the great local goddesses—Mīnākṣi...of Madurai, Nīli, the goddess of Ālañkāṭu, Kāmākṣi, goddess of Kancipuram...'[65]

Texts such as *Tiruttoṇṭarpurāṇa Vaṟalāṟu* (authored by Umapati Sivacariya), Cēkkiḻār's *Piḷḷaitamiḻ* and *Periyapurāṇam* (Śaivite texts), interestingly, highlight the story of the veḷḷāḷas jumping into the fire.[66] In this sense, one would tend to agree with Chakravarti that the central concern—with Cēkkiḻār, for instance—was to praise the seventy veḷḷāḷas who 'kept their word'.

In the text, *Periyapurāṇam* too, the greatness of the veḷḷāḷas, rather than the story of Nīli, is the highlight: "*naṟṟiṟampuri paḻayanūrc ciṟuttoṇṭar navai van(tu) uṟṟapōtu tamuyiraiyum vaṇikaṉuk korukāl coṟṟa meymaiyuṅ tūkki ac colaiyē kākkap peṟṟa meṉmaiyil nikaḻntatu peruṅ toṇṭaināṭu*"[67]

['The greatness of Tonṭaināṭu shines with the greatness of those of Paḻayanūr who sacrificed their lives for the word they gave to the merchant.']

Nīli is also mentioned in Kamba Ramayanam in Tamil—"*nīli taṉatuk kañci niṉṟa vaṇukēcarkkākka kōli yapayañ koṭukkuṅkai!*"[68] ['Nīli granted '*abhayam*' (freedom from fear), to the merchant who stood before her, pleading.']

In *Abhidhānacintāmaṇi*, Nīli is a Brāhmiṇ woman, Navajñāni, who was murdered along with her son. She is reborn into a merchant family in Paḻayanūr, and avenges her death, murdering Darisana Ceṭṭi (her husband of the previous birth) and also leads the veḷḷāḷas to their (honour) suicide. In Cekkiḻār's *Piḷḷaitamiḻ*, we have a different version of the Nīli story wherein the man (brāhmiṇ, as in other versions) goes after the 'other' woman and his wife objects to the same. On the pretext of taking his wife to another village, this man abandons her in the forest. The wife avenges this in the next birth as a *pēy*, Nīli. Again, the self-immolation of seventy veḷḷāḷas is mentioned in this version.

Apparently, Nīli's story spreads as far as the northern part of Kerala, where *Pañcavañkāṭṭu Nīlippāṭṭu* (in the traditional genre of Tekkanpāṭṭu) narrates the story of Nīli; it is called Nīlikata.

So these have been, largely, the prisms for Nīli, the possessing spirit/woman's confinement, in a sense, within traditions. In the following sections, she moves ahead in her journey from these paths into a scenario with a possibility of freedom, of a certain kind.

Nīli's story in different sources and another Jaina Nīli story

Nīli's story, thus, is mentioned (in different periods), in *Kamba Rāmayāṇam, Tiruppukaḻ, Cēkkiḻār Piḷḷaitamiḻ, Toṇṭaimaṇṭalacatakam*, etc.[69] A story of one Nīli, whom we may call a mere namesake (for this protagonist is not the same Nīli), appears in the Jaina ācārya Sāmantabhadra's *Ratnākaraṇṭaka Śrāvakācāra*[70] and Prabhācandra, who is the commentator of the work, narrates the story of this Nīli as follows:

A devout Jaina woman was married, on the sly, to a Buddhist man named Sāgaradatta, and later, when she learnt of the deceit, she took out her 'revenge' by serving food cooked with leather slippers to visiting Buddhist bhikkus.[71] She then (as a result) faces accusations by her husband and father-in-law of being unchaste. As it happens, the gates of this city of Bhrgukaccha are shut all of a sudden and a deity appears in the king's dream saying that they will re-open only at the touch of a chaste woman. Nīli becomes that woman who opens the gates and her husband welcomes her back home since her chastity is proven. It doesn't stop at that. The husband and father-in-law both become practising Jainas.

Incidentally, Samanthabhadrācārya was a Jaina monk who lived in Jinakāncipuram in the 2nd century CE, in which period this story is set, according to Chakravarti. But, he says, 'Here Neeli is distinctly a human being and has nothing to do with the Neelakesi of Pazhayanur...'[72] Chakravarti offers his analysis on the Nīli stories appearing in the Śaivite traditions and the Jaina Nīlakeci. He writes

> ...the Kāli temple of Pazhayanur must have been a very old well-known place where animal sacrifices were offered to Kāli. Probably as result of Jaina influence the Kāli temple was converted into a place of worship according to Jaina doctrine of ahimsā. The story of Neelakesi evidently suggests some such reform...[73]

After a few years, during the Śaivite revival period, this temple, 'reformed by Jaina teachers' was 'taken over by Śaivite reformers and the goddess of the place elevated to the status of Śiva's consort, still retaining the old name Neelakesi translated into the vernacular of the Dravidian people as Vandarkuzhali which term is one the synonyms found in our work denoting Neelakesi.'[74] The reason for this being that Tondaimandalam, where Pazhayanur is situated, 'was completely under the influence of the Jainas...The Saivite reformers had to contend against the opposition of the Pallava king of Conjeevaram who was a staunch Jaina and who evidently wanted to stem the tide of Saiva reformation....'[75]

Vijaya Ramaswamy notes that

> The story of Neeli occupies a whole trope of literary genre ranging from ballads and tales to the dramatic poetic form known as Villuppāṭṭu and the folk theatre... (And)...the versatile Neeli goes through a range of imaging from a prostitute to a proselytising Jain nun to the saintly Shaivite Nayanar 'Pēyar' (of Karaikkal)...Neeli at the social level represents reprehensible social and moral behaviour but continues to exist in the religious psyche of the south Indians, predominantly the non-Brahmanical, largely Dravidian groups, as a figure to be feared and worshipped.[76]

Comparing the Two Versions of Nīli Story

Both *PN* and *NN* are performative texts. But the audience aimed by the two seems at variance with each other. One can understand this by the obvious reference to the Ekāmbaranātha temple precincts in Kancipuram as a place of worship in the *NN* text. The *villuppāṭṭu* is performed in smaller, local village shrines and most certainly has a different kind of audience, with different cultural symbols incorporated in the performance. In the *NN*, each character, and the scene, is described in detail and there is a fair amount of moral discourse, too. For instance, the young *dāsi/dāci* (in *NN*) reminds the priest, her lover, of his '*dharma*', asking him to be with his wife and only pay her (the *dāsi*) an occasional visit:

> ...kēḷīr pirāṇanātarē....vēroruttiyai vaittukoṇṭu avaḷutaṉē vāḻntiruppatu oṟukālattilum tarumamalla....
>
> atu uḷakattir perumpaḻikku iṭamākkum ākaiyālnīrumum muṟaimaṉaiviyiṉ maṉamnōkkāmal avaḷōṭuñcantocamāy vāḻntiruttu ovvoruvēlai eṉṉiṭalum vantu pōvatu caṟṟokkuṟaya tarummāyiruppatuñtavira eṉakkum umakkum apakīrtikkum iṭamillātirukkum kurukkaḷē...[77]

> [Listen oh, my dear one! Never has it been righteousness in any age to keep another woman and stay with her alone. It will bring forth great accusations in the world; hence, if you, too, stay with your wife without wounding her heart and come to my house once in a while, it will be right and, besides, will not bring dishonour to either of us, oh priest!]

In the *villuppāṭṭu* version there is the love aspect (love of the courtesan for the brāhmiṇ). The stress in this version is on brāhmiṇical ritualism—like the performance of sacrificial rituals (*yajña*) to beget children, which both Nāgendraceṭṭi's wife and Paccaiyammāḷ resort to. The brāhmiṇ priest's wife takes a vow on *pañkuṇi viḻā* (a festival celebrated in the month of April–March) at her parents' home in Mayilapur for her husband to return to her. Patriarchal value systems abound in this text. For instance, an argument wherein the brāhmiṇ priest tells his wife to stay behind since women cannot walk so easily in the forest and might not find a way out from there. While in the *villuppāṭṭu* version the Cheṭṭi does not get married in his second birth, here he does. Perhaps *NN* also aims to portray it as a mighty tragedy for more innocent people: the Cheṭṭi's wife and child, for instance, who are introduced in the *NN* version and have no role to play in the *villuppāṭṭu*. The *villuppāṭṭu*' s essential focus is on Nīli (who returned as a goddess on earth), the feared and (hence) worshipped, '*pēy*'. While in *NN*, the revenge itself is seen as a cruel event (in terms of the words used to describe it) and the seventy elders jumping in the fire seems to be the more important event. Even this incident is described in shades of awe, pity and sadness. Besides, here Nīli does not leave even the womenfolk of Paḻayaṉūr, and kills them with poisoned curds (as a curd seller), an aspect altogether missing in the *villuppāṭṭu*. Somewhere *NN* portrays the *pēy* with some amount of disgust—she is a *pēy* at her cruel best. While in the bow-song version, Nīli has some empathy forthcoming and subtle veneration, as a *pēy* who had avenged a wrong done to her. The wronged woman in the villuppāṭṭu version is the *dāsi* herself (who does not evoke the disgust and contempt shown to her in *NN*) who was done to death cruelly. She is not the wife of the priest, as in the *NN* version.

There is a fair amount of valorising of events and personalities in *NN*. The midwife has to be the woman who has supervised the birth of major mythological characters (very importantly, characters with negative shades) such as Indrajit, in the Rāmāyaṇa, son of Rāvaṇa, Suyodhana (Duryodhana), of Mahābhārata. Both women suffer labour pains for inordinately longer duration and both deliver their respective babies in their tenth month. The *NN* seems to be in the manner of a Greek tragedy, with every event being awe-inspiring. There is no such intonation in the *villuppāṭṭu* version, which is simpler. There seem to be several 'extra-textual' elements in the *NN*—in terms of incorporating elements not part of the folklore of Nīli. One says this, assuming the folk tale as 'the text' with its complete story. The narrative revolves around a lot of 'other' things than Nīli and her pathos-filled story by itself. In *NN* all these 'extra' elements—the moralising, the rituals, and the temple—are important inasmuch as the Nīli story merely fits into this well-made structure of a tragedy/play. It could, in other words, be the story of any other folk/mythological character within the same structure. In this sense, *NN* may be considered a codified, structured performative tradition inhering brāhmiṇical values and mores. The *villuppāṭṭu* is a folk tale, of Nīli (also performative), a local persona later deified, familiar to the area around (present-day) Tiruvalangadu and Palayaṉur, and may be few other villages in the north Arcot region, depending on how far the tale travelled. Interestingly, in the *villuppāṭṭu* version of Nīli story, 'the 70' who jumped into the flames are mentioned merely as '*ūrār*' and their caste is not mentioned.

The common motifs in both (or all) versions of Nīli story or events connected with Nīli, however, are the following: the sacrifice of 'seventy of Paḻayaṉūr' by jumping into the burning pyre; the murder and revenge of Nīli; in all versions, the brāhmiṇ (priest) is re-born as a person from the 'Chettiar' community and perhaps is has something to do with his 'act' in a previous birth that gives him a definitely 'lower' caste status in the next birth. In all versions again, Nīli has supernatural powers. She is feared and hence worshipped. It is quite interesting that in the *villuppāṭṭu* version the courtesan Candananaṅkai and her brother are reborn to a Chol̠a queen, or wife of a vassal in the Chol̠a kingdom. The term used for him is merely, *chol̠aman̠n̠an*, without a name. There is also the instance of the two *pēys*—Nīli and Nīlan̠—eating up all the livestock of the region.

Notes

1. Su. Shanmugasundaram, edited, *Pal̠ayan̠ūr Nīli Nāṭṭuppāṭal*—(henceforth *PN*)—villuppāṭṭu version—published by Kodumudi Shanmuga Biragadam, Tinnevelly, 1978. I thank Venkatesh Chakravarty for this reference, and Roja Muthiah Research Library, and Theodore Bhaskaran for the kind permission to utilise the only available copy of this villuppāṭṭu in their library.
2. Ibid, p. 3.
3. Though the villuppāṭṭu version I refer to, does not follow this structure. It is, in fact, in the *Nīli Nāṭakam*, that one finds this exact nature of child birth. But the performance context therein is quite different from the villuppāṭṭu tradition.
4. Stuart Blackburn, 1981, p. 213.
5. Blackburn, 1985, p. 267-268.
6. I combine the two—*Cantana Naṅkaiyin̠ Al̠aku* and *Nampiyin̠ Kātal* in my translation here.
7. Both the Tamil terms, *vēcai* and *dāci makaḷ* (daughter of the *dāci*) are used, which may be understood as *devadāsi*.
8. I will not give the Tamil verses in the entire book, but only where I find it useful for the argument. The verses referred to are from the villupāṭṭu, *Pal̠ayan̠ūr Nīli (PN)*.
9. For present-day place-names I refrain from using transliteration marks.
10. Verse 101, p. 8, *PN*. There is, incidentally, a Ponnur, not far from Vandavasi, near Kanchipuram, which is also famous for its Jaina

association. Today one can find a shrine dedicated to Tiruvalluvar, author of the *Tirukkuṟaḷ* on a hill-shrine here, and also a few Jaina *ashramas* for the laity and monks, nearby.

11. "*Maruntūṭṭi*" is the term used under the head, '*kiḻaviyiṉ keṭuceyal*'. This version of *villuppāṭṭu* seems to highlight the popular belief of 'bringing someone under an influence' through means such as (presumed) magic portions, etc. Even to this day, *maruntukuṭuttal* is used in different contexts: where a husband showers a lot of love on his newly wedded wife, or caters to the new woman in his life much more than to others around him; where a man falls in love with a woman, who is otherwise not acceptable to the family—the woman is portrayed as someone who 'administered the portion' to the man.
12. Interestingly, the song writer mentions Chitragupta (*Cittiraputtira nāyaṉār*) who decides (makes 'calculations') on the fates of each of these characters, based on their respective karmas—"*avarkaḷuṭa kaṇakkeṭuttu aḷavākattāṉ pārtāṉ...*" (He made their calculations as per the birth chart) and places them in different women's wombs.
13. A mercantile community in southern India.
14. '*Nīliyin Tōṟṟam*', v. 279-282, *PN.*
15. A term peculiar to the larger south Indian social custom of consanguineous marriages, wherein *attāṉ* denotes cousin and husband at the same time.
16. There is a *double entendre* in this; she is establishing intimacy by asking for *cuṉṉāmpu* for her *veṟṟilai.*
17. This is the only point in the song when we get a sense of the time of the reunion of Nīli and Ceṭṭiyār Ānantan.
18. The term used is *kaliyāna parisu.*
19. V. 497 to 508. *PN*, pp. 22-23.
20. Referring to the splurge plant which oozes a white substance which is poisonous; but the same words can also mean a child with body soft as milk-cream. There is a pun on the use of '*pāl*'.
21. One who was killed when the *Neem* tree he resided in, was burnt down by the people of the village.
22. April-May.
23. She is referring to tearing through the Ceṭṭi's heart, which she aims to do.
24. *PN*, v. 567; 573, p. 25.
25. Ibid, v. 574.

26. Ibid, v. 580-583, p. 25.
27. Ibid, v. 583-586, p. 25.
28. Blackburn, 1985, p. 272.
29. *PN*, pp. 34-35.
30. Ibid, p. 38.
31. Ibid, p. 27.
32. The story of Kāraikkāl Ammaiyār, the Tamil 'saint'-poet (of the Śaiva tradition) is described later.
33. The Tamil goddess films show this kind of tension—but usually in a fixed, patriarchal mode, and hence under-explore the inherent meanings of sexual intent or sensuality, in different cases.
34. *Nīli Nāṭakam* (*NN*), author unknown, date unknown. Folk theatre version. From copy at RMRL Chennai. Title page missing. From the collections of Roja Muthaiah of Kottaiyur, Ramnad district.
35. Ārumukaṉ/Subrahmaṇya.
36. At the RMRL, Chennai.
37. He played an important part in the Indian independence movement in south India and was a very prolific writer-poet.
38. This invocation is set to *Rāga Curuṭṭi* and *Tāla Aṭa; NN*, p. 2.
39. In the section, *maruttuvakiḻavi paccaiammāḷaippārttuccollutal* set to *Ragam Todi; NN*, p. 40.
40. Interestingly, Mottur near Arani is also a Tamil Jaina settlement. A negligible number of Tamil Jainas live here at present. One of the more prominent among them was the orator of the Tamil Jaina epic, *Civakacintāmaṇi*, Santhakumar Nainar, who was popularly known as 'Cintamani Navalar', who is no longer among us today. I discuss him and how I discovered the history of U.Ve.Ca's Jaina encounter, thanks to him. See Umamaheshwari, 2017, pp. 274-278. Could one conjecture that these '70' may have been Jainas, considering that most Tamil Jainas in this region held the caste title of Mudaliyar, and names of villages mentioned here also have strangely Jaina associations?
41. Set to *Ragam Pantuvarāḷi* (*potuviruttam*); *NN*, p. 75.
42. *NN*, p. 95. '*aivaruṭaiya peṇṭāṭṭikaḷaiyum tiruṭṭutanamā vaittukkoṇṭu irākālattil vīṭukkum varāmal taṉiyāyviṭṭuppōvār itaikaṇṭunāṉ anta aintupuruṣarkaḷaiyum vaittukkoṇṭēṉ atilennattappu...*'
43. My mother actually directed my attention to this phrase, in the course of our engagement with Nīlakeci. The phrase, my mother said, was something she heard often, and it was popular

in the region around Karur, Tiruchi, Udumalpet. And perhaps elsewhere too.

44. Shanmugasundaram, *PN*, p. 39.
45. Ibid, p. 37 & p. 39.
46. Ibid, p. 39.
47. The *LIFCO Tamil-Tamil-English dictionary*, Chennai, 1996, p. 416 below.
48. Rev. M. Winslow, 2004 (originally published in 1862), p. 685.
49. Srichandran, 2000, pp. 220-221.
50. Hameed, 1968 (pp. 196-204); p. 203, fn. 6.
51. Shanmugasundaram, p. 40.
52. Po.Ve.So, 1973, p. 24.
53. Ibid, pp. 24-25.
54. *Pāyiram 15*, Ko<u>r</u><u>r</u>avankuṭi Umāpati Civācāriyār's *Tiruttōṇṭarpurāṇam*, *Cēkki<u>l</u>ār Purāṇam*. Accessed at http://www.projectmadurai.org/ [Open Source]. Also, Shanmugasundaram, *PN*, p. 28.
55. *āraṇi-ceñcaṭai* refers indirectly to the dance of Śiva and Kāḷi at Tiruvalangadu in the Śaivite tradition. Incidentally, there is also a place called Arani, which has been a Tamil Jaina settlement since centuries; a Jaina temple is located here. Interestingly, one of the versions of the Nīli story reveals (as mentioned elsewhere) the names of places from where the veḷḷāḷars hailed and nearly all of them had been ancient Tamil Jaina villages and some continue to be, even today.
56. Campantar 1.45.1 *Pa<u>l</u>aiya<u>n</u>ūr Ālankāṭu*, as cited in Indira Peterson, [1991] 2007, p. 203.
57. Kamil Zvelebil, 1989, p. 297-298.
58. *Cilappatikāram*, edited by U. V. Swaminatha Aiyer, Dr. U. V. Swaminatha Aiyer Library, Chennai, [1892] 1990, p.319 & 328. Henceforth, *Cilap* (U.Ve.Ca).
59. Zvelebil, p. 297.
60. Ibid. p. 297-298.
61. Zvelebil, 1989, p. 298. He has translated the verses 138-169 of *Maduraikkāṇṭam, Kaṭṭu<u>r</u>ai katai*; See *Cilap.* (U.Ve.Ca), p. 506.
62. Chakravarti, 1984, pp. 14-15.
63. Ibid, pp. 11-12.
64. Ibid, pp. 12-13.
65. Zvelebil, 1981, p. 6.
66. One notes that possibly the veḷḷāḷa suicide motif is part of another

folklore and tradition which has at some point blended with, or merged into, the Nīli story—which, on its own, is a simple tale of wrong-doing and revenge. At the same time, the death of Nīlaṉ (Nīli's brother) being avenged does not, somehow, seem to fit into the 'basic' structure of the Nīli story.

67. Shanmugasundaram, *PN*, p. 29.
68. Ibid, p. 28.
69. Ibid., p. 27.
70. A. Chakravarti, 1984, pp. 15-17.
71. I will return later to this common motif—feeding leather slippers—in south Indian folk stories—and the idea of 'pollution' of being married (always on the sly) to a person outside the caste / community.
72. A. Chakravarti, op.cit, p. 17.
73. Ibid, p. 19.
74. Ibid, p. 19.
75. Ibid, p. 19.
76. Vijaya Ramaswamy, 2003, pp.163-171. This work looks at the general image of women in south Indian myths and folklore. A point needs to be made here that there isn't much here on the internal transformation of Nīli within the Jaina story *Nīlakeci* against the socio-cultural backdrop (the veḷḷāḷar 'suicide' motif, for instance) in her work; but that is not the intent of her work. She looks at incorporations and transformations of folklore with in what seems to be an overall 'little' and 'great' traditions-discourse. The problematic point, of course, is this: whose traditions would be deemed 'little' or 'small', and whose would be the 'great', and why at all? M. N. Srinivas' paradigm, if not irrelevant (it had its moment) is no longer tenable.
77. *NN*, p. 9.

3

BECOMING, OR FREEDOM AND REDEMPTION

Nīlakeci the Philosopher

Scenario 3

> *'āynīla vuṇka ṇavaḷā yaṭaṅ kāmai ceyyum*
> *pēynīla keci periyoṉaṟaṅ koṇṭa piṉṉait*
> *tīnīla vuḷḷan tirin tēṟu tiruvattaḷāy*
> *mañāla mellā maṟa māṟṟiya māṭciyaḷā' (verse. 4, 'avaiyaṭakkam')*[1]

> ['Behold this transformation
> unyielding, poisonous fury
> shrivelled to nothingness
> when pēy nīlakeci
> gained right knowledge from the wise one']

According to Chakravarti, "We know absolutely nothing about the author of the text though we know the commentary is written by Vāmana-muni. Since there are references to the *Kuṟal* and the *Nālaḍiyār* in this work, it must be later than the age of the *Kuṟal*."[2] The text itself is meant to be a counter to the Buddhist text *Kuṇṭalakeci*, in that it uses the concept of philosophical debate and polemicising with non-Jaina systems, just as non-Buddhist systems are contested in Kuṇṭalakeci. But the story and the way the author constructs the text is distinct. The genesis of the text, as the author reveals right at the onset, apparently, lies in a dream where a deity (whose name is not mentioned) appears in the dream urging the author to write this text. The story, then, is part of what occurred in a dream.

TARUMAVURAICCARUKKAM: The Process of Transformation and the Jaina Path

The site is the land of Pāñcāla, ruled by king Samudrasāra, whose capital city was Pundravardhana—in Tamil, *Puṇṭaravaruttaṉam*. Now, on the outer fringes of this city was a cremation ground called Palālayam, with a Kāli temple. A Jaina monk (*muṇi*), named Muṇicandra was doing penance in this place. He used to watch several people of the villages nearby bringing goats and sheep for slaughter as offerings to the goddess Kāli. He accosts them one day and tells them there is no use sacrificing the lives of these creatures and dissuades them from doing so. But the people, who do understand him, are afraid it might evoke the displeasure of the goddess and it might incur her wrath. He gives them an alternative, which is to offer her clay models of goats and sheep or other creatures. This, he tells them, would please the goddess and also save the lives of these animals. Convinced, the people adopt this practice. The goddess Kāli, however, is upset with this turn of events. She decides to enlist the help of the *pēy* Nīli 'of the south':-

> *'ācu miṅkirun tiṉiyeṉṉai yeḻukaveṉ ṟayala*
> *kāci nāṭṭinuñ cēṭiya nāṭṭiṉuṅ kāṇā*
> *tēcan tāmpala tiriyavat teṉṟicai nīla*
> *kēci mātaivan talaippaṭuk kiḷarntiṉṉa vuṟaikkum'* (v. 44)[3]
>
> [what is the use of being here in vain
> quickly she (Kāli) searched in the nearby lands of Kāci, Cēṭi and others
> and found Nīlakeci the great goddess (*mātaivam*) of the south (*teṉṟicai*; teṉ ticai) to whom she prayed...]

On reaching the cremation ground Nīli first tries to scare the monk in many ways. But he does not budge from his penance.

She then assumes the form of Samudrasāra (the king)'s beautiful daughter, princess Kāmalekai and tries to act coy, in order to seduce him.

> *'yāma nīṅkalu maracaṉṟa ṉorumaka ḷuraicāl*
> *kāma lēkaitaṉ ṉuruvoṭu tiruveṉat toṉṟit*
> *tāmañ cāṅtutaṇ malariṉṉa palakoṇṭu tuṇaicāl*
> *cemaṅ kāvala cēvaṭi pōṟṟeṉac ceṉṟāḷ.'* (v. 59)[4]

> ('After the first half of the midnight hour, Nīlakeci, assuming the form of Kāmalekai, the beautiful daughter of a king named Samudrasāra, adorning the best of jewels and with flowers of lovely fragrance and sandal paste.... reached the place' (where the monk resided).

Muṇicandra, however, tells her that he is well aware of her real form. She is amazed at his ability to stay so peaceful amid all her efforts to seduce him and trying to scare him. She now wishes to learn from him as to how he is able to be so peaceful and calm. It is then that he speaks to her about the nature of existence and the theory of the bondage of *karma*. The monk explains to Nīli the nature of reality and cosmology as expounded in Jaina tradition. He speaks of the different realms and kinds of existence within each realm. So there is the existence (*gati*) of *devas* (godly beings), *makkaḷ* (humans/people), and hell beings in each realm—in the higher (heavenly), middle (earthly) and lower (hellish) realms, respectively. A class of demigods (*vyantara devas, yakṣas* and spirits) dwell in a space between hell and earth. In the *madhyaloka*, the middle world inhabited by humans and various kinds of animals, birds, insects, tiny, microscopic organisms, these beings are characterised by their different sensory capacities. This biological categorisation, unique to the Jainism, incidentally, is also referred to in the ancient Tamil grammatical text, *Tolkāppiyam*.

> *'uṇṇi mukuṭṭai yeṟumpeṟi tēṇmuta lāvuṭaiya*
> *veṇṇilpal kōṭṭiya vāyav viraṇṭōṭu mūkkuṭaiya*

kaṇṇiya mūvaṟi vāmavai peṟṟōṟ karuṇamilā
naṇṇiya vaṇṭōṭu tēṉi yaṉaiyavu nālaṟivē' (v. 79)[5]

> [There are thousands of beings/organisms with two senses (*iraṇṭaṟivu*), such as ants, scorpions, and so on. There are those that have three senses (*mūvaṟivu*) including that of sight, without the sense of hearing and there are those with four senses (*nālaṟivu*). There could be organisms/beings with a sense of touch alone, or those with the sense of touch and smell and not hearing, or those with the sense of sight and smell and hearing, or those devoid of hearing, and so forth. Honey bees and beetles are categorised as having four senses]

Then there are beings with five senses (*ayyaṟivuyirkaḷ)* and those that have strong sense of hearing, those with strong legs, some with six legs, four and some with two legs. There are many kinds of beings that dwell on trees, in the seas and on islands and so on. (v. 80)

Clasification of *jīva* (soul):

> 'The Jain thinkers...first made a distinction between animate (*jīva*) and inanimate (*ajīva*) objects. These two categories were further analysed and classified [originally] from a purely scientific point of view. This was made solely on the basis of the number of sense-organs the Jīvas was supposed to possess. Ekendriya or one-sensed Jīvas possess only the sense of touch. They are subdivided into earth-bodies, water-bodies, fire-bodies, air-bodies and vegetable-bodies...Next we come across Dwindriya or two-sensed Jīvas, possessing the organs of taste and touch. To this category being the animalculae, worms, things living in shells, leeches, earth-worms, etc. The Trindriya Jīvas have three senses. Besides the senses of touch and taste, they have the additional sense of smell. In this are various kinds of ants, moths, etc. The Caturindriya Jīvas are possessed of the four senses of touch, taste, smell and sight. To this class belong the wasps, scorpions, mosquitoes, flies, locusts, butterflies, etc. The Pancindriya Jīvas have another extra sense, namely, that

of hearing. To this category are included the quadrupeds and bipeds. The animals which possess five organs of sense are of two kinds, those which originate by generation acquivoca (*samucchana*, coagulation) and those which are born from the womb. Each of these [is] again of three kinds—aquatic, terrestrial and aerial. Fishes, tortoises, crocodiles, Makaras and Gangetic porpoises are the five kinds of aquatic animals. Quadrupeds and reptiles are the two kinds of terrestrial animals. The former are of four kinds—solidungular animals, as horses, etc, biungular animals like cows, etc; multiungular animals, as elephants, etc, and animals having toes and nails, as lions, etc. The reptiles are of two kinds—those which walk on their arms, as lizards, etc., and those which move on their breast, as snakes, etc. Both are again of many kinds. Winged animals are or four kinds—those with membranous wings, those with feathered wings, those with wings in the shape of a box and those which sit on outspread wings. Men are of two kinds—originating by coagulation (this is a dogmatic imposition; to this category belong the gods and other supernatural beings) and born from the womb. Those who are born from the womb are of three kinds—those living in the Karmabhūmi, those living in the Akarmabhūmi, and those living in the minor continents (*Uttarādhyāyanasūtra*).'[6]

Someone like Nīli also has a place within the minute categorisation that the Jainas texts delineated. Thus:-

'Gods and hell-beings, although they occupy widely separate worlds, share many charactersistics. They are born spontaneously (*aupapādika)* that is, they simple appear, with no need for parents, and can alter the appearance of their physical bodies at will. In addition to possessing the five senses and reasoning powers seen in many earthly creatures, they are naturally endowed with special "super-knowledges" (*avadhijñāna)* such as clairvoyance, memory of prior incarnations, and the ability to see objects at great distances. The real difference between a birth in heaven and one in hell revolves around the effect produced by these special powers; whereas they increase the pleasures of a god's existence (he may remember, for example, his good deeds in a former life), they bring nothing but greater suffering to the hell-being (for he will recall only the evil of his actions, the hatred of his enemies and so on). Jainas believe that in every such state, no matter how low or simple, there will always be some residue of qualities that define the soul: perception, knowledge, energy, bliss, and so on. Thus even the huge mass of karmic matter which oppresses the lowest being will not keep its soul at such a level forever; the potential for spiritual growth (progress to higher states) is never eliminated completely. It should be noted, however, that this is not a theory of necessary evolution; the Jaina also accepts the possibility of retrogression, and thus of eternal bondage.'[7]

Nīli, who is one of the 'hell-beings', within the Jaina discourse on soul, has the possibility of reprieve. Thus:

> 'For a Jaina, the knowledge, bliss and energy of the soul can never be totally extinguished, whereas karmic influence is subject to complete elimination. Hence the soul possesses a sort of built-in advantage, an everpresent tendency to develop its qualities and temporarily reduce the influence of the karmas. When the Jainas say that a soul is free to work for its own salvation, it is this inherent tendency towards self-improvement that it is referred to...Jainas have given us a detailed picture of the ladder one must climb...from the depths of delusion and entrapment to the pinnacle of omniscience and freedom. This ladder has fourteen rungs, called *guṇasthāna*, stages of perfection. The state of *mithyādṛṣṭi* (the incorrect view of reality) is designated as the first of these rungs; it is here that every embodied soul must dwell until it undergoes the momentous shift described above. This event is followed very quickly by the experience called *samyak-darśana*, having the correct view, in which the soul for the first time glimpses its true nature. Such an experience is compared to that of *a blind man who is suddenly able to see...*'[8]

Muṇicandra tells Nīli that the subjects of the three realms or regions are bound by the laws of transmigration according to their conduct in life and can attain the final liberation only in the middle world. And here, too, there are certain geographical regions, *karma bhūmis*, where, with the performance of meditation, penance, it is possible to destroy the *karma.*[9] Pain and misery is part of life for beings in this middle world and for those in the hellish realms. Only the *deva-gati* (realm of gods) is free from suffering and pain. Someone like Nīli too, the monk tells her, resides in her own place in this scheme of things and is bound by actions that cause pain and suffering to others (*pēykaḷ piṟarkkuc-ceyyum tuṉpañkaḷ):-*

> *'tīyē yeṉavevarkkuñ cellal palavākki*
> *vēyē puraitōḷāy mikka viṭameṅkum*
> *pēyē yeṉappaṭṭup pēṉā taṉaceyvar*
> *nīyē yeṉṉillai niṉpōlva raṉṟō'* (v. 115)[10]

> [Oh, with a bamboo-like skin, aren't you one of those, who cause people to burn with suffering and pain, being hailed as a *pēy* travelling in air-borne vehicles to people's world, inflicting harm on noble people?]

Municandra urges Nīli to understand the futility of adding to her bad karmas by scaring people and being a despised one as a result. He then tells her of the *mukkūṭṭu maruntu* (v. 116) 'three-way medicine' that will rid her of these bad deeds of her *pēy* life, expounding on the basic three principles (*mukkuṭai*) of the Jaina doctrine, namely, *naṟkāṭci, nallaṟivu* [*naṉñānam*] and *naloḻukkam* (right faith, right knowledge and right conduct)[11] as the means to get rid of the pain and bondage of this life / existence. He advises her to avoid causing pain and hurt to living beings and teaches her about *koḷḷāmai* (non-killing).

Having listened to Municandra with great devotion, Nīli is truly transformed and decides at that moment to spend the rest of her life propagating the Jaina doctrine that allows her the space to get rid of her previous form or existence or the pain of it.

Nīlakeci's Invocation to the Jina

For someone like Nīli, used to living in a *pālai tiṇai*-like situation, the *pālai* of her life itself, and the *pālai* of the place—both an internal barren space and an external scrub-forest of thorny plants, the only species to grow here—which was land only a few people just about passed through, the world was now seeming suddenly so beautiful. She could now smell flowers and appreciate the beauty of ones she had never seen before. That is the kind of 'movement' that the poet of *Nīlakeci* gives to Nīli; in the internal movement of the text you can also find Nīli's sudden realisation of different sensations (for the world of flowers, which the poet is seeing through Nīlakeci as she travels across). In many places you have the description of the place before the debating verses begin. There is also the description of the variety of flora and fauna when Nīlakeci offers worship—to the Jina-tīrthankara image at the *Cittakūṭa Caityālayam*—which is located within pristine environs.

And thus begins pēy Nīli's journey into the realm of philosophical/metaphysical discourse and debate. It has been a long journey for a woman forced to become a pēy, possessing, vindictive, murderous; or a deity feared, hence venerated, to a woman challenging the various philosophical/religious systems of that time—the Buddhist, Ājīvika, Vaiseṣika, Sāṁkhya, Vedic, Bhūtavāda (Materialistic) and so on. From a 'scenario' where Nīli tore the flesh of the Ceṭṭi who had murdered her in the previous birth—"*ceṭṭiyārmel vil̲untu verikoṇṭu paḷḷināl toṇṭiya par̲r̲ikkaṭittāḷ...*"[12] *(pouncing on the ceṭṭi she sunk her teeth into his throat and bit him...)*—to one of humble submission to the tīrthankara at the jinālaya.

> *'yā a taṭika ḷataruḷā laruntuya rakalvakai yatan̲ān̲*
> *mā a tuṭaiyaṭi yivaitā mar̲avale n̲en̲avalaṅ koṇṭu*
> *vē e taṭaviyan̲ malaimēl virīkatir maṇviḷak kāti*
> *tī itaṭu talai viḷankuñ cin̲akara muvakaiyir̲ cen̲r̲āḷ* (v. 149)[13]

> [Blessed by the monk (aṭikaḷ) she entered joyously at the
> feet of the Jina at the excellent mountain Vellimalai,
> lit with brightness (a halo) of gemstones,
> to worship the Jina (at cittakūṭa caityālayam)]

Speaking of transformations, meanwhile, Karen Pechilis writes

> 'A bodily transformation demands that we consider, or reconsider, what the body was in the first place, thus inviting critical refection on the conventions governing the perceived nature and significance of that body.'[14]

Of course, this was said in the context of Kāraikkāl Ammaiyār, but the same could be said for the story of Nīli, as well. Nīli, metamorphosed into Nīlakeci, is now 'possessed' of the thirst for knowledge and philosophical rumination and an urge for a higher plane of existence. And I will try to assess this long journey of hers and see what this journey holds. The next section engages with the actual journey of Nīlakeci, or some of the more important places in her itinerary where Nīli or Nīlakeci discourses and debates with (and defeats) teachers of other systems of thought.

The author of *Nīlakeci*, as has been mentioned before, is not known and we only know of the commentator, Samayadivākara Vāmanamuṇi, who has been identified as the Vāmanācārya who authored the Jaina text *Merumantarapurāṇam*. Vāmanācārya is also referred to Mallisenācārya and is among the most revered of Jaina ācāryas of the old Tamil country. While there is general agreement on this aspect of the authorship among scholars of Jaina literature, there is no informed consensus on the date of *Nīlakeci*. Scholars assign anywhere from 1st century to 10th century CE for the text, but give no ample historical evidence for the same. There has been no attempt (or hardly any attempt, so far as I have observed) to study *Nīlakeci* from a historical angle, in terms of placing it in the context of the history of the Tamil Jainas. Perhaps this has a role to play in giving different dates to this text—since the matter contained therein, and not the date of the matter, as it were, became the prime concern among scholars. Sometimes, the dating has been done on the basis of literary usage and terms appearing therein. In many cases, the only point where consensus has been arrived at is that *Nīlakeci* must date later than the Buddhist *Kuṇṭalakeci*, since it is modelled after this Buddhist text. Po.Ve.Somasundaram[15] is of the opinion that *Nīlakeci* should have been written in the 5th century CE. He reasons that some of the names of Buddhist monks/teachers mentioned in the works of the Pallava ruler, Mahendravarmaṉ of the 6th century CE, seem to correspond to the ones mentioned in Nīlakeci's debate with the Buddhist thought in the text. So, he avers, *Nīlakeci* may have been written prior to the works of Mahendravarmaṉ, somewhere around 5th century CE. A. Chakravarti assigns *Nīlakeci* between 1st and 5th century CE.

> 'The only thing that we can be certain of is that the author of Neelakesi must belong to a later period that the composition of the great grammatical work, "Tholkappiyam" and the two ethical works "Nāladiyār" and "Kural". There is reason to believe that these three were written by Jaina teachers. The other Jaina works were not in existence. These three works are quoted by the author of "Neelakesi". Hence it follows that he must be of a later period... If the Jaina tradition about Kuṟaḷ is recognised to be valid, then we have to accept its age to be the 1st century AD. Elāchārya is supposed to be the author of Kural. Elāchārya is another name of Kundakundācārya who lived partly in the 1st century BC and partly in 1st century AD...'[16]

Hence the upper limit of the date, he takes as 1st century CE. Again,

> 'The author of Neelakesi locates the Ājīvaka teacher and his conjugation in a suburban village called Samadhandam—somewhere near Kukutanagar which is another name for Worayur, a town in Trichinopoly.... In Harshacharitra of Bāna there is a reference to the several religious schools at that time. King Harsha...[in the] forest Asrama of Divākaramitra...meets

> several congregations...(of) religious orders such as Bauddhas, Jainas... In this group he finds the Maskarins. Maskari was the founder of the Ājīvaka school....Maskarin school or Ājīvaka sect was a living faith about the time of Sri Harsha in the early part of the 7th century AD. [Thus] in the south, the Ājīvakas were flourishing only in the early centuries of the Christian era and disappeared afterwards. This will put the lower limit for the composition of Neelakesi somewhere about the 5th century AD.'[17]

Another important question he raises (in connection with assigning these dates) is 'Evidently the author [of Nīlakeci] was not acquainted with the later Vedānta schools of Śankara, Rāmānuja and Mādhva. Only the earlier schools are mentioned and criticised in the work...'[18]

One is inclined to agree with the last point, especially considering the fact that the largest part of the text is the debate with Buddhism which was apparently a big force / thought system to contend with/reckon with at that point and the need for such a work. Verses 150 to 658, a total of 508, are dedicated to the debate with Buddhism. Of these, the largest section is Nīlakeci's debate with the Buddha himself, in verses 463 to 658, that is, 195 verses in all. Moreover, one would be inclined to wonder as to how, in terms of conflict with the Śaivite tradition—so crucial to the Tamil Jaina history—the Śaivite tradition, and later, Śankara, would not even find mention in the text challenging all the major religious/philosophical systems. Also, by the 8th and 9th centuries CE, there was no immediate context to take issue with the Buddhists, since by that period, they were well on their way to neglect and marginalisation in terms of political and economic patronage in Tamilnadu. Thus, devoting a large section to Buddhism—in a text dedicated to 'revealing' as it were, the lacuna in each of the major systems at that point, and highlighting the superiority of the Jina doctrine—would have been more of an anachronism. One would agree with A. Chakravarti's larger arguments in this context, and not enter the dating debate further; while be inclined towards 5th century CE as the period of its composition.

As for the author of *Nīlakeci*, importantly, Chakravarti says (based on internal evidence from the text) that

> '[The] author of Neelakesi was a direct student of the author of Kuṟaḷ from whom he learnt the several philosophical systems included in this work. I would also follow that the author of Neelakesi was a convert to Jainism and that he learnt the fundamentals of Jaina philosophy from his guru—the Thevar—the author of Kuṟaḷ. This influence we are constrained to have from...the 3rd stanza of Neelakesi where the author confesses that his story is not based upon accepted religious agamas of old."[19]

The stanza that is referred to above reads:

> *'paṇṭākamattuṭ payilāvurai yeṉṟu mikkār*
> *vīṇṭtiṅ kitaṉai vekuḷārviṭal vēṇṭu vaṉ yāṉ*
> *taṇṭā maraimē ṉaṭantāṉ ṟaṭantāḷ vaṇaṅkik*
> *kaṇṭēṉ kiṭantēṉ kaṇaviṉṉitu kaṇṭa vāṟē' (v.3)* [20]

> ['One day, as I was worshipping the one who walked on a lotus (the Jina, 'vēṇṭu vaṉyāṉtaṇṭāmaraimēṉaṭantāṉṟaṭantāḷ vaṇaṅkikkaṇṭēṉ), I saw the events that unfolded here in this text as in a dream. Hence, I admit (or urge) to the discerning and knowledgeable ones that this text does not claim to be based on our old āgamas (*paṇṭākamattut....*)]

Irrespective of the fact that the author dismisses, in a sense, all that is said of the events—leading to—the conception of *Nīlakeci*, the text, it may still be considered a fact that the author was well aware, as also a part, of a socio-cultural context which related to Nīli (as) the *pēy* and her story. The Nīli story was deep rooted in the context the author came from, and which is what made him (re)consider a character such as this for a treatise on the Jina ideals. One agrees with Chakravarti that the author was a convert to Jainism (and came from a milieu where Nīli 'loomed large'); he became influenced by the Jaina doctrine of karma and the '*ratna-trayam*' ('three gems'—right faith, knowledge and conduct). The author had an immediate 'base', and it had to be one that convinced readers of the idea of 'becoming'. It had to be a character from the author's own immediate environs, which could convince people that if a '*pēy*', a dreaded possession woman such as Nīli, could become a philosopher and preacher of Jainism, surely, anyone could accept the Jaina doctrine and transform into better human beings. At another level, the author's admission (or confession?) that this text did not follow any of the old āgamas (almost as a confession of going 'against the grain') happens because the author has to show—as a new entrant into Jainism—twice the respect for the old āgamas of Jainism, especially since the author is going out of the way to bring in a possession spirit as a central character in the text. Thus, the author chooses to call the sequence of the text, as a part of a dream. Moreover, a folk tale of the region gives *Nīlakeci*, the text, a certain rootedness in the region, to be able to debate with the systems of thought then prevalent in the area.

Interestingly, and intriguingly too, however, the locale, the 'site' of the story, the setting of *Nīlakeci* happens to be in the 'north' (in Pāñcāladesa) and the places where she debates each system of thought are not all of them in the Tamil country. However, in the period that *Nīlakeci* is believed to have been composed, these are the systems of thought popular in the old Tamil country. It may not be a totally unrelated matter that *Nīlakeci* also happens to be a text of the Tamil Jainas and does not find a special place in the pan-Jaina (or pan-Indian Jaina) textual tradition. Of course, it is also written in Tamil, and obviously, had a certain audience in mind. Funnily enough, though, the place, as the events unfold, in Pāñcāladesa, the goddess of Palālayam temple (i.e. Kāli) has to look far and wide and ultimately choose '*teṉṟicai Nīlakeci*'—Nīlakeci of the Southern region—to help her scare away the Jaina monk Muṇicantiraṉ. This is obviously on the one hand to give sanctity and importance to the character of Nīli the *pēy* (dreaded across Toṇṭaimaṇṭalam for her cruelty) as also to give that much more potency to the doctrine of karma and becoming. The three gems of Jaina faith, and the doctrine of *koḷḷāmai* (non-killing), retrieve Nīli from a life of violent retribution.

As noted earlier, Nīlakeci devotes the largest part of her mental engagement to Buddhism. The debate with Buddhist philosophy sees Nīlakeci take up issue with instances from the dhamma as preached by the Buddha, the eight-fold path, the doctrine of nirvāṇa, an elucidation of the Jātaka stories and so forth. She does not merely debate with Kuṇṭalakeci, but also with the Enlightened one himself, to prove the moral and philosophical superiority of the Jaina doctrine, especially that of the Jaina idea of non-killing in ideology and in praxis.

The sites of Nīlakeci's debates, and her movement in that process, are interesting. It starts of course with Pāñcāladesa, the beauty of which place is described in truly lyrical poetic style. Very importantly, it uses the conventions of Tamil Caṅkam poetry in using the five *tiṇai* (*aintiṇai*)—five ecotypes, which are the hilly (*kuṟiñci*), riverine (*marutam*), pastoral (*mullai*), littoral (*neytal*) and deserted/barren land (*pālai*)—concept to describe the country ruled by one Samudirasāraṉ. The *tiṇai* concept itself, as scholars have shown, may not be seen merely as a literary convention of early Tamil poets but a reflection of, or extension of, the socio-cultural and political situation then prevalent. Zvelebil points out that the *tiṇai* concept (he only talks of four, not five *tiṇais*, leaving out what's been seen as rather ambivalent/abstract construct, the '*pālai*'):

> '[The *tiṇai* concept] was elaborated, formalised and conventionalised by Tamil sages of the early classical age, but it was most probably founded on the actual state of affairs when some centuries earlier, the ideal eco types were still rather separate as different concrete types of habitat of various tribal and demi tribal communities.'[21]

According to Murton, the *tiṇai* concept signifies actual landscapes of the Tamil country (which) became the 'interior landscapes of Tamil poetry'.[22]

Coming back to *Nīlakeci*, the early part of the text is substantially devoted to describing Pāñcāladesa and these verses use the kind of imagery and 'sense' of the geography one sees in the *akam* poems of Caṅkam corpus. For instance:

> *'māñcōḷai poṅki marutaṅkiḷip piḷḷaikaḷ vāyt*
> *tīñcā ṟoḻukun tiṇaiyiṉ ṉaṇī taṅkī yeṅkun*
> *tāñcāla vaḻnā ṭaḷirīṉun takaiya tūṇṭu*
> *pāñcāla meṉṟu palarum pukaḻ pārttī nāṭē'* (v. 10)[23]
>
> [The country called Pāñcāla, celebrated for its fame and prosperity
> exemplifies the beauty of all the tiṇais
> of these, the *marutam tiṇai* excels
> with its profuse mangroves and parakeets perched atop trees
> feasting on the juices of sweet mangoes...]

Again, there is a description of the *kuṟiñci* part of this land:

> *'niṉaiciṉaiyaṉa rakuviraiyaṉa nalaṉuṭaiyaṉa nākam*
> *viṉaiyuṭaiyaṉa poḻutivaiyeṉa virivaṉakaṇi vēṅkai*
> *kaṉaicuṭarviṭu katirmaṇiyaṟai kaḷaṉayarvaṉa kānta*
> *ḷiṉiyaṉapala cuṉaiyayalaṉa viṟuvaraiyaṉa kuṟiñci'* (v. 16)[24]
>
> [Here in this *kuṟiñci* flourish trees such as the jambulina
> numerous fragrant flowering plants abound, like the kino tree
> here the *kuṟavar* spend time picking millets while the mountain glistens with the sun's rays and moonlight and there you see space laid out (*kaḷam*)
> it is (where) the *kuṟiñci* (flowers) blossom by the spring pools of water by the mountainside.]

It must be mentioned here that the making of the *kaḷam* (space/context) for *veṟi-āṭal* (where the shaman dances in frenzy of being possessed by divinity) is a very typically *kuṟiñci* eco-type motif of the *akam* of the Caṅkam corpus. A beautiful context of laying out space for *veṟi-āṭal* in some of the *akam* poems have the heroine's family—fearing that she is unwell, while she is love-sick—lay out the *kaḷam* and make the shaman dance to rid her of the bad spirit. Here let me refer to Vijayalakshmy on the interaction between Sanskrit and Tamil Jaina epics. She takes the instance of *Cīvakacintāmaṇi*, one of the major *kāvyas*, especially on the descriptive elements present there. She says, 'Though such descriptions arise out of the mahākāvya tradition in Sanskrit, the way in which the fauna and flora are described is in accordance with the Tamil conventions.'[25]

However, there is no explanation of the reason for looking at *Nīlakeci* and the influence of Sanskrit *kāvya* on the same. Moreover, Vijalayalakshmy dates *Cīvakacintāmaṇi* around 8th century CE, and mentions *Nīlakeci* as a text that was composed post-*Cīvakacintāmaṇi* (and influenced by Sanskrit literature and poetics) in Tamil. But looking at the evidence stated by Chakravarti, discussed earlier, it would be difficult to concur with Vijayalakshmy's explanation. However, the fact that she accepts, that the descriptive elements (flora and fauna) fit the 'Tamil' conventions may substantiate the point about the use of the *tiṇai* concept in *Nīlakeci* (with related concepts) coming from a poetic convention immediately preceding, or corresponding with it. In the entire text, wherever Nīlakeci announces her challenge, there is a description of the place within the *tiṇai* poetic device or convention.

However, fascinating though it would be to focus even purely on the literary convention and the descriptive elements of *Nīlakeci* within the Caṅkam paradigm, my own focus here, for the moment (of this book), is more on the way the text re-interprets a local idiom—or use of a prevalent cultural metaphor—to suit a purpose very different from the one the idiom/metaphor is confined to, both literally and metaphorically. And that too, adapted from yet another counter (to the larger Vedic) tradition, the *Kuṇṭalakeci* of the Buddhists. It is also important to reiterate the fact that the cultural idiom of Nīli has in it something so significant that it has given itself to so many versions and re-interpretations in its long wandering existence. And in all these interpretations (or despite them) certain motifs remain forceful and powerfully intact, such as the *pēy* form of Nīli. A point where, even for a brief moment, even in Nīlakeci that starts off with an all new meaning for Nīli, redeeming her, as it were, from her '*pēy*-ness', the *pēy* Nīli figures, albeit for a brief moment in the text.

Nīlakeci's Debating Journey

It begins with the invocation to the Jina-tīrthankara ('*nallār vaṇaṅka....*') 'Exaltations to the Supreme being, who is beyond the four, birth, disease, death and decay, worshipped by the good (to which Chakravarti adds these—Narendra, Surendra, the devas of this world).' Having gained the knowledge of Jina ideals, Nīlakeci is moving onward in life. What is this place she crosses through, like?

For someone used to living in the *pālai* tract, with just the *kaḷḷi* plants for company, the world suddenly looks so colourful; she can smell the fragrance of the flowers, see the wide variety of trees and creepers and shrubs she had not known of before. That is the kind of 'movement'—within the text and in Nīli's newfound form—that the poet wishes to bring out; so there is an elaborate description of the greenery that Nīlakeci encounters when she goes forth to offer worship at the feet of the tīrthankara at the *cittakūṭa caityālaya,* right after she has been ordained by Muṇicantiraṉ. The shrine is located amidst abundant natural beauty, and rich biodiversity, which is described by the poet as if Nīlakeci were seeing and relishing it all. In most of the sections in *Nīlakeci* prior to the debates, the poet gives similar description of the landscapes she will see, not all of them beautiful; but each giving her a sense of the space and the world around her that she will see in the course of her travels to different places.

Incidentally, it is in *Kuṇṭalakecivātaccarukkam* that we find the verses describing the worship of the Jina-tīrthankara by

Nīlakeci. So what is this place like, which she crosses, before she will halt at Kāmpili?

But prior to the actual debate, there are many verses dedicated to the worship of the Jina-tīrthankara. Nili experiences freedom, and hence, a rejuvenation of the sensations of sight and smell, which you find in the description of the place.

> *'kollai mullaippaṅ koṅku kuruntaṅ kōtaraṇ kurava*
> *nalla mallikai naṟavam ñāḻal tāḻaipuṉ ṉākam*
> *palli taḻappaṉik kuvaḷai pāṉal pātiri piṟavu*
> *mellai yiṉmala rēnti yiṟaivaṉ tiṭavakaik keḻuntāḷ'* (v. 150)[26]

Here is an expansive field of jasmines in bloom; there she sees the *koṅku* (cotton-tree), is enchanted by the fragrant foliage of the *kuṟunta* (*Trichilia*) tree and the Gloriosa blossoms, and the date tree. The fragrance emanating from the various flowers blossoming delights her mind; there are the Peacock flower plant (*naṟavam*),[27] the *puṉṉākam* (*puṉṉai; Rottlera tinctora*), and the *panal* (blue lotus, *Pontideria*) and crossing through all this, Nīlakeci reaches the shrine where the idol of the lord (*iṟaivaṉ*[28]) is consecrated.[29]

And what does this *cittakūṭa caityālayam* look like to Nīlakeci? She saw the height and expanse of the place; looked at it from all sides (in amazement) and walked around that magnificently beautiful cave, and worshipped the lord of great penance in the path of right conduct seeking that all the doors be opened, which the lord did, following which she was able to look at the beautiful image of the lord, free from obstacles, and folded her hands, seeking blessings for all the three worlds (realms). She then prayed to the tīrthankara with the various kinds of flowers she had gathered, which were blossoms from fruit trees in the forests where reside various kinds of birds, and prayed to the image of the lord who walked in the path of right knowledge.

Perhaps the poet wishes to portray Nīlakeci's plea to opening the doors as a plea to open the doors of knowledge and self-realisation that were hitherto closed for her pēy Nīli form.

And perhaps this was the first time that Nīli was praying to a tīrthankara, offering worship instead of being worshipped by people out of fear. Incidentally, there couldn't have been a Buddhist reinterpretation of Nīli because Buddhism would not recognise the pēy form.

What is so interesting is the manner in which Nīlakeci worships the Jina—with the flowers and sandal paste and lime, fragrant incense smoke (*tumam*); singing the 108 names of the Jina set to melodious musical notes (*nātakītam*). She addresses him as the most valiant of all, most knowledgeable of all and the most excellent, at whose feet she bows down in respect; for he has stopped the influx of desires, who has crossed the ocean of birth, death and rebirth and caused the destruction of the cause of suffering for the benefit of all living beings. What is fascinating in the section of Nīlakeci's Jina worship is the constant use of alliterations in the many verses when describing the Jina-tīrthankara—*vīrartana vīrarkkum virā; pulavartam pulavarkkum pulavā; periyavarpperiyavarpperiyāy*, etc. Further she addresses the Jina as the most learned of all, who imparted the right knowledge to people to be able to cross over the unending cycles of birth and rebirth on account of bad deeds (bad karma/*tīviṉai*) through one's own individual action, just as a boat takes people to the shore across a trubulent ocean (of unending births).

The 'site' of the *Nīlakeci* text, of course, is Pāñcāla, as has been said before, a country in the 'north' (*vaṭaku*). It begins with the author's prologue, that the events occurring in the text are all based on his dream. In this Pāñcāla country then, at a cremation ground with a temple of Kāli, begins the story of 'southern' Nīli's encounter with, and finally submission to, Muṇicantiraṉ, and Jaina ideals. It is interesting to see that both figuratively and literally there is 'movement' here from a local to a larger Jaina sacred (?) geography and movement for Nīli from the south to meet the Jaina monk in the north, and inspire a text in her name! Once enlightened, Nīlakeci, as is usual with any new convert, takes up her 'vocation' with great fervour and her first debate would obviously be with the 'next' most important/influential/ prominent system, namely, 'Buddhavāda', Buddhism. It begins with Nīlakeci challenging Kuṇṭalakeci. This may be both to challenge the text *Kuṇṭalakeci*, as well as the character, the Buddhist nun.

The sites of Nīlakeci's debates are, respectively: Kāmpili, capital of south Pāñcāla (Kuṇṭalakeci, *Kuṇṭalakeci vātaccarukkam*); Ujjain (*Arukaccantiravātaccarukkam*); Padmapura (*Mokkalavātaccarukkam*); Kapilapura (*Buddhavātaccarukkam*); Kukkuṭanakara (*Ācīvikavātaccarukkam*); Hastinapura (Cānkiyavātaccarukkam/Sānkhya); again, Hastinapura (*Vaicēṭikavātaccarukkam*/Vaiseṣika); Kākaṇṭi (*Vetavātaccarukkam*); and finally, on the way, *Pūtavātacarukkam*, which is, perhaps the same place, for the text does not mention the same of the place for this section, except that it is in the royal court of Madanajit. The people she debates with in each of these places are, respectively: Kuṇṭalakeci, Arukaccantira, Mokkala and the Buddha. Maskari, Parāsara, Lokajit, Pūtika (Bhūtika) and finally, Picācakaṉ (Piśācaka). Only one among these happens to the founder of the school of thought—Gautama Buddha—while others are great teachers of their respective schools. The author seems to have done this with a purpose, namely, to establish the superiority of Jaina perception of non-killing and non-violence, as against the Buddhist, and what better way than to debate, and win over, the very founder? It is meant to give the text, as much as the character (or the author of Nīlakeci), a certain celebrated antiquity, as well as to give sanctity to the long-standing difference of perspectives on two pressing issues: meat-eating and existence of the soul. For, obviously, *Nīlakeci* (the text) cannot claim to belong to the time of the Buddha. But in including a separate section within the larger Jaina-Buddhist debate—Nīlakeci (or the author, through the character) is only establishing the potency of Jaina ahimsā over Buddhist (what the Jainas call 'pseudo') ahimsā. And this is the first non-Jaina system Nīlakeci is debating with. Establishing her prowess in philosophical enquiry and debate with the Buddha, would give her the aura that will precede her arrival in each place where she will throw open the challenge.

I deal briefly here with a few salient points for discussion from Nīlakeci's arguments with the systems of thought important to one's own study—here, Buddhism, Vedic system and Bhūtavada (materialistic system). The idea is also to bring out some crucial points concerning the Jaina identity question and the identity of Nīlakeci and her past, both of which are subtly expressed in these arguments, and intrinsic to my own discussion on 'redefining' of Nīli in the section that follows this one. Before moving on to the debate, there is yet another aspect that is part of dedicating an entire text to debate with non-Jaina systems. As Phyllis Granoff says,

> 'Jain reactions to the fact that they lived in a world marked by religious plurality and one in which their own faith was not the dominant one must have been as many as, and as varied as the local circumstances of their lives. But one consistent Jain response seems to have been that Jains exhibited an eagerness to study and understand the various religious groups around them was virtually unparalleled in classical and medieval India. Jaina monks read and studied every major work of literature, philosophy, poetics...'[30]

The last point, of course, is clear from even a casual perusal of *Nīlakeci.* In order to debate and refute each philosophical / religious system, it is important to have known and grasped the finer details of each of these systems. Granoff further asserts,

> '...We have many accounts in the biographical and story literature of Jain monks engaging their opponents, and of course, defeating them...Many Jain philosophical texts are also debates, and give evidence of the fact that Jains did not withdraw into the seclusion of their own community, but actually sought to engage with other groups or intellectual issues that concerned them.'[31]

In *Nīlakeci*, it is interesting that in each section dealing with different schools of thought / philosophy, we have extended dialogues between Nīlakeci and the teachers, giving equal importance to the teachers of other schools to define their systems and defend, or vouch for, them and Nīlakeci tackles every single point of each system separately in order to quash each of their theories. The poet/author, thus, has deep knowledge of each of these philosophical/religious schools.

I. Nīlakeci Meets Kuṇṭalakeci (Kuṇṭalakecivātaccarukkam)

> '...Train yourself strictly, don't let
> what can hold you back, overwhelm you,
> When you are free from everything that holds you back
> You can love in the world
> Without the depravities that ooze from within
> [Buddha to the nun Tissa, in *Therigāthā*][32]

It seems rather intriguing that Chakravarti devoted only five pages (in the English section of his book) to the Nīlakeci-Kuṇṭalakeci debate, for reasons one cannot fathom.

It is, perhaps, for the first time that this particular debate between the Buddhist and Jaina 'transformed' women will find public expression (within this book, of course); so, I seek some indulgence and a few concessions towards my attempt here. Before moving to the women's dialogues, it might be useful to dwell a bit on the Buddhist-Jaina antagonisms and trajectory of contradictions between the two.

Bahm points out that:

> Gotama is reported to have argued against the Jain view of gaining merit and removing demerit by austerities. The Jain view, as reported is that if there is 'an evil deed that was formerly done by you, wear it away by this severe austerity... Thus by burning up, making an end of former deeds, by the non-

> doing of new deeds, there is no flowing in the future...'Gotama's supposedly devastating rebuttal of the Jain view is recorded thus: 'But do you know that you yourselves were in the past, that you were *not* not?' 'Not this, your reverence.' 'But do you know that you yourselves did this evil deed in the past that you did not *not* do it?' 'Not this, your reverence.' 'But do you know you did not do an evil deed like this or like that?' 'Not this, your reverence.' 'But do you know that so much ill is worn away, or that so much ill is worn away, all ill will become worn away?' 'Not this, your reverence.' 'From what you say you do not know, then whether you yourselves were in the past, whether you were *not* not; you do not know whether in the past you yourselves did this evil deed; whether you did *not* not do it; you do not know whether you did an evil deed like this or like that; you do not know so much ill is worn away, or that when such much ill is worn away al ill will become worn away...Since one cannot rely on this knowledge, or ignorance, of the way the law of karma works, if he is to achieve salvation with assurance, it must be by some other means. Evil consists in anxiety, which is caused by craving. Now regardless of whether one's present craving is caused by past karma, one still has the task of stopping craving, and this task requires present effort. Why not concentrate upon what is necessary and ignore matters which are irrelevant? In fact, interest in karma involves interest in future rewards, hence in rebirth, attachment to a persisting soul, a demand for justice, and taking sides regarding explanations. To the extent one is attached to karma, he deviates from the middle way.' Did Gotama believe in rebirth? 'All beings, sire, are mortal; they finish with death.'[33]

What is the Jaina view of karma then? Padmanabh Jaini writes:

> 'In its embodied state, the soul (*jīva*) experiences—and, indeed, must experience—both pleasant and unpleasant feelings (*veda*). The former are referred to by the Jainas as *sāta* and are understood as both the mental and physical states of ease, happiness, pleasure, etc. Their opposite is *asāta.* Like the *sukha*

> and *dukkha-vedanā*, of the Buddhists, both *sāta* and *asāta* are the fruit (*vipāka*) of karma; good karma (puṇya) produces *sāta*, bad karma (*pāpa*) produces *asāta*. Unlike the Buddhists, however, the Jainas distinguish different kinds of karma[34] which affect the soul differently. Thus, the karma productive of good (śubha) and evil (aśubha) bodies (in the human, heavenly, animal and infernal existences) is known as nāma-karma. The nāma and vedanīya karmas are always present to the jīva as long as it is bound to a body; hence the embodied soul is never free from pleasant and unpleasant feelings. Consequently, the Jainas recognise that in our ordinary life we have no choice but to act in such a way as to bring about the production of asāta. Since these two arise in accordance with our own actions (such as compassion, charity, asceticism and their opposites) it is possible for us to follow a moral course which will maximise our happiness and reduce our suffering. Yet it is not possible for us, so long as we remain in this body, to free ourselves entirely from unpleasant feelings. Like the Buddhists, the Jainas believe that an existence characterised by the incessant fluctuation of pleasant and unpleasant feelings is basically unsatisfactory and an expression of man's karmic bondage... According to the Jainas the jīva in its pure isolated state (kaivalya) is characterised by the qualities (guṇa) of infinite knowledge (jñāna), perception (darśana), vigour (vīrya) and bliss (sukha). These qualities are obstructed or defiled by the influx (āśrava) or the various kinds of karmic matter, whose association with the soul represents the bondage (bandha) from which the Jaina path seeks to free man. Once freed from this bondage, the jīva perfectly manifests its inherent qualities.'[35]

For the Buddhists, "it is not stilling of existence, but stilling of craving, which is the goal. Gotama sought suppression of rebirth of craving. The term 'rebirth' ambiguously denotes rebirth of craving, rebirth of desire, rebirth of consciousness, either in a next moment, next hour, next day, etc., or either in this same body only or in another body or bodies..."[36]

That the author of *Nīlakeci* devotes the largest section of his composition to debate not just one but three Buddhists, including the Buddha, is a continuation of the legacy of their fierce opposition to each other, despite their commonalities, which included, rejection of the authority of the Vedas or the existence of a creator. Some of these commonalities also become apparent when you take into consideration their own respective debates with contemporary religions and schools of thought.

> 'The Jains reject the Buddhist view that reality consists in causal efficiency, i.e., an object is real if it is capable of causing any effect. The Jains reject this approach because according to it, even an illusory snake must be called real as it can cause effects like fear, etc. In fact production of effect is with the Buddhists, the only definition of existence. Each unit of effect is different from any other such unit, but a succession of the different units of effect reveals a succession of new substance every moment, and that is why all things are momentary. The Jains refute this view on the following grounds: we can only assert that thing the existence of which is indicated by a corresponding experience. The Buddhist view that each unit of effect produced is not exactly the same at each new point of time and that therefore things are momentary is fallacious because experience shows that not all of an object is found to be changing every moment.'[37]

Sutton points out that

> 'Buddhism embraced right from its very beginning (at least in its written, doctrinal form) a dynamic concept of Self, more like a stream of psycho-physical events, than a strictly defined entity, 'psychic substratum' or metaphysical 'substance'. Its definition was pragamatic and tentative, rather than dogmatic and mandatory. For lack of a better term, they called Self "non-Self" (Pali Anattā, Sanskrit Anātman).'[38]

There are texts that remain liminal within a textual tradition and *Nīlakeci* is one such. Probably because the text deals with a liminal subject who instills fear in people's hearts and is worshipped, or suppressed on account of her ability to kill. However, it has been a long journey and Nīlakeci will meet her nemesis, a fellow traveller. From here, the two traditions, with two female representatives will meet and take it forward, as if, coming full circle—a debate far away from their own once-limiting and dreaded contexts to that of metaphysical and polemical discourse on two traditions holding their own. Two traditions that accepted two imprisoned women into their folds, in fact welcomed them, and gave them identities that allowed their feminine discourse—within an otherwise male dominated tradition—to *be*.

At Kāmpili, where she goes seeking debate, Kuṇṭalakeci has planted her symbolic rose-apple tree challenging people to come debate her. This is the moment for Nīlakeci. She is about to meet a woman who has transformed from a person filled with remorse and pain, having been betrayed in love, then committing a murder in self-defence and wandering around looking for solace initially in the *nirgrantha* Jaina tradition. The Jaina tradition does not give her the peace she seeks and then she finds a teacher who leads her to the Buddha, who ordains her into the sangha as a nun. For her, too, it has been a journey from a path of imprisonment within bondage of love and loss, revenge and murder, to finding her true calling within a redeeming and forgiving tradition: the Buddhist.

Both Nīlakeci and Kuṇṭalakeci are realised beings (by the time they meet): the only difference being that in Nīlakeci's case, within the Jaina system, she would be perceived as a realised 'soul' while Kuṇṭalakeci would be a realised mind within a 'body'. Because, at one level, both Buddhism and Jainism "teach that only one with insight into the basic structure of our existence is really aware that such an existence is unsatisfactory. In Buddhism, only one who is free from avidyā can clearly recognise the universality of anitya; in Jainism only one is free from moha [ignorance] can understand that the true quality of the soul is sukha."[39]

But before moving on to some significant aspects of this debate let me share the 'antecedents' of Kuṇṭalakeci. And based on a few verses of the Buddhist major *kāvya*, *Kuṇṭalakeci*, I share Kuṇṭalakeci's own thoughts as *theri* (from the sisterhood) or nun of the Buddhist order (outside of what is represented of her in *Nīlakeci*). Then there is the important aspect of how Buddhism included women in its order and what it meant. And it may not have been incidental that the actual debate (for which this text was created) of Nīlakeci begins with Kuṇṭalakeci. One, it is *Kuṇṭalakeci*, the text[40], that the author of *Nīlakeci* is refuting, or countering, essentially; and two, there are certain similarities in the way Kuṇṭalakeci took to Buddhism, and in her life-story, though her beginnings are very different from that of Nīli's. The difference, of course, is that Kuṇṭalakeci is considered (and seems to have been) a historical character, unlike Nīli, who is more of a 'construct'—at least her *pēy* form is. But 'transformation from and into' is the binding factor between the two women apart from the commonality in their chosen vocation, once transformed. Hence, it is important to go back to the story of Bhadda Kuṇṭalakesa of the Buddhist sources.

lūnakesī paṅkadhāri ekasāṭi puracariṃ
avajje vajjamatinī vajje cā vajjadassinī
divāvihāra nikkhamma gijjhakūṭamhi pabbate
addasaṃ virajaṃ buddhaṃ bhikku saṅghapurakkaṭam
nihacca jāṇum vanditvā sammukhā pañjaliṃ akaṃ
ehi bhaddeti maṃ avaca sā me āsūpasampadā
ciṇṇā aṅgā ca magadhā vajjī kāsī cakosalā
anaṇā paṇṇāsavassāni raṭṭhapiṇḍam abhuñjahaṃ
puññaṃ ca pasavī bahuṃ sapañño vatāyaṃ upāsako
yo bhaddāya cīvaraṃ adāsi vippamuttāya sabbaghanthehī

[Once I wandered with hair cut off,
covered with dirt, wearing only one cloth,
I thought there was a fault where there was none,
and I saw no fault where there were.
I went out from the day-shelter up Gijjhakuta mountain,
where I saw the spotless Buddha honoured by his monks.
I bent my knees and worshipped,

facing him I joined my hands in honour,
He said to me, "Come, Bhadda."
That was my ordination.
Chinna, Anga, Magadha, Vajji, Kasi and Kosala-
for fifty years I enjoyed the alms of these places,
never incurring a debt.
The name I was called means good fortune,
it now becomes me.
That wise lay Buddhist made a lot of merit
when he gave a robe to me,
this Bhadda, who is quite free from all ties.][41]

The above verses are part of the *Therigāthā* (*Psalms of the Sisters*, as Rhys Davids published them) and these verses are attributed to Bhadda Kuṇṭalakesa (the same as Kuṇṭalakeci of the story) and record her ordainment in the nun order of the Buddhist sangha; Kuṇṭalakesa was already many years into Jainism as a nun and met the Buddha only after she was defeated in a debate by a Buddhist teacher. The Buddha ordained her and that makes her story very special not only to the *Therigāthā* but also to the Jainas and which is why she is the first opponent for Nīlakeci to defeat.

Charles Hallisey points out that 'The *Therigāthā*'s poems are some of the first poems by women in India; as a collection, the *Therigāthā* is the first anthology of women's literature in the world...' [42]

Kuṇṭalakeci's story is given in the 46th section of the *Psalms of the Sisters* (Therigāthā), edited by Rhys Davids, under the heading, "Bhadra Kuṇṭalakeci, the ex-Jain".[43]

'In addition to the verses [*Therigāthā*]...information about Bhadda is contained in a number of later sources...Buddhaghosa's *Wish Fulfiller* (*Manorathapūraṇi*) a commentary on the *Anguttara Nikāya*. There is a source earlier than the *Wish Fulfiller*, viz, the collection known as *Noble Deeds* (*Apadāna*), which is, like the *Verses*, part of the *Khuddaka Nikāya*. The *Noble Deeds* has been defined as a "kind of supplement to the *Thera Therigāthā*" and

> as being "parallel to the Jātaka describing the former lives of the Buddha"...'[44]

Kuṇṭalakeci was the daughter of a wealthy merchant...One day from her grilled window, she saw a convicted thief named Sattuka (Kāḷaṉ in the Tamil version of her story) being led to his execution. She fell in love with him and told her father that she could not live without him. Exerting a sort of emotional pressure, she manages to convince her father to get him married to her, which he does, after getting Kāḷaṉ released by paying a bribe to the guards. One day, a misunderstanding develops between Kāḷaṉ and her, after she calls him a 'thief', casually, in jest. He pledges to avenge this insult. He tells her one day that he had undertaken a vow to offer worship to a hill deity if he was released. And it is time now to fulfil this vow. He asks Bhadda to accompany him, adorned with her best jewels. Unsuspectingly, she goes with him. Once atop the cliff, he commands her to remove all her jewellery and hand it over to him. Her arguments, to get him to act sensibly, fail. He tells her that he plans to kill her after taking all her jewellery. Her presence of mind saves her. She tells him she would willingly give her jewels and her life for him, but would like to circumambulate him one last time as he was her husband and she, his devoted wife. The conceit in him makes him agree. After the second round, she embraces him, and pushes him from the cliff and kills him. Having done this, she is bereft of all desires towards the material world. Bhadda joins the order of the *nirgranthas* (the Jainas), initially, where, in due course, she gets her name as Kuṇṭalakeci, one of curly locks.

> '[Bhadda] chooses the highest ordination, and has the hair of her head painfully plucked out. The story proceeds thus: In time Bhadda grasps all the teachings of the Jains she joined, and eventually, thinking that she has nothing left to learn, leaves and wanders from place to place, meeting and learning from a variety of paṇḍitas. After becoming highly knowledgeable, she travels around villages and towns challenging anyone to debate

with her. Apart from her superior intellectural capacities, the depiction of Bhadda here and henceforth could hardly be more different than that of the young Bhadda. Growing up and undergoing extensive training, Bhadda has turned ino a dedicated mendicant and skilled debator who travels into the villages and towns and, as far as our sources tell us, remains undefeated in spite of issuing her challenges to whomever wanted to accept it... While upto this moment Bhadda is depicted as a young woman embodying standard gender roles and stereotypes, from now onwards Bhadda is there mostly in a mere grammatical sense, that is to say, very little of Bhadda is left that is specifically characteristic of a woman, even though the texts do use female pronouns when referring to her.'[45]

It is in one of these sessions that she is defeated by the Buddhist teacher, Sāriputta. Sāriputta sent her to the Buddha to take refuge in, and the Buddha spoke a verse of the Dhammapada (v.101) to her:

"Though a thousand be the verses
with words of no avail,
better is a single line of verse,
having heard which, one is pacified." [46]

'Bhadda Kuṇṭalakeci attained enlightenment when she heard this verse and she immediately asked the Buddha for ordination. She spoke the first five of her verses at a later time when she recollected her attainments. The final verse she spoke when a lay follower gave her his own robe... Dhammapada interprets these practices in the context of Bhadda's experience among Jains earlier (pubbe nigaṇṭhīhutvā) and he then interprets the ascetic practices named more narrowly: plucking out the hair, not cleaning the teeth, and wearing only one robe.'[47]

In the section that depicts Nīlakeci's debate with Buddhism (including with the Arukaccantiran and Buddha) Nīlakeci picks on flesh-eating and alludes to lack of cleanliness as a counter to what Buddhists said about the Digambara monks and nuns in their texts. The focus in both seem to have been on attacking each other on questions of cleanliness and body in their ascetic practices, besides of course their problems with each other on the question of the soul. The author of *Nīlakeci* only enters the long tradition of intense contest between the two traditions since long.

> 'Bhadda's story ends rather suddenly once she has entered the Sangha. In a way, both in terms of her life and of the pedagogical function of the tale, the mission is, so to speak, accomplished with the double event of attaining Arhatship and entering the Sangha. These show that even someone who has committed such heinous acts as killing her own husband can be fully redeemed to the extent of being able to achieve the highest goal and being allowed to join the Sangha in the very same life as the killing took place.'[48]

Nīlakeci's story too, seems to halt after her debates with various schools and there seems to be no remembrance in popular Tamil Jaina imagination of such a character or woman.

Uma Chakravarti opines that

> 'Although the wider culture of renunciation recognised that regardless of barriers of caste, class and sex, everyone had the potential for salvation, the Buddha was reluctant to admit women into the Buddhist sangha. Permission was finally (and grudgingly) granted because of the persistence of Buddha's foster mother, Mahāpajāpati Gotami, who travelled many miles through heat and dust in pursuit of the Buddha.'[49]

The *Therigāthā*, according to Uma Chakravarti, is 'amongst the most poignant pieces of writing by women...where it is dukkha, the driving motif of Buddhist philosophy, that is movingly expressed...'[50] Given below is one of the verses, attributed to Vassithi who lost her child, but meeting the Buddha, was calmed down:

> 'Now here, now there, lightheaded, crazed with grief,
> Mourning my child, I wandered up and down

Naked, unheeding, streaming hair unkempt...
And then at last I saw him...great tamer of the untamed hearts...
Banisher of fears,
Came back my heart to me...
Now all my sorrows are cast out
I now can grasp and understand
The base on which my miseries were built.'[51]

Similarly, 'the story of Kisa Gotami whose son died and in her grief she went about seeking medicine to revive him. 'The Buddha said to her, "go and fetch me a handful of mustard seeds from any house where death has not occurred." Relieved, Gotami went around the village. Going from door to door and as she did so, realisation dawned upon her that death was inevitable and her crazed mind was calmed... Her verses capture the sorrow and then the wisdom...:[52]

"...I saw my husband die, my baby too...
Yet she, her people slain, herself outcast...
hath thither come
Where death is not...
I am healed of my hurt...
My heart is wholly set at liberty."

It is rather unfortunate that the world has lost out on the entire text of the Tamil *Kuṇṭalakeci*, which would have been as wonderful as the *Therigāthā*, and perhaps one of the only remaining Buddhist works in Tamil from a female voice. But what is left of that text are verses attributed to *Kuṇṭalakeci* in other early Tamil works. It was by accident that I found a compilation of nineteen such verses brought out in a book which gives a brief summary of two other works in the same volume—*Maṇimekalai* (a Buddhist work) and *Valaiyāpati* (a Jaina treatise,which again, is not available in its entirety). J. Srichandiran compiled the nineteen verses from commentaries to the *Tolkāppiyam*, *Yāpperuṅkalavirutti and Vīracōḷiyam*, and commentary of Ñānaprakasar in *Sivañānasiddhi* and of course from *Nīlakeci*'s commentary of Samaya Divākara, where ninety-nine verses of *Kuṇṭalakeci* are alluded to.[53]

It is interesting to see that *Kuṇṭalakeci*'s verses, too, seem to record the pain of living through both her own experiences (from her life, which is not invoked in the verses, but which we know from other Buddhist works) and that of her fellow nuns. And if we compare a few verses of the *Therigāthā*, we can perhaps find reflection of the experience of even Kisa Gotami and Vasitthi.

Though Uma Chakravarti believes that "Despite these rich attempts by women to give meaning to their lives, the Buddhist corpus compiled by a body of bhikkus reveals a lack of appreciation for the bhikkuni...",[54] in case of the Tamil country, *Kuṇṭalakeci* seems to have gained far more respect and centrality since the work itself figured among the five major kāvyas (*ainperuñkāppiyam*) dedicated to Bhadda Kuṇṭalakeci. *Kuṇṭalakeci* was important enough for the Jaina author to model *Nīlakeci* after, considering that Kuṇṭalakeci was also moving from place to place, arguing with men about the superiority of the Buddhist school. Perhaps one of the reasons is also that there were a large number of Jaina nuns in the Tamil country as can be evidenced from inscriptions of the early centuries BCE. The Buddhists could not keep nuns out of their order in the same region and definitely not afford to give them a subordinate status, especially when they had a rival order to contend with. Apparently, one of the debates where Kuṇṭalakeci emerged winner was with the Jaina monk, Nātakuttanār, in a city called Āvaṉam (not identifiable).[55]

I share below a few of the nineteen verses of *Kuṇṭalakeci* collected by Srichandiran, just to give a sense of her mind.

The invocatory verses to the Buddha are as follows:

'We take refuge at the feet of him,
who is our lord
of good thoughts and right speech
who, not possessing anything for himself, thought of others before he thought of himself
and gave up his all for the good of others.'[56]

Here below, Kuṇṭalakeci criticises other ascetic systems, making the case for the Buddhist form of true penance.

'Adorning ochre robes or smearing ash over one's body,
Standing naked in the rain and in blistering winter
or on fiery coal in hard summer
walking around taking alms from the community, growing locks of hair
says he [the Buddha], more than these
exerting oneself in good conduct
is the true penance'[57]

The following few verses seem to have a semblance of the thoughts expressed in the *Therigāthā* and to some extent also seem to reflect the realisation Kuṇṭalakeci had gained from her own experiences.

'Admiring someone's beautiful shoulders
or another's beautiful black tuft of hair
saying these are mere external objects
is like people saying, adding butter into the flames [of passion]
will extinguish the fire [of desire]'[58]

'The burning flame of desire [passion] consumes the body
it is like holding on to a burning piece of wood
and waiting that it will die of its own coition [of wood and flame]
it may be extinguished only by non-desire
can we wait for further floods to stop a flood?[59]*'*

'Species of snakes, the lion[60] *and demons*
may stay for a short while forgetting their inherent characteristics
and show tenderness
but one day shall show no compassion
just as some men'[61]

'We die as embryos in our mothers' wombs[62]
then as a young child we die
later we die as a young woman
we die in so many forms everyday

yet do not cry over all those deaths
wonder why then do we cry over someone else' death!'[63]

'Thinking that this body is mine
you shower love on it
however, like tiny millet mixed with rice
several small and large organisms combine
to produce this body, and to destroy it, too
Oh foolish one, can one really say this body is mine?'[64]

The Two Women's Cerebral Contest

In both the works—*Kuṇṭalakeci* and *Nīlakeci*—the essence of the arguments are for real, in terms of the contemporary discourse of the time, even if the actual place of the debate or 'event' of it, may have been a creation.

Through her clairvoyance (*avadhiñāna*) Nīlakeci saw a rose-apple tree planted to the ground at Kāmpili. When she entered the place, she asked the gatekeeper of the city-gate by the king's palace the reason and learnt that the bhikkuṇi Kuṇṭalakeci was now residing there, since nobody had come forward to accept her challenge for a debate, for which she had planted the rose-apple tree branch.

With Kuṇṭalakeci, Nīlakeci's main points of contestation include the rejection of the Buddhist theory of absence of soul (ātman) and that of impermanence. She also takes issue with each of the *Jātaka* tales of the Bodhisattva, denying greatness and compassion to the Buddha, saying that causing pain to oneself, when it is of no use to another, may not be called greatness. Kuṇṭalakeci recalls the magnanimity of the Buddha in many of his previous births, in the verse titled *puttaṉiṉ vaḷḷaṉmay* (Buddha's benevolence). In *Sibi Jātaka*, Bodhisattva as king Sibi granting his own eyes; *Sasa Jātaka*, as a hare, offered himself to the brāhmiṇ; in *Maitribala Jātaka*, as a king he tore off his own flesh and offered food to the yakṣas; in Viswāntara Jātaka, he gave his own wife and children away. Similarly, the Vyāgri,

Sankalpa and and Mahākapi Jātaka stories each have instances of a great sacrifice by the Bodhisattva signifying self-suffering to relieve the pain of others.[65]

> *'kaṇkoṭuttā<u>n</u> <u>r</u>aṭikoṭuttā<u>n</u>*
> *kayappulikkut ta<u>r</u>koṭuttā<u>n</u>*
> *peṇkoṭuttā <u>n</u>uṭampi<u>n</u>aiyum*
> *piḷantiṭṭup pi<u>r</u>arkkīntā<u>n</u>*
> *maṇkoṭuttā<u>n</u> makkakoṭuttā<u>n</u>*
> *ma<u>n</u><u>n</u>ūnta<u>r</u> cērntārkku*
> *viṇkoṭuttā <u>n</u>ava<u>n</u>koṭutta*
> *viritturaippa<u>n</u> kēḷe<u>n</u><u>r</u>āḷ'* (v. 205)[66]
>
> [Hear what I say, of the greatness of his giving (munificence)
> His eyes, he gave, and his body parts,
> To the tigress suffering from agonising hunger, his own body he gave
> His young children, he gave away,
> And his own wife he gave away
> Thus enduring self-suffering
> He gave, in each of his lives]'

Reiko Ohnuma writes—

> 'Indian Buddhist narrative literature of all ages and schools is full of stories involving paradigmatic acts of generosity in which an animal or human character gives away his entire body or a part of his body to whomever requests it: King Sibi gouges out his eyes and gives them to a blind man; Prince Mahasattva throws himself off a cliff in order to feed a starving tigress; a hare jumps into a fire in order to feed a hungry traveller; and an elephant removes his own tusks and presents them to an evil hunter. The majority of such stories are jatakas, or accounts of the Buddha's previous lives, and serve to demonstrate the great selflessness and compassion cultivated by the Buddha during his long career as a bodhisattva. In terms of the bodhisattva's cultivation of the perfections (paramita), they are almost always classified as preeminent examples of the perfection of generosity or giving (dana).'[67]

Nīlakeci charges that these are more acts of foolishness than munificence and compassion. She points out, "magnanimous gifts must be of some service to the persons who receive the gifts. For a headless trunk to go to the Bodhisattva and ask his head is primarily meaningless...and it cannot live, much less speak; and to satisfy this headless trunk by severing his own head does not indicate the wisdom of the giver..."[68] Nīlakeci rejects each of the instances that Kuṇṭalakeci narrates, as meaningless.

Kuṇṭalakeci speaks of the Buddha as having travelled through the *samsāra* for several *kalpas* (times / time-zones / unit of time) for the welfare of others. The three *piṭakas* revealed by him are the Buddhist scriptures, but Nīlakeci expresses amusement that if the Buddha is supreme and perfect from the beginning, then why he should wander through samsāra for several *kalpas*, unless it is due to his past karmas. The most crucial point she raises is about meat-eating, which is not condemned in Buddhist teachings.

> 'While preaching mercy to all living beings, it did not condemn flesh eating...while preaching ethical conduct or *śilācāra*, it rejects the doctrine of the ātman. There is no meaning in insisting on moral life, while rejecting the very basis of morality.'[69]

There are 81 verses on this debate. I am only taking selectively of these. I shall come to the content of their debate, shortly. Here, let me bring direct attention to the fact that Chakravarti, for whatever reason, in his English summary, devotes only five pages in all to the Nīlakeci-Kuṇṭalakeci debate. In the Tamil section, he does not give any editorial inputs to the verses 150-174 and only begins to do so from verse 175, when the actual debate begins. Perhaps he considered the rest 'fluff' one could do without, since there is elaborate description of Nīlakeci offering worship to the Jina, among other things. Po.Ve.So, of course, gives detailed editorial inputs and comments for all the verses. However, in the English summary of Chakravarti's edition, we find a long discussion regarding Kuṇṭalakeci as a woman and as to why she may have entered the Buddhist sangha.

'Buddha himself, when he organised the Order, was very reluctant to admit women into the Sangha. But finally he yielded to the importunate requests of his friends and disciples. He was willing to admit women into the Order and they formed an important section of the Buddhist Sanga. But in the case of Nirgranthas, women were admitted into the Order of ascetics from the very beginning. Women had no diffuculty in securing admission. But from the very beginning they were under a disability due to an important Nirgrantha doctrine which became later a bone of contention between Digambaras and Svetambaras the two later sections of the Jainas due to a schism about the time of Bhadrabāhu. This Nirgrantha doctrine is that since women are not fit to adopt the Nirgrantha *tapas* they could not become Arhats in the same birth. The Nirgrantha *tapas* referred to consists in complete renunciation of worldly things including clothes...and the early Nirgranthas evidently emphasised this aspect and included in their teachings the doctrine that women were not fit to attain Mukti as women. Learned in all the Sāstras, Kundalakesi was evidently not satisfied with this inferiority of women according to the Nirgrantha doctrine. She must have been too proud to acquiesce in such an inferior status. But in the case of the Buddhists, when once they admitted women into the fold they treated them as equals, provided the women kept up all the *silāchāras*, they were also equally qualified for Arhatship. This being the case, Kundalakesi who was on her debating tour visiting all the learned men of the country met Sāriputta at Śrāvasti. Sāriputta who must have known the Nirgrantha doctrine very well must have exploited it to the full advantage. Knowing that the lady...was thoroughly learned in all important philosophical doctrines of the day, he evidently wanted to bring to her consciousness, how with all her scholarship she was not given the status that she deserved, by the Nirgrantha teachers to whom she owed allegiance. Hence the question which he put her[70] must certainly have reference to Arhatship. *Ekam nāma kim* must be interpreted to mean the state of perfection...the state of conquering of the karmas and the state of perfect knowledge and perfect bliss... Kundalakesi brought up under the traditions of the Nirgrantha school must have been taught about the inferior status of women in the Order and must have accepted the doctrine as a Jain female ascetic...with her firm conviction that it was not her lot to know anything directly of the state of Arhatship... But when Sāriputta began his exposition of his Buddhistic doctrine, he must have certainly emphasised the fact that the goal was within the reach of women also and this particular lady Kundalakesi was eminently fit to be one of the Arhats... From the point of view of intellect, certainly, the male members of the Nirgrantha Order associated with her were not in any way superior to herself. From the point of view of moral discipline and devotion to truth she was quite their equal. In spite of such equality she was assigned only an inferior status merely on the strength of difference of sex. When the Buddhist teacher Sāriputta pointed out that sex was no disqualification to Arhatship she must have perceived her opportunity. It is no wonder that she immediately offered herself as a candidate to be admitted into the Order. Knowing her eminent culture, Sāriputta naturally suggested that she must have her ordination directly from Buddha himself...It is just this doctrine of the Nirgranthas that is one of the disputed doctrines by Swetambara Jains who also believe that women are quite qualified to attain Moksha as women.'[71]

If one reads *Nīlakeci* with some level of intensity one can't help notice a different attitude or approach of Nīlakeci towards Kuṇṭalakeci when compared to the others she contests. There is a definite undercurrent of female mutual respect and certain calmness to the way Nīlakeci takes up each of the points Kuṇṭalakeci elaborates upon, even if, at the end of it, Nīlakeci is denouncing the Buddhist doctrine and rubbishing the *Jātakas* and all claims of the Buddha being perfect.

Having set her mind of the path of Jina dharma Nīlakeci now takes the form of a woman of mighty penance, an ascetic and seeks the blessings of the *pañca paramēṣṭis*[72] to take on Kuṇṭalakeci. Kāmpili was looking deserted when Nīlakeci landed there (she had flown to that place with her special powers); she learnt from the gatekeeper of Kāmpili as to the reason for that appearance. He told her about Kuṇṭalakeci who was at that moment resident there, and gives a symbolic description of how everyone (including the horses) is confined within their homes and in the palace because they cannot face the debating challenge posed by Kuṇṭalakeci who had firmly planted a rose-apple tree branch as a signifier of being open to challenge. It was as if people were imprisoned. Nīlakeci asked the gatekeeper to inform the king that a female ascetic (she) had arrived and would like to accept Kuṇṭalakeci's challenge. The gatekeeper then pointed Kuṇṭalakeci out to her. Seeing the woman with large, beautiful eyes "shaped like tender green-mangoes", Nīlakeci asked her (feigning innocence, as it seems, from the queries she puts to her opponent) as to what could be the purpose of her planting the rose-apple tree branch in this place? Was it to amend the present system ("*muṟai tiruttal*", or rule or governance), or conditions, or was it to start some sort of battle, or is there an enemy there who needs to be killed, [which was obviously pun-intended, aiming at the Buddha's idea of ahimsā or non-violence]?

Kuṇṭalakeci, in her response, said to Nīlakeci that she had asked the ruler of Kāmpili to bring forth ascetics of other religious schools to challenge her in a debate, for which purpose she had planted the rose-apple tree [which was to be crushed if someone accepted the challenge]. She told Nīlakeci, if she was here as a visitor to the king's palace, she should better be carrying on with her own job and leave, unless, of course, she would dare to engage with her in a debate by responding to her questions. [Verse. 169][73]

Hearing that, Nīlakeci remarked, with a tinge of sarcasm, to the gatekeeper: let the passages of the palace be open, and anyways, it is time for the elephants and horses in this palace to move about free; with her lips red as ripe coral and voice of a cuckoo, Nīlakeci asked the gatekeeper to let the king know that she accepts Kuṇṭalakeci's challenge and he should ready the place for setting up the debate.

Incidentally, it may be mentioned that it was commonplace in those times to conduct open philosophical / religious debates in the king's court, and the victor of the debate could also convert the king to her or his own school of thought.

Learning of this conversation, the king, pleased, invited the two women over with great respect and due preparations, in keeping with the tradition, and honoured the two female ascetics before commencing the debate (v.171) and he prepared to welcome the women, asking them to examine, individually, if they so wished, the various texts/scriptures he had. (v. 172)[74]

Meanwhile, the indisputable/incontestable Kuṇṭalakeci [referred to in the verse as *kuṇṭalamākeci*] set forth a condition before commencing the debate that whosoever will win the debate, should be felicitated/celebrated and the loser should be sufficiently humiliated/disgraced, as a punishment of sorts. The king agreed to this condition (v.173)[75]

Kuṇṭalakeci starts the cerebral duel with the "one with honey-tipped voice", as Nīlakeci is referred to here. (v. 175)

She eulogises the Buddha:

ātitāṉ periyaṉā yaṟakkeṭu maḷavellā
mūtiyamē yuṇarntava ṉūṟutaruma mēyuraittāṉ
yātaṉaiyum tāṉvēṇṭā ṉayalārkkē tuṉpuṟṟāṉ
pōtiyā ṉemmiṟaivaṉ poruṅtiṅṉā ruyakkoḷvāṉ (v.176)[76]

[Being supreme from the beginning,
he, having attained omniscience,
thinking of the good of all living beings, propounded a faith
He endured suffering, for the sake of others, not thinking of himself
He protects all who take refuge in him, that Buddha, is our god]

Kuṇṭalakeci then goes on to elaborate on her religion, on the Buddhist scriptural tradition, the nature of elements and existence. She says,

> 'First he [the Buddha] created the three texts
> Wherein he spoke of the elements five,
> Form, sensation [pleasure/pain], consciousness, volition and perception
> Non-permanent is the birth and death of each of these
> They die, even as they are born, like a flame of a lamp extinguished.' (v. 177)[77]

Kuṇṭalakeci just says *muṉṉūl* but it is to be understood (since she does not name them) as the three *piṭakas—Vinaya Piṭaka, Sutta Piṭaka* and *Abdhidhamma Piṭaka.* Again, she just says, *poruḷ* (*muṭiporuḷ*) which are *uru, uḻappu, aṟivōṭu kuṟi, ceykai,* which are the Tamil terms for the kandas (or Skandas, which is explained below)—*uruvakkantam (rūpa), nukarccikkantam (vedana), aṟivukkantam (viññāna), kuṟikkantam (samjña), ceyaṟkkantam (samskāra).*[78]

Sutton explains the Buddhist concept of Self, which Kuṇṭalakeci in this verse is alluding to as the first point in her exposition of her system. We may remember that both Sāriputta and the Buddha held an important place in the life of Bhadda Kuṇṭalakeci.

> '[The] "factors" (Khandhas) of personality are usually translated as "aggregates", "elements", "classes", "groups", or "heap" of qualities, or constituents. They are of two kinds: material (*rūpa*) and mental, or immaterial (*nāma, arūpin*). The latter are further subdivided into four categories pertaining to specific activities of the mind, such as sensation or emotions (*vedana*), perceptions (*sañña*), volition, predisposition or impulses (*samkhāra*) and cognition or consciousness (*viññāna*) A comprehensive presentation of the *rūpa* elements is given in the *Mahā-Hatthi-Padopama-sutta* of the *Majjhima -Nikāya,* where Sāriputta speaks about the attachment to visible shapes. The realm of visible forms is here explained as being constituted of the four principal elements, that is, water, fire, wind, and earth. Each of these can be either personal or external (to the physical person). Through a detailed analysis of all possible identifications with such elements, or with their adjectival derivatives (that is fluidity,

heat, breath, and solidity, respectively) Sāriputta arrives at the conclusion that no self-identification is acceptable with the physical substances on account of their continuous transformation...'[79]

Further,

> 'The Buddha...described (in his first sermon) the psycho-physical complex, known as the human personality, along five different strands, or streams of events, bundled together in a dynamic river of energy, accessible to everyone through self-observation. These five strands (Sanskrit Skandhas, Pali Kandhas) were classified in the Theravadin *Abdhidhamma Piṭaka* under three headings: (1) physical body (*rūpa*); (2) sense-perception and reaction to it, that is, sensation of feeling (*vedana*), perception (*samjña*), volition or impulses (*samskāra*) and (3) consciousness (*viññāna*). These three groups were also called; "form" (*rūpa*), "concomitants" or "conditioning factors of consciousness" (*cetasika*) and the "state of consciousness proper" (*citta*).' [80]

B.K. Matilal interprets the Buddhist concept of Self, in this manner:-

> '[In] the Buddhist way...there is no real subject, no real 'I'. There is only a conglomerate of five aggregates, each element of which is pushing ahead on its own, but which jointly falsely create a sense of unity that plays the role of the subject. The continuity or flow of these five phenomenal series allow for the identity of the person over time. If the liberating insight shatters the unity of the subject in this way, desire, etc are thereby shattered altogether. And if the unity of the subject is lost into the multiplicity of fluctuating phenomena, the object to be grasped by perceptions and intended by desires, etc are also automatically shattered into phenomenal pieces...'[81]

Nīlakeci now tells the people assembled to witness the debate that she will now take up, one-by-one, the inconsistencies in the doctrine so far laid out by Kuṇṭalakeci. (v. 178)

She starts off by saying—

'mu̱ṉṉeṉap paṭuvatutāṉ mutallit taṭumāṟṟa
maṉṉataṉkaṭ periyaṉē laṟaṅkoṇṭa tavamākum
piṉṉataṉkat periyaṉēṟ piṟaḻveytuṅ kālacco
leṉṉeṉṟāṉ periyavā ṟirumaiyiṉun tirinteṉṟāḷ' (v. 179)[82]

[There is an inherent confusion in what you say
That your preceptor (the Buddha) was supreme from the beginning
Was he then, supreme even prior to the doctrine he founded,
having attained enlightenment?
If, having created his doctrine, he was supreme,
then how could that be the beginning (of time), and be not, a defective statement?]

Nīlakeci then moves to the perpetually contested subject of non-violence.

'Oh woman, endowed with beauty that can drive even the deer away,
You say he is the virtuous one, with mercy for all living beings
At the cost of his own destruction
But, consider this, when all beings experience suffering in their lives
By destroying himself could he end their destruction forever?
Did he not kill them, too?' (v. 181)[83]

Perhaps, this may be an allusion to the Jātakas where, by undergoing suffering while assuming the form of different beings, to end others' distress, did he not cause (self) destruction of these beings? It can also be a reference to the inconsistency in the doctrine with regard to eating flesh, thereby causing pain to living beings. By the way, what exactly was the Buddha's opinion on consumption of meat? Bahm has noted that:

> 'Gotama advised against 'the eating of meat in these cases—if there is evidence either of your eyes or your ears or if there are grounds of suspicion. And in these cases I allow it—if there is no evidence of your eyes or of your ears and if there is no

ground for suspicion...' Battling with an animal victim intended for food, especially if accompanied by an attitude of fear, hatred, brutality, or even of pity, is not conducive to calmness. In seeking calmness one should avoid such killing. However, also killing animals for food is a custom. One who follows the middle way is neither attached to nor repulsed by customs, is unanimous about any custom. It is also a custom to believe that killing of animals is an evil. If this is paradoxical, then it is a customary paradox, and one with which those who are willing to accept things as they are must be prepared to live. One may wish to stop the killing of animals, but if this desire grows into desirousness, generates restlessness, willfulness, regarding interfering with the lives of others, then this desire to stop the killing of animals has become evil.'[84]

In what I found a particularly challenging (in spite of the two editions I referred to), but interesting verse, with a fascinating use of metaphors, after many readings I thought it appropriate to infer that Nīlakeci was commenting both on the idea of the Bodhisattvas (former births), as well as the Buddhist idea of momentariness and impermanence of the moment, but Chakravarti (and Po.Ve.So, too) interprets this as her critiquing Kuṇṭalakeci's statement about the Buddha striving for the good of others and having committed bad deeds.

'nuṉaittalaiya nuṇmayirai nuṉiyuṟī-i vitirttiṭṭā
laṉaittuṇaiya tataṅkaṭalu maṟakkiṭanta piṟantuḻappu
niṉaikkuṅkāṟ piṟarkēyā meṉṟiyā nīyaṉṉā
yaṉaittuṇaiya perumpāva mavaṉceyta nākāṉō' (v.183)[85]

[if you pierce the sharp ends of hair (follicles?) into the sea
how many wave-particles (ripples) would be produced (born) therefrom?
countless would be the births and deaths (there, of waves / wave particles)
those many bad deeds, seems to me, the Buddha committed
who, you say, strived for others]

One way to also understand this is to say that (Nīlakeci is pointing out to Kuṇṭalakeci that) just as the Buddha speaks of momentary-ness (in the context of the five kandas/skandas) which are born and die as a continuous process, so too are waves/ripples produced in the sea, that are born and die the next moment and if you were to count these, how many births and deaths would there have occurred in the world and if you used this analogy, how many Bodhisattvas were born and died, as per your (Buddhist) doctrine, so (as per our, Jaina order of things) those many rebirths meant that the Buddha must have committed those many bad deeds to be born and re-born, just as there are waves in the sea; but you say he was born to strive for others' welfare, whereas you also say that everything is impermanent (*anitta*)!

What isn't clear to me, though, is the use of the metaphor of piercing sharp-ends of the hair into the sea (*nuṉaittalaiya nuṇmayirai nuṉiyurī-i vitirttiṭṭāl*).

In the following verse it is very interesting that Nīlakeci invokes Kuṇṭalakeci's life-story for the first time (in the text). The tone of her invoking, however, is rather demeaning of Kuṇṭalakeci and it appears as if, for a moment, she has forgotten her own past life!

> '*paruvaralōṉ ṟilaṉṟāyaip paḻūpparittāṉ ṟalaivaṉivaḷ*
> *karuvaraimēṟ ṟaṉkaṇavaṉ kāḻaṉaiyuñ kaviḻttiṭṭā*
> *ḷiruvaraiyum polvāriv virunilattiṉ mēleṅkum*
> *peruvaḻiyār poruḷār piṟaryārē veṉaṅkkāḷ* (v. 192)[86]
>
> [He leaves his mother to turn grey by age[87] inflicting pain[88]
> while she kills her own husband, Kālaṉ, pushing him to death
> from a high cliff
> would we find anywhere great path-makers like these two!]

Then there are a series of verses where Nīlakeci does some scathing critique of the Jātaka tales—their conception and the nature of Bodhisattvas in those stories. I refer to just a few.

As for the *Jatakas*, these are 550 stories of former births of

Śākyamuni Buddha compiled in the collection (in Pali language) *Jātakatthāvaṇṇanā*.

> 'The belief of orthodox Buddhists on the subject is this. The Buddha, as occasion arose, was accustomed throughout his long career to explain and comment on the events happening around him, by telling of similar events that had occurred in his own previous births. The experience, not of one lifetime only, but of many lives, was always present to his mind; and it was this experience he so often used to point a moral, or adorn a tale. The stories so told are said to have been reverently learnt and repeated by his disciples; and immediately after his death 550 of them were gathered together in one collection, called the Book of the 550 Jatakas or Births; the commentary to which gives for each Jataka, or Birth Story, an account of the event in Gotama's life which led to his first telling that particular story. Both text and commentary were then handed down intact, and in the Pali language in which they were composed, to the time of the Council of Patna (held in or about the year 250 B.C.); and they were carried in the following year to Ceylon by the great missionary Mahinda...[89]

Meanwhile, Kuṇṭalakeci proceeds with exalting the Buddha's generosity and self-suffering.

> *'ēti lāriṭar tīrkku memaviṟai*
> *cāta kammivai yeṉṟu talaittalai*
> *yōti ṉāṉiṉ ṟorupaka lellaiyuṅ*
> *kōtai vārkuḻar kuṇṭala kēciyē'* (v. 206)[90]
>
> [Kuṇṭalakeci of the long curly tresses
> distressed by the opponents, exalted our preceptor (the Buddha)
> in one after the other of the Jātakas (stories) so that his fame
> be everlasting
> who was born and died through one hundred thousand *kalpas*
> (of time)
> so others' sufferings may cease]

An additional verse delineates the different forms the Buddha took in his former lives while abstaining from killing and having subdued his passions:

'vāṉūṭum pariyāyu mariṇa māyum
vaṉakkēḻaṟ kaḷirāyu meṇkār puṇmāṉ
ṟāṉāyu maṉaiyerumai yorutta lāyuṅ
taṭakkaiyiḷaṅ kaḷirāyuñ caṭañka māyu
mīṉāyu muyalāyu maṉṉamāyu
mayilāyum piṟavāyum vellaluṅ ciṅka
mānāyuṅ kolaikaḷavu kaṭpoy kāmam
varaintavartā muṟaintapati maṉā vūrē' [91]

Hearing this, the 'large-eyed Nīlakeci' says—

'nūlu nāru micaittaṉa vottalā
nīla keci neṭuṅka ṇūḷcollu
mālum pēyu muṭaiyavar ceykaiyē
pōlu nīcoṉṉa puttar caritaiyē' (v. 207)[92]

[Oh do you weave a long thread, said the large-eyed Nīlakeci
Extolling the eminence of the Buddha,
Like (weaving tall tales of) being possessed by a *pēy* and being
in delirium]

It is quite a pun on the word, and the very idea of—and her former form—'*pēy*'. Nīlakeci soon takes on the Jātaka tales.

'yāva ṉāyiṉu maṉṉava ṉiṉmayiṟ
ṟēva ṉeṉṟu teḷiyun teḷintapiṉ
cāva ṉeṉpatōr caṅkaiyu miṉṟiyē
yīva ṉeṉpatō riccaiyun tōṉṟumē' (v. 210)[94]

This verse refers to the *Maitribala Jātaka*. Bodhisattva was once Maitribala the king, who was known for his righteousness and generosity. Once, five yakṣas, passing through a forest in the guise of brāhmins, saw a happy cow-herd who extolled the virtues of his king to them. By nature mischievous and wicked, the yakṣas desired to check out on the king and also made plans to bring about his fall. Knowing that he was mighty generous, they went to him, still disguised as brāhmins, and begged for food. But they did not want just any kind of food. They told the king they wanted human flesh, blood that was fresh and hot, since that is what they were habituated to. They revealed their true form and even though the king knew their unreasonable request, he felt it was his moral duty to give what was requested for, since he was a righteous king who had never refused anything that was asked from him ever. So he decided to give his own flesh and blood to the yakṣas, but not as a dead body, since they asked for fresh and hot blood and flesh. So he told the yakṣas: 'this body made up of flesh and blood exists only for the service of mankind. If I can satisfy you by offering my flesh and blood from this body it would immensely satisfy me. Hence this body is yours.'[95]

He sent for a surgeon to cut open five main arteries and gave the blood to the yakṣas to drink, and offered pieces of flesh cut open, as well. Gradually, seeing his selflessness and purity, the yakṣas begged of him to stop cutting himself up and became transformed. Maitribala spoke to them about universal love. The yakṣas offered worship to the Bodhisattva and Indra, too, came down to praise him, and restored his body to its original glory.

Now this is the story which is picked up for criticism in the verse (210). Nīlakeci tells Kuṇṭalakeci—

> 'Anyone, knowing that the person before him
> was a deva, in an illusory form, and in spite of knowing,
> willingly deciding to die
> is, beyond doubt, committing suicide.'

Yet again, aiming at the *Matsya Jātaka*, and its redundancy, Nīlakeci points out—

> '*yāṉai yuḷḷara ceṅkuḷa taṅkelām*
> *vāṉa niṉṟu vaḷipaṭal kāṇṭumāṉ*
> *mīṉu mallavum vētaṉai yeytuḷi*
> *tāṉa tātar ṟōtākatar taṉmaiyō*' (v. 220)[96]

Before translating this verse, let me give a brief summary of the *Matsya Jātaka* story. In one of his births, Bodhisattva was a fish in a pond near Śrāvasti. At one point the place was hit by drought and the lakes and ponds were drying up. The fish and tortoises in the pond were dying and eaten up by birds of prey. Bodhisattva decided to save the fellow fish in the pond and began to pray to the king of gods, Pārjanya, who, pleased, sent a downpour of rain and saved all other fish. The verse above refers to this tale. Nīlakeci says—

> 'When we already have, elsewhere, stories of
> an elephant[97] standing and praying for the rains
> Does it behove the Tathāgata[98] to prove his own greatness
> To repeat the same (story), be born as a fish and taking pains
> bring down the rains?'

The following one is about Bodhisattva as a monkey (*Mahākapi Jātaka*) which Nīlakeci critiques:

> *'cīla nallavar nīḷkuvar cēṇeṉiṟ*
> *kōla milkuraṅ kāṭṭikol vārkaḷaik*
> *kāluṅ kaiyu meḻaṟkeṉak kāṇkilāṉ*
> *Vālai nīṭṭik kiṭattaṟaṉ māṭciyō'* (v. 222)[99]

Briefly, the story:

> 'The Bodhisatta's pontifical function is the theme of this story, where he is the king of the "monkeys", who are resident in a tree on this side of the Ganges, where they are in danger of a royal hunter, who would kill and devour them; it is only on the other shore that they would be safe; but they cannot cross the torrent. The Bodhisatta, therefore, "makes of himself a bridge" (attānam saṁkamaṁ katvā), by which they can cross. He first springs, as they cannot, from shore to shore "sped, as it were, by the Gale" ... On the farther shore, he attaches a rattan rope to a tree, and the other end of it to his own waist, and so makes the return leap, and is able to reach the tree on this side, and to grasp it, but can do no more; in this way he bridges the flood. Across his body and by the rattan rope the monkeys escape; but

> the Buddha's enemy, Devadatta, finally springs on his back as he hangs on the tree, and breaks it, so that he falls and dies. The body falls on this side of the river...'[100]

The Bodhisattva, of course, is captured by the king's servants and the king was pleased with his sense of self-sacrifice. While preaching to the king the duties of a ruler, the Bodhisattva died and a shrine was built for him where he was buried.

Nīlakeci has this to say about it:

> 'Being the good and lofty [the Buddha] could have, through his greatness, caused the hands and feet of the killers of those beautiful monkeys [sent by the king] to stop moving
> Did his greatness consist [instead] in lying there, lengthening his tail?'

There is intended pun on the word, *nīḷkuvar,* used for the Buddha, which can mean both 'long' (indicating the length of his tail as a monkey in the story) and lofty (in character).

Nīlakeci's 'fault-showing' (critique) of the Jātaka stories ends with the story of the yakṣas drinking blood out of the Bodhisattva which, Nīlakeci charges, is akin to the Buddha killing his own mother, though I am not very clear about the analogy used here, which is not clear from the verse (v.223). Perhaps, indirectly, there is the invoking of the blood or womb connection with the mother which Bodhisattva, in his moment of generosity and self-denial, sets aside. Chakravarti interprets it as a fault in the Buddha's non-killing (ahimsā) doctrine, which is being rubbished in the nature of blood sacrifice of the Self, to please a set of demons and making it 'impure' because it is being consumed by the demons; hence it is akin to killing (figuratively) his mother. While I am not totally convinced of this interpretation, it will need further dwelling on this verse (and others, such as this one) to find the perfect meaning, originally intended.

Nīlakeci also takes issue with the Buddhist notion of *kṣanapaṅkam* (momentariness) and tells Kuṇṭalakeci that their ideas are unacceptable, and in valid propositions. At the end of the debate, the king tells Kuṇṭalakeci that her preceptor, the *ēkāntaṉ* (referring to the Buddha as an *ekāntavādin*, a monist, in a sense, which is intriguing as it is interesting, because the monism is about Buddhist *savvam dukhata* or *anittā*—suffering as being the quintessence of reality and that permanent is nothing, or, all is impermanent); the king also mocks at the 'imaginary' tales of the Jātakas, which were critiqued by Nīlakeci with no proper response from Kuṇṭalakeci. The king implores Kuṇṭalakeci to become more conscious of these aspects and announces an end to the debate, and Kuṇṭalakeci is sent away, sufficiently disgraced. Before leaving, Nīlakeci learns from her of Arukaccantiraṉ, the Buddhist monk, with whom she will sharpen her verbal swords next. But I am skipping the next two Buddhists for there is the pre-eminent one, following.

II. Meeting the Buddha at Kapilapura (Puttavātaccarukkam)

By now, Nīlakeci has already won over two Buddhist opponents; so one presumes there is relative calmness, as well as confidence in her, to be ready for the rendezvous, with the 'supreme being'. The poet describes the environs in which Nīlakeci meets the Buddha, reflecting the attitude the early Jainas had towards the Buddhists, though same is the case in Buddhist texts, about the Jaina monks.

> *'kayaṉmī ṉiriyak kaḻunīr viriyum*
> *vayaṉmāṉ puṭaiya vaḷamait teṉavum*
> *muyaṉmī ṉeṟiyum muṟiyuṅ kaṟiyā*
> *tayaṉmē yuṟaiyā taṇiyiṟ ṟeṉavum'* (v. 467)[101]
>
> [Carps (fish) and red water lily blossoms abound
> In this expanse, adorned with rich vegetation
> There you see leftovers of broken ribs of hares and fish
> There is proximity (*ayal*) to stuff to gorge on and become
> strong]

And further,

> *'kaḻukiṉ ṉiṉamuṅ kaḻutiṉ ṉiṉamum*
> *muḻutum maṟuvai paḻamu ṭiṉaruṅ*
> *koḻutiṉ ṉiṉaṉum piṇṇuṅ kulavi*
> *iḻuteṉ ṉelumpā riṭukā ṭeṉavum'* (v. 468)[102]

> ['a swarm of eagles and a gathering of demons
> full of robed monks
> with a multitude of fattening things, carcasses,
> fat / grease bones, akin to a burial ground']

And as Nīlakeci walks ahead, in the market streets:

> *'cātiyē mikka taṭumāṟṟa ventuyara*
> *mōtiyē vaittārav vōttelā mīkkiṭanta*
> *vītiyē kāṇalā meṉṟuḷā ṉiṉṟārum*
> *pōtiyā rīṇṭaip pulālpaḻiyā reṉṟalum'* (v. 469)[103]

> [One can see on these streets
> shops selling different kinds of meat
> People buying meat from the street markets
> are followers of the Buddha
> who propagated this wrongful doctrine (of flesh-eating)]

Moving ahead, she meets the Buddha at this kind of place:

> *'aṇiccey kōḻarai yarainiḻa laḻakaṉaip porunti*
> *maṇika ṭāmpala katirvīṭu malaruṭai maṇaimēṟ*
> *ṟuṇivu tōṟṟiṉai yeṉaccilar tutiyōṭu toḻutu*
> *paṇiya yātumōr parivilaṉ paṭamputain tiruntāṉ'* (v. 476)[104]

> [By the thick shade of the peepul tree was he seated on
> an ostentatious-looking pedestal, made beautiful with pearls and flowers
> Some said, it seemed as if a phosphoric light emanated from him
> It seemed like he was concealed behind a screen of people
> worshipping him with affection and some bowing down in obeisance.]

'ātta n̲eyen̲at teḷintava ṇamarntirun tavarkkuc
cūtti rammitu vin̲aiyamu mituvitu pir̲itāñ
cātti rammivai mūn̲r̲en̲a van̲r̲avat tōn̲r̲al
pāttu raikkuntan̲ patapporuḷ palavakai patavē' (v. 477) [105]

[There, to the people thus gathered
he gave a sermon about the sūttas (Sūtta, Vinaya and
Abhidhamma piṭakas)
saying, these are the three scriptures and
there are different kinds of gross material elements.]

Nīlakeci accosts the Buddha and requests him to elaborate on his doctrine so she can critique it in a debate with him. With the Buddha, Nīlakeci has a long argument, running into many verses, but I am only presenting a select few, reflecting the basic Buddhist concepts, some of which have been mentioned earlier here.

Buddha discusses his doctrine with Nīlakeci:

'uruvē tirive tan̲aiyā r̲uṇarvum
maruvā tan̲amāṇ kur̲iyut tuṇaicey
kuruvē r̲avaicey kaiyiru patumāt
tiruvē yivaiyem poruṭē ren̲avum' (v. 484)[106]

[Rūpaskanda, three vedanāskandas, six vigñānaskandas
six sajñaskandas, kuyalam (kusala) and akuyalam (akusala)
twenty samskāraskandas, these comprise elements in our
doctrine, said he.]

Matilal elaborates on the Buddhist 'analysis of Self' (which seems appropriate to recount here; also because much of what the Buddha says, in ten verses starting from v.484, more or less cover a lot of how well it is explained here:-

'The Buddhist analysis of self is usually given in three different ways. The three analyses are somewhat independent of each other. The first and the most common one is the terms of five aggregates or groups of elements which are also in perpetual flux themselves. (Groups)—aggregate of material forms or visible forms (*rūpa*) [which] covers the physical elements;

aggregate of feelings; that of perceptions; that of dispositions or (mental) forces; that of awareness or consciouness in general... The theory states that a member of any group is in perpetual flux... Each is also connected with a member of its own kind of a causal nexus. (Bases)—faculty of vision; hearing; smelling; taste; touch; mind; colour and shape; sounds; odours; tastes; objects of touch and; mindable objects...[this last one] comprise[s] an assortment of entities, volitions, feelings, birth, decay and even the unconditional elements such as space; (Base Elements)... being same as before [plus] visual awareness, auditory, olfactory, gustatory, tactile [and] mental awareness.'[107]

The Buddha explains to Nīlakeci each of the skandas in detail, which I shall not dwell upon here, but will move over to just a few more points of their debate. Chakravarti gives a summarised version of the general Buddhist doctrine that the Buddha discusses with Nīlakeci, which is as follows:

> '[A]part from the five skandas which constitute the puruṣa, we do not accept the existence of any independent reality called ātmā. These five skandas, which constitute the reality, are intrinsically characterised by—anityā (impermanence), dukha (pain, suffering), aṣuchi (impurity), and anātmā (non-soul)... momentary and vanishing... The idea of permanent substance is due to ignorance of the nature of reality. When you bend the fingers of your hand, you give it the name first. But where is the substance called first apart from and independent of the five fingers?... Similarly, apart from the five Skandas which constitute the Purusha, we do not accept the existence of any independent reality called Ātma... One who realises the true nature of reality, will be free from evil, escape from samsāra and will obtain mokṣa, nirvāṇa.'[108]

Following the Buddha's exposition, Nīlakeci asserts that she will demolish his theory.[109] She tells him:-

> *'piṇṭam pirivila vēyeṉaccolluta lālavaṟṟuk*
> *kuṇṭaṅ korukuṇi yāṅkavaitāṅkuṇa mākumaṉṟēl*

viṇṭaṅ kavaiyavai vēṟuḷa tātalum vēṇṭumaṉṟō
paṇṭaṅku nīcoṉṉa muṭṭiyiṟ pañcāṅ kulikaḷumpōl' (v. 495)[110]

Chakravarti interprets it thus:

> 'You compare the Pancha Skandas to the five fingers which constitute the first when closed, and to the building materials used to raise a house. But still your analogy is incomplete. In the case of the five Skandas, you say, that they are inseparable, that they must die together and be re-born together. But this characteristic is absent in the case of the five fingers or the building materials. The latter are separable from one another, one element may get destroyed without the others being destroyed. But in the case of the Skandas which are distinct from one another, and yet which are inseparable from one another, you have to postulate some kind of force or a cohesive principle which keeps all the five together in a cluster whether they get destroyed or whether they are re-born. Without such a postulate, the group appearance and the group destruction of the five Skandas which are in themselves distinct, would remain unexplained. Hence in order to clearly explain the behaviour of the Skandas, you have to postulate an underlying permanent substance as the sub-stratum for these five Skandas and that is exactly what we call Ātma, of which the five Skandas would be related as different Guṇas to a single Guṇi, the qualities inhering in the substance... Similarly, the elements vēdana skanda, vigñāna skanda, sagñā skanda and samskāra skanda must presuppose a consciousness being capable of having these experiences...'[111]

Another interesting argument relates to the Buddhist definition of killing, which Nīlakeci finds fault with.

āynta vaintiṉu māmviṉai yārppeṉiṉ
vīyanta tīṉmaiyiṉ veyya vavīcitāṉ
kānti pāli yiraṅkak kalakaṉaip
pōḻuntu kōṭal poruttala tokkumē (v. 546)[112]

'The five *angas* of killing, as enumerated by you, are (1) that it must be a living being, (2) it must be known to be a

> living being to the person who kills, (3) there must be the intention to kill, (4) there must be the act of killing, and (5) as a result of the act, the animal must die. Unless these five *angas* are present together, there can be no killing... According to this definition, it would be no murder to kill a stranger under the impression that he is your enemy.'[113]

Further into the debate, the Buddha says:

> *'vittiṉ vaḻivaḻit tōṉṟum muḷaikiḷai*
> *cattiyi ṉāyacan tāṉattai māṟṟeṉpaṉ*
> *vettava vittiṉiṉ veṟaṉṟu vīṭitu*
> *tattuva mākko ṭaḷiriya lāyē'* (v. 573)[114]

> [Just as the seed embodies the germ, which embodies the plant
> consecutive series reflects change
> this I call the phenomena of existence (*citta santānam)*
> conditioned by change
> ceasing of the germination is liberation
> this is the essence, oh woman, with skin the colour of a tender
> mango shoot!][115]

In the context of the above verse, let me revert back to Matilal:

> 'The origin and disappearance of the phenomena of existence [just as the Buddha's analogy of the seed given to Nīlakeci, in our case] is governed by the fixed law of what is called dependent origination (*pratitya-samutpāda)...* The conditionality of suffering (by which is meant all the phenomena of existence) presupposes its cessation also, through the removal or dissolution of its condition [which in the analogy referred to above consists in the non-germination of the seed or to stop the seed from germinating].'[116]

In continuation of the previous argument, Buddha says:

> 'There is karma and fruit of action, both
> but it is not about the doer of action
> for the kandas are impermanent
> all elements die the next moment (they are born)' (v. 574)[117]

Nīlakeci critiques the Buddha's statement:

> *'kuṇamporu ḷeṉṟi koṭaiporu ḷeṉṟi*
> *yuṇarntucey tuṇpā ṉoruvaṉi leṉṟi*
> *kaṇantaṉi lēnilai kantamu māyakkāṟ*
> *piṇañkuva tokkuniṉ pēremak keṉṟāḷ'* (v. 575)[118]
>
> Moral quality (right conduct) you accept, so too, you acknowledge (the act) of giving, yet you say the doer or the result (of that doing) is inconsequential
> Only the momentary *kandam* (skandas) matter
> But pray, tell me, what is the name for that thing that binds (the skandas)?]

Buddha responds, giving the analogy of colouring a pomegranate seed, and the resulting flower born of it (in his attempt to explain the non-affect of a 'soul-substance':

> *'tītuḷḷa mēlatu tīyuḻamp pēceyyum*
> *yātuḷḷa māṇpuḷa mēliṉpa māmeṉṉai*
> *mātuḷam pīcamuṇ māṇarak kiṉṉiṟam*
> *pōtuḷḷaṅ kāṇpatu pōlamaṟ ṟeṉṟāṉ'* (v. 576)[119]

Nīlakeci responds to this (v. 581, as interpreted by Chakravarti) with this argument:

> 'Shellac, with which you coat the pomegranate seed is an external thing, and not one of the components of the Ashtaka, whereas Kuśala and Akuśala which are to produce the happiness and misery, are distinctly internal to the Purusha Santāna series, and are included in the five Skandas. Again, the flower, whether black or red, must appear in the tree grown out of the seeds. If the plant dies, there is no chance of the flower appearing at all. There must be an unbroken continuity of the series from the seed to the flower. But in the case of Purusha Santāna, it is just the opposite. Kuśala, element of good conduct, or Akusala, the element of evil, present in the Purusha Santāna, can produce the happiness in Swarga, or misery in Hell, only after the death of the individual. If the tree dies there is no chance of a flower.

Whereas in the case of man, unless the man dies there is neither Swarga happiness, nor Hell misery...'[120]

What is the general Jaina perception of the momentary-ness concept of the Buddhists?

> 'In criticism of the *kṣaṇika* (momentary) doctrine of the Buddhist thinkers, the Jainas point out that *smṛti* or Recollection is impossible if the soul be denied. Sensations, according to the Buddhists are absolutely self-identical or particularistic (*svalakṣaṇa*), so that if it were possible for one such sensation to revive another, it should also be possible for the perceptions of one man to be recollected by another man.'[121]

Nīlakeci also engages with this issue. As she does with several others, including the Buddhist idea of eating meat, the conduct of Buddhist bhikkus, and each skanda; the numerous verses between the Buddha and Nīlakeci can, in fact, be a single book by itself and hence, unfortunately, cannot be tackled in this section. Nīlakeci then, towards the end of her long discourse with the Buddha, highlights the superiority and feasibility of the Jaina idea of *anekāntavāda* (many-ness). She points out that:

> 'No absolute point of view or Ekāntavāda (non dualism / monism) is logically possible. If you maintain the "*savvam anityā*" (all is impermanent) doctrine then even the person speaking must be anityā and there will be no time for him to preach his doctrine, no knowledge is possible for him, either to have or impart. Hence there can be no philosophy at all. So also when "*sarvam nitya*" is held. Then everything will be unchanging and permanent and... no experience, no acquisition of knowledge, and no imparting of the same, for, all these imply activity and change...The only logical course....is to recognise the truth of anekānta view, to accept that the reals have different characteristics from the different points of view...'[122]

Thus:

> *'ni<u>n</u><u>r</u>ē nilaiyume<u>n</u>i <u>n</u>ittiyamē yāyo<u>l</u>iyu*
> *ma<u>n</u><u>r</u>ēy-i tāyi lanittiyamā mavviraṇṭu*

me<u>n</u><u>r</u>ē yuraikki liruva<u>l</u>ik ku<u>r</u><u>r</u>amumā
me<u>n</u><u>r</u>ē yuraikki<u>n</u><u>r</u>u yēkānta <u>n</u>ākutiyō' (v. 656)[123]

[That all existence is permanent (*nityamē*) or all is impermanent (*anityamē*), that these are the only two (truths) helps no one. Only the anēkāntavātis (Jainas) show fault in both these doctrines of reality. You must realise that you are *ekāntavāti*, accept this.]

Nīlakeci urges the Buddha to accept the anekānta view, outside of the extremes of *anityā* and *nityā,* and the existence of a permanent entity (ātmā)... The Buddha says (of course, in the perception of the composer of *Nīlakeci,* perhaps also giving the Buddha the benefit of an introspective mind and heart), "yes, I acknowledge/accept"—"*yān meccuva<u>n</u>ē*" (v. 657).

As Matilal says,

'The Jainas carried the principle of non-violence from the physical and practical plane to the intellectual plane. Thus, 'respect for the life of others' was eventually transformed into an obligatory respect for the views and beliefs of others. The Jainas claim that when two or several parties are seriously and sincerely arguing regarding the truth, it is seldom that one side is absolutely wrong, while the other side is absolutely right. The world is not divided only into black and white, for there are innumerable shades of grey in between. The Jainas contend that one should try to understand the particular point of view of each disputing party if one wishes to grasp completely the truth of the situation. The *total* truth, the Jainas emphasise, may be derived from the integration of all different viewpoints (*nayas*).'[124]

III. Nīlakeci on caste, authorship, God: Takes on Pūtika<u>n</u> of the Vedic School (Vetavātaccarukkam)

Nīlakeci meets Pūtika<u>n</u> at the town called Kākaṇṭi. Before moving into this debate, a few words about what the Jainas think about the concept of a creator/god. The Buddhist, Jaina, Ājīvika, and the materialists were all a-theistic or even anti-theistic or non-theistic religions, to begin with. In spite of the changes that crept into some of the more organised/structured systems among these (for instance, Buddhist and Jaina), the basic concept of 'god' as the creator of the universe was one point they strongly opposed and even condemned. According to the Jainas, that the world was brought into being by a creator/god-principle 'had no logical foundation'. Chakravarti discusses the Jaina response to this belief of the non-śramaṇic tradition.

> 'The world [for the Jainas] is constituted with the following six Dravyas or reals: Jīva, the life; Pudgala, the matter; Dharma and Adharma, the principles of motion and rest; Ākāśa, the space... [The] creator is assumed to be a permanent unchangeable entity and yet he is engaged in the activity of creation. If the creator by his manifestation brings into existence the created things, then he must be identified with created objects. By this charge, he will lose his true nature of unchanging permanency. The creator being himself uncreated, may have created the world. If so, where was his existence before the creation of the world?... Further, is the creator an embodied entity or one without a body? If the latter, how can a pure spiritual entity create corporeal bodies? If on the other hand, he is assumed to be having a body of his own, then is his body created or uncreated? Is the creator a completely liberated being or an unliberated being? If his nature was completely liberated and perfect, then he could not indulge in the activity of creation. If he is a sāmsāric being, then he cannot create the world and nature by the fiat of his will as it will be be far beyond his power.'[125]

And being a religion that asserted its textuality, the question of authorship was important to the Jainas. Then there is, of course, the very crucial critique of meat-eating which the Vedic system propagated through sacrificial rituals involving killing of animals (following which the meat was obviously consumed) and the sacrificial rituals are critiqued by Nīlakeci as developing a class of people who amass wealth. These we find in some of the arguments of Nīlakeci in this section. I am only taking some of the most significant points of this interesting debate, some of which seem so very relevant and appropriate for today's time and context.[126]

If there are places where Nīlakeci really gets angry it is in the debates with both the Vedic teacher and the Bhūtavādin (materialist), more so with the former; you almost feel she might re-enter her *pēy* consciousness or form, which she does, briefly in the case of the Bhūtavāda, not in anger but to prove a point. For, while in each case, I found (in terms of interiority of *Nīlakeci*, the text) a certain readiness by the defenders of each school of thought to debate with, or be challenged by, Nīlakeci, *vetavātaccarukkam* shows the Vedic teacher Pūtikan̲ condemning Nīlakeci, whom he considers incapable and unqualified to criticise the Vedic tradition as (as he says) she is a śūdra.

This is the first (and only) instance in the entire text where caste as a question comes up for discussion, showing also the kind of intrinsic association of caste and hierarchy with the Vedic system. At yet another level, it is interesting for the *Nīlakeci* author to mention Nīlakeci's (while in effect, it is Nīli's) caste here to commence the actual Jaina-Vedic debate, without mincing words (being pretty scathing in the critique) because we then come back to the social context of the Nīli *pēy* stories and the bow-song tradition where one has noted the caste context of the same. The composer-author of *Nīlakeci*, in bringing out this factor, has also registered a personal comment on the Vedic system, which is not merely a Jaina engagement, as one finds in other sections.

Nīlakeci's caste is almost thrown at her face (as one senses, quite suddenly, as one proceeds to the near-end of the treatise) when, after hearing out Pūtikan̲ about the 'timeless' Veda and philosophical system emanating from the same—including Sāmkhya, Vaiseśika, Brahmavāda, Pāśupata, the sub-sects within these and so on—Nīlakeci points out that this Mīmāmsa system is a *nāstika* system, not recognising the omniscient *puruṣa*, unlike what they claim.[127]

Hearing Nīliakeci's comment, Pūtikan is raging mad and says:

> *'nāttika mallatu collalai yāyiṉmu ṉāṉpayanta*
> *cāttira māvatu vētamaṉ ṟōvatu tāṉ cayampu*
> *cūttiri nīyatu vallai yalāmaiyiṟ collukilāy*
> *pōttanti yōvataṉ ṟimaiyeṉ ṟāṉpoṅkip pūtikaṉē'* (v. 826)[128]

> [(Dare) you call the tradition I belong to *nāttikam*
> challenging (the fact that) the Vedas are primordial/self-created
> śūdra woman, you have no eligibility to understand that,
> no right to find faults either, said Pūtikaṉ, in fiery rage.]

Angered by his casteist remark, Nīlakeci commences a long argument rubbishing the concept of non-authorship of the Vedas (that it was *cuyampu*—self-created, and existed primordially), and caste and raises issues with various contradictions and illogical statements, as she perceives them, within the Vedic texts. I found her analogy of human excreta fascinating both in terms of the exact reason she might have used such examples for (to deliver a strong punch) and that this is the first time in the entire text that this device is used for lampooning. One may also add that using the example of human excreta comes as a deliberate attempt to annoy the (obviously) brāhmiṇ Pūtikaṉ, whose idea of purity and pollution and his gender bias was reflected in his anger against her. That she should mention 'shit' (*malam*) is also to do with the caste question. So there is an element of subversion here, as well. The voice of the composer of *Nīlakeci* (or of Nīlakeci, who becomes the voice of the composer/author) seems to be quite a 'located' voice, when you analyse the nature of metaphors and analogies used in each of the systems she debates with. But this one, for me, is fantastic.

> *'yāratu ceytava raṟiyiliṅ kuraiyeṉi laṅkoruva*
> *ṉūratu naṭuvaṉū ruṟaiyuḷil malampeytiṭ ṭoḷittoḻiyiṟ*
> *pēriṉu muruviṉum peṟalila ṉutaliṉ ṟukkuṟittut*
> *tēriṉu miṉiyatu ceytava rilleṉac ceppuvavē* (v. 829)[129]

[Your claim that no one authored them (the Vedas) is like this
One night, unknown to people, someone dumped his faeces in the middle of the village outside a house and left
The following day, unable to find out the name, shape and form of who did it, would people conclude that nobody did this?]

She goes on, further, regarding 'high' and 'low' birth:

'tōṟṟamu nāṟṟamuñ cuvaiyuṭa ṉūṟivaṟ ṟuṟṟoṭaṅki
yāṟṟavu māyiru vētamval lārkaḷ i taṟinturaippa
mēṟkulat tārō ṭiḻintava reṉpatu meymaipeṟu
nāṟṟiṟañ ceytava raṟikuvar nuḻaintaṟi vuṭaiyavarē' (v. 830)[130]

[Specialists of the Āyurveda, who examine excreta by appearance, odour, taste and touch might judge sickness or health
not whether it is shit of a high-born or a low-born
So, too, is a text examined by its content
not whether it was written by a 'high-caste' or a 'low-caste' person][131]

The use of the term Āyurveda specialists (*āyiruvētam vallārkaḷ*) seems to me to have been used deliberately and with an element of sarcasm. The use of scatological examples may also seem to be a subtle (but in this case, very direct) use of the satirical, and it should be noted that Nīlakeci pours forth all these (and more) examples, quoting from the *Mahābhārata*, especially in response to the caste question (her caste status, which infuriated her) which is the highlight of the Jaina debate with the Vedic teacher/thought; and only after a long argument establishing the futility of caste and social status, does Nīlakeci move on to the other important issues, namely, animal sacrifice in the Vedic ritual. The prioritisation of this debate is the most important element in the entire text.[132]

Next, there is Nīlakeci's critique of the concept of the four castes being born out of Brahmā:

'cātikkaṭ payavā tavappayan tavumeṉat tanturaippa
vātikka ṉuṉvaḻi nālvara tamaitiyai yamarnturaippa

cūtitta tōṟṟamum piḻaippeṉac cūttirap piṟavikoḷḷār
vātitta vāreṉṟu teruṇṭavark kivaiyivai mayāmayakkē' (v. 834)

[Saying that birth to a caste status follows from deeds in a former birth,
And hence penance and action in this birth will not change the status
And that from Brahmā's body parts emerged the castes
And that the śūdra (*cūttira*), born out of his feet, is ineligible for
Debate, Penance, because of low birth
Are mere delusions (*mayāmayakkē*, arguments meant to delude)]

There is a long commentary following this verse in the text (in both Chakravarti's and Po. Ve. So's editions of *Nīlakeci*) and Chakravarti refers to this also in the English section of his book.

> 'Speaking about creation by Brahma, you arrange the creatures into four grades of importance according to their sources from the Body of Brahma. Arranging the people according to four castes of lower and higher, would be meaningless when you remember that all of them are created from the very same body of Brahma. But, you cannot justify this classification on the ground that what proceeds from the head must be certainly higher than what proceeds from the feet; for a member of the body of Brahma has neither greatness nor smallness in itself. Ganga water proceeding from the feet of Vishnu is considered pure and sacred, whereas the perspiration from his head is considered impure and useless. Brahma born from Vishnu's Navel becomes the chief of Gods; whereas Madhu and Ketabha born from his ears are not so. Hence the position of the organs higher or lower cannot be an adequate ground as to the worth of things created through them.'[133]

Nīlakeci cites specific instances from the scriptures to substantiate her point. She also forcefully negates the notion that the Vedas have no authors; and cites names of authors mentioned therein (which of course Pūtikaṉ refutes).

'[She] enumerates the following defects in the Vedas:

1. Veda distinctly bears the mark of having been produced by somebody.
2. It bears the mark of recent production.
3. Veda is incompatible with experience.
4. It contains a number of false statements.
5. It promotes inordinate desire for 'worldly' things.
6. It promotes undesirable conduct.
7. It creates confusion of the intellect.
8. It contains self-contradictory doctrines.
9. It instigates man to cruelty, and ultimately leads him to degradation of life.'[134]

She points out that "Veda contradicts concrete experience... It contains statements relating to the birth of a person from an ant-hill, from a pot, from the ground, from a fish, from an animal... It narrates the story of Indra and Sūrya, having intercourse with Aruna, a male who is said to have brought forth as his sons Vāli and Sugrīva, the two monkeys. It narrates the story of Indra who lost his generative organ and who cut the penis of a ram and had it tacked on to himself... All these statements refer to events which are quite impossible and in conflict with ordinary experience..."[135]

Nīlakeci takes issue with the killing animals for sacrifice and shows the inherent contradictions in the Vedic system where, on the one hand, there is talk of killing of living beings as a bad deed, and on the other, there is perpetuation of the practice of sacrifice. Thus:

> *'kolvatu tīteṉap poruḷvaḻi vēḷviyiṟ kolappaṭuva*
> *vellaiyoṉ ṟilateṉpa viṇaiviḻaic coḻikeṉpa vammukattāṟ*
> *celkati yuḷateṉpa tīrttika neṟiyeṉṟun tīyaveṉṟu*
> *pallavar tuṇivumem vētatti nuḷaveṉp payiṉṟuraippa*" (v. 833)[136]
>
> ['It is wrong to kill, you say, yet you perform sacrifices
> to amass material possessions
> Control (your) desires, you pontificate, yet you seek gifts of
> house and fame

Most branches of philosophy are in our Vedas, you say,
but your own Vedas are split into systems']

And she points out the various ways that are conceived for exploitation and appropriation in this system:

'maṟutalai tattamu ḷākki mayakkamuñ ceyatamaiyāṟ
peṟutalai yeṉṉaiko ṟattuvan taṉaiaṉṟu pērumuṇṭē
yuṟutiyuñ cālpu muṭaiyaṉa yāvaiyu muṇmaiyiṉāṟ
ceṟutalai yēvilla cīrttaṉa ceyvikkuñ ciṭṭituvē' (v. 835)[137]

She says that the doctrinal form (Vedas) is created (by men) craftily (*ciṭṭitu*), to delude (*mayakkamuñ ceytamaiyāṟ*), out of some excuse of antagonism (from others—*maṟutalai*)[138], to obtain wealth through practices that involve killing. And this doctrine has assumed name, prestige and authority. Chakravarti however, in his interpretation qualifies 'wealth' as land grants, grants of horses, cows, *kanyādānam* (giving of the bride), eating meat and drinking liquor.

Finally, after a long debate, the people (his contemporaries there), seeing the defeat of the great teacher Pūtikaṉ, said

'Indeed you (Nīlakeci) were right when you said our Vedas are false and it is wrong to say there is nothing compared to the Vedas. Hearing that, Pūtikaṉ, too, asked her to enlighten him about her system, which people from all sides gathered there listened to, and Pūtikaṉ accepted.' (v. 852)[139]

But did he accept to delete the caste aspect? We will never know.

Nīlakeci would hope he would, as she would now move on to yet another opponent, Picācakan, the materialist on matters of this world, where no such problem of caste, nor even god, appears.

Incidentally, Chakravarti notes that eight stanzas of the Vedavāda (*vetavātaccarukkam*) section are missing from among the original manuscripts. He says he was unable to secure those manuscripts[140]—which are probably lost to the world now.[141]

IV. An Encounter with Materialism: Nīlakeci Meets Picācakaṉ/Picācikaṉ (Pūtavātaccarukkam)

In the assembly of king Madanajit, described as the one with shoulders broad and strong as a mountain, and as a peaceful and joyous-looking one, etc.[142] Nīlakeci starts her debate with Picācakaṉ, also referred to as Picācikaṉ, in some verses, chose this particular debate with the contention that in this section the 'identity' of Nīlakeci as '*pēy*' returns, used as a device by the composer to prove a point to the Bhūtavādin. Her supernatural/ paranormal 'skills' are brought to play in this section. For me, this directs attention to the fact that at a basic level, despite the affirmative status, Nīli's 'pey' identity—in the Tamil cultural idiomatic sense—overwhelms, or at least pervades the larger 'universe' of this creative enterprise, namely, the philosophical form of Nīlakeci. Even momentarily, the Nīli concept is relived; and it is important that she does so to make a Jaina point, as it were, about perceptions of reality and life. And only to make that point, she has to go beyond reality itself and what is 'perceived'. And in this, she seems to have validated or vindicated the text's creator in choosing, appropriately, a discourse on the superiority of the Jina doctrine over all others, through her own transformation.[143]

Before moving to their debating space, perhaps a few words about this school of thought and their points of contestation with Jainism are in place here.

According to N. Bhattacharya

> 'The philosophical views of Pūrana, Pākhuda and Ajita, who were contemporaries of the Buddha and Mahāvira, must have contributed to the growth of a purely materialistic philosophy which later came to be known as the Cārvāka system... The Jaina criticism of the Cārvāka was directed mainly against their theory of knowledge... According to the Cārvākas, there is no soul. This conclusion is based upon the following argumens. There is no soul apart from the body. Thus, the soul is nothing

but the living body itself with the quality of consciousness. But this consciousness is not the quality of any unperceived non-material or spiritual entity. It exists in the perceptible living body composed of the material elements and hence it must be a quality of the body itself... What is called consciousness is nothing but epiphenomenon or by-product of matter, which has no existence independent of the body. But the Jains are not ready to admit that there is no soul apart from the body or that consciousness is the effect of matter, resulting out of the combination of material elements that constitute the body. If that be the case, there will be no absence of consciousness so long as the body exists. Loss of consciousness in sleep, fainting or in a dead body will then be impossible... Jain atheism has some common features with that of the Cārvākas. The supposition of god as a creator is unnecessary, according to the Cārvākas, since the world comes into existence by the spontaneous combination of material elements... According to the Jainas, neither perception nor inference can prove god. The substances by their interaction produce a new set of qualities. The diversities of the world are due to cooperative conditions inherent in the nature of things. If things can function only in obedience to the will of god, there is no reason why they should be endowed with distinct attributes.'[144]

Chakravarti writes

'Jaina thinkers criticise this school for its materialism... They further emphasise the fact that our experience was not altogether confined to sense perception. Our present-experience is based upon our past experience and it is certainly projecting into the future. Having its root in the past and projecting into the future, it is the essential characterisitic of consciousness and this phenomenon cannot be explained purely by mechanical activity of matter. Our consciousness is not confined to sense presented experience of the present. Memory of the past and its recognition all go beyond the sense-present experience...'[145]

Hari Satya Bhattacharya points out that

> 'In criticising the Cārvāka position the Jain philosophers point out that if consciousness were an outcome of the physical body, it would have continued to persist in a dead body. For the body remains as usual even when the animal dies; rather, on account of the subsidence of fever, etc, the body of the dead animal may be said to be in a healthier state. The physical body cannot be said to be the cause of consciousness... Nor can you say that the physical body is the Material Cause of consciousness. For, in that case every modification in the body would have been followed by a corresponding modification of consciousness.'[146]

To a substantial extent these are the arguments which can be found in the Nīlakeci-Picācakaṉ debate, as well.

At Nīlakeci's behest, Picācakaṉ enumerates the basic tenets of his school of thought (Lokāyata or Cāravāka school). He tells her that *reality*, in their doctrine, comprises the five elements—air, water, earth, fire and ether. It is these five elements that lead to the sense perceptions of taste, colour, smell, touch and sound. Pleasure, pain, intelligence, perception, etc., are aroused by a confirmation of these five elements and with the disintegration of these, everything else disappears.

'ulake lamavai yēyuyi ruṇṭeṉac
cola valāraṉa coṟṟelin tēniṉṟu
pala kalāṅkaḷuñ ceyyap payaṉilār
pulava rāvataṉ ṟōvaṅkup pōntatē' (v. 859)[147]

[The world is but these (five elements)
Those that insist on the soul
Only stir up arguments
From which there isn't much to gain]

'ceṉṟa kālattuñ celkiṉṟa kālattu
niṉṟa kālatti lummin nikaḻcciyē
yeṉṟu mivvula kittaṉmait tēyitu
vaṉṟa teṉṟuraip pārayarp pārkaḷē' (v. 860)[148]

[In all times (past, present, future)
This is the real(ity), these five elements

and naught else prevailed
Ignorant are those who speak of another beyond/above these]

Nīlakeci gives a lengthy argument about the difficulty in accepting the fact that all is composed of five elements. What about those without an organ of a body? Is it that they cannot possess intelligence since they do not have the corresponding sense perceptions that, according to you, are connected to the five *bhūtas* (elements)? She also points out that there are experiences that cannot be explained going by the pañca-bhūta principle—such as dreams, hallucinations, etc. She proves the existence of *uyir* and an intelligence beyond the five elements and also speaks of the Jaina—Tamil concept of living beings with one, two, three, or six senses; ātma and ñāna, thus, she says, are essential.

Nīlakeci tells Picācakaṉ:

'pēyummilai piṟappatu milleṉpāy
vāyuṅ kiḷḷip puṭaippa varuvateṉ
māyat tālaṉṟi mantirat tāṟṟeyvaṅ
cūyak kālaṟaṅ kōṭalai yoṭṭeṉa' (v. 887) [149]

[You say there is no after-life or spirit (*pēy*)
Let me excite you a bit now/give you a 'pinch' of how it really is
with my magical powers and incantations
May you come in agreement with our religion]

But Picācakaṉ is wondering what is the use of her bringing up this subject of *pēy*. He tells her, if you show me, with the help of your powers, a *pēy* right now, I will believe you. And then...

'ōṭṭi ṉēṉeṉ ṟuraippa vuṇarvilā
muṭṭai kāṇkeṉa muṉkai muṟukkiyē
cuṭṭi nāḷaṅkut tōṟṟamu nōkkeṉa
viṭṭut tāṉṟaṉ vikurvaṇai kāṭṭuvāḷ' (v. 888)[150]

[Saying, so you shall see,
she twisted her elbow and said, there, look at that!
She showed him her *pēy* form]

'kal̲utuṅ kāṇala rākik kalaṅkiyē
yal̲utuñ cāpa vakaliṭat tārivan̲
mul̲utuṅ kāṇin̲ muṭiyu men̲amuṇṇi
val̲uvil vāyum vaḷaipallun tōr̲r̲alum' (v. 889)[151]

Thinking that normally people tremble upon seeing a *pēy* and if he were to see that he might die, the leader of all *pēys*, Nīlakeci, produced a form of one with a face and mouth, and teeth, without the whole body.

'kaṇ putaittuk kavil̲untan̲an̲ vīl̲avē
tiṇ patattir̲ r̲eruṭṭi yeṭuttirī ip
paṇpu takkan̲a collipp pariyan̲in̲
naṇpa ten̲r̲u naṭukkamun tīrttapin̲ (v.890)[152]

Seeing this form, with teeth and a face, he cupped his eyes with his hands in fear, and fell unconscious. Nīlakeci held him up and, comforting him, said, don't be afraid, that *pēy* was that of your beloved mother; and after he caught his breath, getting rid of his fear, she said to him—*"pēykaṇ ṭāyatan̲ per̲r̲i yur̲aiyen̲a..."*[153]—"now that you have seen a *pēy* (of your mother) you may believe in its existence...."

Picācakan̲ is sufficiently affected by all this. He pays respects to the all-knowing Nīlakeci and accepts the doctrine of right knowledge, right faith and right conduct, giving up his own doctrine of materialism.

For our purposes, Nīlakeci assuming, or reverting, to the older form (*pēy talaivī*—chief of *pēys*) to prove a point of the existence of forms beyond materialistic comprehension is important. Incidentally, it may be mentioned that Nīlakeci, throughout the text, goes to each site of debate aerially. Her inherent power (even within the Jaina cosmos of 'infernal being') of transforming herself for the benefit of redeeming her status, and perhaps seeking release in her form as a Jaina philosopher, thus, is not 'meddled' with by the author of the text.

Thus ends not only Nīlakeci's debate with Picācakan̲, but also her entire journey of philosophical discourse. *Pūtavātaccarukkam* is the last section of the text, so in a sense, beginning from her pēy form, the text comes full circle with the last momentary flash of *pēy*-ness in order to prove a Jaina point.

Notes

1. A. Chakravarti, 1984, p. 15 (Tamil section). Po. Ve. Somasundaranar (Po.Ve.So.), 1973, ('*avaiyaṭakkam*'), p. 15. Hereinafter, Chakravarti (English/Tamil, because the page numbers are different for the English and Tamil sections of the book); Po.Ve. So, with relevant page numbers. Translations, unless otherwise mentioned, are all mine.
2. Chakravarti, 1974, p. 109.
3. Chakravarti (Tamil), p. 22; Po.Ve.So, p. 41. She is Nīli-Nīlakeci of Pal̲ayan̲ūr.
4. Ibid, p. 25,; Po.Ve.So, p. 49.
5. Ibid, (Tamil), p. 28; Po.Ve.So, p. 64.
6. N.N.Bhattacharya, 1976, pp. 125-126. *Nīlakeci*, Verses 79-81; Chakravarti, (Tamil), p. 28-29; Po.Ve.So, pp. 64-66 both delineate this classification.
7. Padmanabh Jaini, 1998, pp.110-111. Chakravarti (Tamil), pp. 29-30; Po.Ve.So, pp. 66-70, Verses 82-88, give us some of these details.
8. Jaini, 1998, pp. 141-142.
9. Chakravarti, 1984 (English), p. 139.
10. Ibid (Tamil), p. 35; Po.Ve.So, p. 83.
11. By the way, the Buddhist *triratna* (three gems) comprises the Buddha, Dhamma and Sangha. The Tamil Jainas have the concept of *mukkuṭai* or *mummaṇikaḷ*, right faith, right knowledge, right conduct.
12. *PN*, villuppāṭṭu, lines 520–524, p. 23.
13. Chakravarti (Tamil), p. 56; Po.Ve.So, p. 112.
14. Pechilis, 2006, p. 169.
15. Po.Ve.So, p. 21.
16. Chakravarti (English), pp. 5-6.
17. Ibid (English), pp. 7-8.
18. Ibid, p. 6.
19. Ibid, p. 10.
20. "*Avaiyaṭakam*", Chakravarti (Tamil), p. 15; Po.Ve. So, p. 15.

21. Zvelebil, 1981, p. 7.
22. Brian J. Murton, 1975, pp. 93-94. Scholars such as Stein, Sivathamby, Rajan Gurukkal, R. Champakalakshmi, Selvanayagam and many others have excellent hypotheses on the *tiṇai* concept.
23. *Tarumavuraiccarukkam-Nāṭṭucciṟappu*, Chakravarti (Tamil), p. 17; Po.Ve.So, p. 21.
24. Po.Ve.So, (*tarumavuraiccarukkam—kuṟiñci nila varuṇai*): v. 16, p. 25, which does not occur in Chakravarti, p. 18.
25. R. Vijayalakshmy, 1981, p. 114.
26. Chakravarti (Tamil), p. 58; Po.Ve. So, p. 116.
27. Also called naḻal; *mayiṟkoṉṟai* in Tamil.
28. Iṟaivaṉ (lit. god), in this case, has to be understood to be the Jina tīrthankara.
29. *Cittakūṭa caityālayam*, where she offers her worship.
30. Phyllis Granoff, 1994, pp. 242-243.
31. Ibid, p. 242.
32. Charles Hallisey, 2015, p. xxii.
33. Bahm, 1968, 126-128.
34. In the Tamil Jaina texts, the term usually denoting karma (deeds) is *viṉai: nalviṉai* (good deeds) and *tīviṉai* (bad deeds).
35. Jaini, 2001, p. 135.
36. Bahm, 1968, pp. 129-130.
37. Bhattacharya, 1976, pp. 173-174.
38. F.G.Sutton, 1992, p. 112.
39. Jaini, 2001, pp. 137-138.
40. This Tamil Buddhist text—one of the five major kāvyas—as a whole text, is considered more or less lost to time. All we know about *Kuṇṭalakeci* is through references from other texts, such as even *Nīlakeci*, which devotes a large part to it. In 1996, J. Srichandran brought out some sections of *Kuṇṭalakeci*, based on these references and extracts from elsewhere, in a book titled, *Maṇimēkalai, Valaiyāpati, Kuṇṭalakeci: Mūlamum, Telivuṟaiyum* (Vardhamana Patippakam, Chennai). One has taken some references of Kuntalakeci's life, etc, from this book.
41. An alternate translation goes thus: 'With hair cut off, wearing dust, formerly I wandered having only one robe, thinking there was fault where there was no fault and seeing no fault where there was fault. Going out from my daytime resting place on Mount Vulture Peak, I saw the stainless Buddha attended by the

Order of Bhikkus. Having bent my knee, having paid homage to him, putting my raised hands together, I stood face to face with him. "Come, Bhadda", he said to me. That was my full ordination. I wandered over Anga and Magadha, Vajji, Kesi and Kosala. For fifty years without debt, I have enjoyed the alms of the kingdoms. Truly wise was that lay follower who gave a robe to Bhadda, who is now completely freed from all bonds.' [Todeschini, 'The Maiden who Fell in love with a Thief: Considerations on the Story of the Nun Bhadda Kundalakesa', Dharma Drum Journal of Buddhist Studies, no. 13, pp. 153-188 (2013)].

42. Hallisey, 2015, p. vii.
43. Chakravarti, 1984, p. 75; for her story, J. Srichandran, 1991, pp. 512-531.
44. Todeschini, 2013, p. 161-162.
45. Ibid, pp. 171-172.
46. Hallisey, 2015, pp. 259-260.
47. Ibid., p. 260.
48. Todeschini, 2013, p. 180.
49. Uma Chakravarti, 2015, p. 40.
50. Ibid, pp. 46-47.
51. Ibid, pp. 46-47.
52. Ibid, pp. 47-48.
53. Srichandiran, 1996, p. 513.
54. Uma Chakravarti, 2015, p. 50.
55. Srichandiran, 1996, p. 513.
56. Srichandiran, 1996, p. 515. Translations, unless otherwise specified, mine, with cross-reference to Srichandiran's comments in his book. The rest of the nineteen verses should be part of a separate discourse, hopefully for a later time, dedicated to her, even as seeking the entire text itself should be an important exercise in itself.
57. Ibid, p. 517.
58. Ibid, p. 518. Kuṇṭalakeci was herself attracted to the physical beauty of Kālaṉ/Suttaka, whom she desired, after one glance from a distance.
59. Ibid, p. 519.
60. The term used is *yāḷi*, which is explained in the dictionary also as a mythical creature with the head of a lion and elephant's proboscis (Winslow, p. 905).

61. In other words, keeping some bad friends is like giving space to species mentioned here, who will one day assume their original form and show no compassion whatsoever. Kuṇṭalakeci suffered the consequences of trusting and loving the thief, Suttaka/Kālaṉ, similarly, who attempted to kill her, in spite of her love.
62. With every new form created, something of the old dies.
63. Ibid, p. 522. The obvious inference is to the *kṣanikavāda* (momentariness) theory of the Buddha.
64. Ibid, p. 526.
65. These are some of the Jātaka stories alluded to, when Kuṇṭalakeci speaks of Buddha's munificence and compassion.
66. Chakravarti (Tamil), p. 78; Po.Ve.So, p. 171.
67. Reiko Ohnuma, 1998, p. 323.
68. Chakravarti, 1984 (English), p. 144.
69. Ibid, p. 143.
70. The question was: *Ekam Nāma Kim* (what is that one thing/what do you call that one/what is its name).
71. Chakravarti, 1984 (English), pp. 81-84.
72. These are the five invoked by all the Jainas in all rituals and at the beginning of every auspicious work. They offer salutations thus: *ṇamo arihantāṇam, ṇamo siddhāṇam, ṇamo āyiriyāṇam, ṇamo uvajjhāyaṇam, ṇamo loye savva sāhuṇam.* There is no mention of these in the relevant verse, where only the term *pañca paramēṭṭikaḷ* is used.
73. Chakravarti (Tamil), p. 61; Po.Ve.So, p. 132.
74. Ibid, p. 61; Po.Ve.So, pp. 133-134.
75. Ibid, p. 61; Po.Ve. So, p. 135.
76. Chakravarti, p. 62 (Tamil); Po.Ve.So, p. 137.
77. Chakravarti, p. 62 (Tamil); Po. Ve. So, pp. 138-139. This refers to the Buddhist concept of momentariness. The five kandas are supposed to constitute reality which is impermanent (*anitya*), full of suffering/pain (*dukha*), and there is no Soul (*anātmā*).
78. Po.Ve.So, p. 139. Chakravarti sticks to the Skanda/Kanda occurring in Buddhist Pali scripture, whereas the verses mention the Tamil equivalents of each of the five Skandas/Kandas, which Po.Ve.So retains.
79. Sutton, 1992, pp. 87-88.
80. Ibid, p. 113.
81. B.K. Matilal,, 2002, pp. 219-220.

82. Chakravarti (Tamil), p. 63; Po.Ve.So, p. 142.
83. Ibid, pp. 64-65; Po.Ve.So, p. 144.
84. A.J. Bahm, 1958, pp. 142-143.
85. Chakravarti, p. 66 (Tamil); Po.Ve.So, p.148. See both the authors' interpretation of this verse.
86. Ibid, p. 72 (Tamil); Po.Ve.So, p. 158. Strangely, Chakravarti does not make any editorial comments on this particular verse. And the way Po.Ve.So interprets it, is also problematic when he refers to the Buddha 'killing' his own mother. Po.Ve.So writes, '*īṉṟu tāyinatu paḻuvēlumpiṉaip paṟittu koṉṟāṉ; aṉṉaiyiṉun ciṟanta taivam illaiyākavum ivaṉ aṉṉaiyayē koṉṟāṉ enbadu karuttu.*' He is saying—'there is no higher god than one's mother and he killed this mother, which he infers from the word *paḻūparittāṉ*. Though he makes an additional comment saying that what is really meant by this word is *koṉṟunkālattum koṭumaiceytu koṉṟāṉ* (killed through causing pain to the person who is about to die).
87. The interesting metaphor used is *paḻūppu*, used in the context of crops, fruit—to ripen. *Paḻūpparici* is used for 'rice turning yellow or brown by neglect in drying': Winslow, Tamil-English dictionary, 1862; 2004 reprint, p. 744, below. *Paruvaralōn* means 'one inflicted by pain'.
88. By separation, since the Buddha, Siddhartha Gautama, renounced home and all attachments.
89. V. Fausböll, T. W. Rhys Davids, 1880, p. ii.
90. Chakravarti, p. 78; Po.Ve.So, p. 172.
91. Ibid, p. 79 (Tamil); Po.Ve.So, p. 173.
92. Ibid, p. 79 (Tamil); Po.Ve. So, p. 173.
93. *Nūl*—thread; *nāru*—rope, fibre.
94. Chakravarti, p. 80 (Tamil); Po.Ve.So, p. 175.
95. Chakravarti, (English), pp. 107-108. The entire story in detail, along with other *Jātaka* stories that are referred to in *Nīlakeci*, are also given by the author.
96. Ibid, p. 84 (Tamil); Po.Ve.So, p. 182.
97. Ibid, p. 84. Chakravarti writes that the elephant referred to here is the elephant king Gajendiran who brought forth torrential rains by his prayers. He does not mention which Gajendiran is referred to here, and whether it is the story of Gajendira Mokṣam where the elephant, whose leg was caught by the crocodile, prayed for years to Viṣṇu who then released him. But in *Nīlakeci* we just have

the word, *yāṇai* (elephant), without the name. Nīlakeci means to say that when there are so many tales about similar feats in different religions, what was the need for using the same template by the Buddha to prove his greatness.

98. This is the first verse in this section that calls the Buddha *Tathāgata*.
99. Chakravarti, p.84 (Tamil); Po.Ve.So, p. 184.
100. Doña Luisa Coomaraswamy, 1944, pp. 199-200.
101. Chakravarti, p. 198 (Tamil); Po.Ve.So, p. 403.
102. Ibid, p. 198 (Tamil); Ibid, p. 403.
103. Ibid, p. 198; Ibid, p. 404.
104. Ibid (Tamil), p. 201; Po.Ve.So., p. 410.
105. Ibid (Tamil), p. 201; Po.Ve.So, p. 411.
106. Ibid (Tamil), p. 203; Po.Ve.So, p. 415.
107. B.K. Matilal, 2002, pp. 221-222.
108. Chakravarti (English), p. 197-198.
109. '...*vēṭṭak kurampai cuṭupavarpō lalliyaṅ kōtainiṉ kāṭci yaḻittiṭu vēṉeṉattāṉ*' (v. 494. Chakravarti, p. 207 (Tamil); Po.Ve.So, p. 422).
110. Chakravati, p. 207 (Tamil); Po.Ve.So, p. 423.
111. Ibid, pp. 197-199.
112. Ibid (Tamil), p. 232; Po.Ve.So, p. 467.
113. Ibid (English), pp. 211-212.
114. Ibid., p. 245 (Tamil); Po.Ve. So, p. 488.
115. I managed this translation referring to interpretations of both Chakravarti and Po.Ve.So (the fomer seems far more lucid) and use of the dictionaries.
116. Matilal, 2002, pp. 282-283.
117. Chakravarti, p. 245 (Tamil); Po.Ve.So, p. 489.
118. Ibid, p. 245; Ibid, p. 490.
119. Ibid, p. 247 (Tamil); Po.Ve.So, p. 491.
120. Ibid, English summary, pp. 218-219.
121. H.S. Bhattacharya, 1966, p. 273.
122. Chakravarti, *Nīlakeci* (English summary), p. 229.
123. Ibid (Tamil), p. 272-273 (Tamil); Po.Ve.So, p. 543.
124. Matilal, 2002, p. 58. But then, what should one say for an entire poetic treatise critiquing other schools of thought!
125. Chakravarti, 1957, p. 25 & p. 27.
126. Let me point out here that Tamil (Digambara) Jainism was far more critical—over a longer period of time, thanks to the historical experiences of the religion in the Tamil historical context—of the

larger 'Hindu' tradition than its counterpart in the north. The Tamil (Digambara) Jainas had their own experiences of religious persecution, and temple worship paradigm, blending with the bhakti tradition, doing them in; the Tamil Buddhists did not remain (as far as one knows, as of now), to tell their part of this story, while the miniscule Tamil Jaina population does, today. Secondly, there doesn't seem to exist one single poetic treatise such as *Nīlakeci* in the northern or western Indian Jaina context countering the other traditions (so far as I know, since I have yet to come across such a poetic treatise in comparative philosophy), though there may be many separate texts. If there is, one has not encountered any scholarship that speaks of such a singular text (in verse).

127. Chakravarti, 1994 (English summary), p. 306.
128. Ibid (Tamil), p. 337 (Tamil); Po.Ve.So, p. 575.
129. Ibid (Tamil), p. 344; Ibid, p. 612.
130. Ibid (Tamil), p. 344; Ibid, p. 683.
131. Strangely, Chakravarti's English summary skips this particular segment of Nīlakeci's argument completely. One cannot help but wonder if the nature of this entire set of arguments (parody) on excreta has anything to do with this choice of his, writing as he was early in the 1930s.
132. Unfortunately, the issue is more or less brushed aside in books on *Nīlakeci*—few that are there. B.Saroja does not as much as mention a subject as important as this, talking of the text.
133. Chakravarti (English), p. 317.
134. Ibid, English summary, pp. 308-309.
135. Ibid, p. 311.
136. Ibid (Tamil), 346; Po.Ve.So, p. 685.
137. Ibid (Tamil), p. 348; Po.Ve.So, p. 688.
138. Else, an antagonistic system is created/crafted? Chakravarti translates *tattamu lākki* as created a *tattuva swarūpam* (doctrinal form) and Po.Ve. So interprets it as *tattu vandanai peṟutal.*
139. Chakravarti (Tamil), p. 353; Po.Ve.So, p. 698.
140. Incidentally, Prof. Chakravarti'son, Mr. Jayavijayan in Chennai (whom I had the chance to meet many years ago during the course of my PhD research) had lost the only copy of his father's original 1936 book, which apparently had been lent to someone who did not return in. There was a single copy of the original print, donated

by someone to the U.V. Swaminatha Iyer library in Chennai, which is also in a delicate condition. The Tamil University edition, thankfully, has made the work accessible to people, though after 1984, even they did not print this work.

141. And one will never know if during the time of religious persecution, many such manuscripts (or parts of the larger ones, of the Jainas and Buddhists) would have been deliberately wiped out, though popular lore does believe that to be the case. Which would also explain the vanishing of *Kuṇṭalakeci* from Tamilnadu.
142. v. 855-856, Chakravarti (Tamil), p. 354; Po.Ve.So, pp. 699-700.
143. At the same time, the author also gives Nīlakeci her 'feminine' identity; at various points in the text, following literary conventions, Nīlakeci is described as one with fish-shaped eyes, or one with tresses like the clouds, and so forth.
144. Narendranath Bhattacharya, 1976, pp. 170-180.
145. Chakravarti, 1957, pp. 199-200.
146. H. S. Bhaṭṭacharya, 1966, p. 271.
147. Chakravarti (Tamil), p. 355; Po.Ve.So, p. 702.
148. Ibid (Tamil), p. 355; Po.Ve.So, p. 702.
149. Ibid (Tamil), p. 365; Po.Ve.So, p. 722.
150. Ibid, p. 366; Ibid, p. 723.
151. Ibid, p. 366; Ibid, p. 724.
152. Ibid, p. 366; Ibid, p. 724.
153. Ibid, p. 366, v. 891; Ibid, p. 725.

4

NĪLI-NĪLAKECI

Text and Alter-Text

The purpose of looking at Nīlakeci was two-fold: one, to urge attention and focus of scholarship on the use of folklore in Tamil Jainism; and two, to read the text in a context, and look for meanings hitherto not seen, or read. It is important here to note that firstly, not too many Tamil scholars have focussed on this text, perhaps also because of heavy interest in other Jaina Tamil works such as *Cilappatikāram.* Scholarship from outside India, too, has almost with singular attention focussed on the story of the 'Lay Anklet'. The few scholars who have, at least, mentioned *Nīlakeci*, have been those based in Tamilnadu, and mostly those concerned with Tamil literature, broadly, more than Jaina philosophy, *per se*. There are, unfortunately, very, very few (if not none at all) people who have actually worked on *Nīlakeci* the text in a comprehensive manner. Part of the reason for this also lies in the fact that at one point the manuscripts of *Nīlakeci* were scarce and it had taken the labour of the Tamil savant U. Ve. Swaminatha Aiyer to retrieve and add to his huge collections, for posterity. For a long while thereafter, despite the availability of the manuscript, there were few—even among the educated Tamil Jainas—to bring it out in published form. One of the manuscripts (in palm leaf/*ōlaiccuvaṭi)* was also with the Melcittamur Jaina maṭham (monastic institution) in Cenji in Tamilnadu. Fortunately, *Nīlakeci* survived to see its printed version.

Prof. A. Chakravarti, a student and teacher of political philosophy, was the Principal of the Government College at Kumbakonam. He got hold of the manuscript and decided to bring out a printed version of the same as early as 1936—its first print edition. He not only brought out the text in the original Tamil but also included a scholarly, though summarised, translation and editorial notes in English. His 1936 work, too unfortunately, has very few copies left in libraries today. In 1984, the Tamil University in Thanjavur came out with the first reprint of the entire work without changing any part of it. Later, in 1994, the Prakrit Bharati Academy of Jaipur decided to bring out the second print edition of this work. But they published only the English section of the text, and not the entire work in its original form. It must be said, therefore, that the context in which these works appeared and the aim with which these were brought out were very different and one may not rightfully critique them. The concerns one is raising today in this work and the ways of seeing it today—equipped as one is, in whatever limited manner, with critical historical and methodological concerns and ideas in a different world context—are bound to be far removed from the year and context when these early editions were published. However, a few points need to be made here about these works and their focus and why was there a need to re-locate *Nīlakeci* as a text in a different context than has merited attention so far.

Prof. Chakravarti was looking at, essentially, a Jaina text *par excellence*—a text that highlighted some of the most influential, contemporary religious/philosophical/metaphysical systems of thought. He was looking at the essence of this Jaina work and being a Tamil Jaina himself—and one of the educated and professionally qualified Tamil Jainas of a period in Indian history that was addressing 'modern' questions—he saw in this work, as he says in his Preface (which has been mentioned earlier), something that needed to be shared towards an altruistic purpose. His interest in the whole enterprise was more to bring out of the closet, as it were, a Tamil Jaina literary work. Hence, one can see the consciousness—of this larger aim—throughout his work. He also adds to the text, in his translation, by inserting critical comments on matters where necessary. For instance, in the chapter on Bhūtavāda and Nīlakeci's debate, he adds a note that in some texts, the Bhūtavāda doctrine only spoke of four bhūtas (elements) and not five, as stated in *Nīlakeci*. And to make this point he refers to other works which deal with Bhūtavāda, such as Sarvadarsana Sangraha of Mādhvācārya and Sarvasiddhānta Sangraha of Sankarācārya.

And he also writes,

> ...The author of Neelakesi introduces as the teacher of this Bhūtavāda one Piśācaka. Probably this is a fictitious name. But why should he introduce the five Bhūtas instead of four? Is it really a problem to be investigated? Does it mean there was a special branch of this Chārvāka school which recognised the five bhūtas as the fundamental elements instead of four?...At a period in the history of thought there must have been a belief that all the five elements combined to form the organic bodies. But later on, to make the system consistent with the logical foundations, Ākāsa must have been dropped out since it is not within the direct reach of sense perception.[1]

Comments such these are added as notes which set the context to the actual text; he has also added some Jaina inscriptions from Tamilnadu and he discusses the history of Ājīvakas in the Tamil country. At places one finds traces of a pre-independence era engagement/concern with European philosophy and classical metaphysical traditions of the West. As also a generation that was tackling issues of science and modernity and seeking these elements in Indian thought systems. Thus in the introductory pages he notes

> He [the author of *Nīlakeci*] has adopted the famous method of philosophical dialogue so splendidly used by Plato... Plato's dialogue has arisen to the literary eminence of a drama, because of the human elements introduced on the stage. The author of

> Neelakesi similarly sustains the same dramatic element while trying to present the various philosophical systems and to critically examine them.[2]

Again,

> In the controversy with the Buddhist thinkers who reject the doctrine that plants are living organisms, Neelakesi marshals elaborate arguments to establish the Jaina attitude towards the vegetable kingdom. This is referred to by the technical term Ekendriya jīva—living beings having one sense... Enumeration of other characteristics which the plant world shares with the animal world, such as plants are subject to disease...that they behave quite like other living organisms with a characteristic re-action in response to adequate stimulus, that they are capable of curing themselves by internal re-adjustment and the quoting of the very instance of the plant Mimosa which figures so much in the recent researches of Dr. Bose illustrating the extreme sensitivity in plants are details which would be emphasised in any modern treatise on plant biology. It is interesting to note that these ideas are contained in a Tamil classic several centuries old.[3]

Elsewhere, he had compared and contrasted Jainism with Western thought[4] and Classical Greek thought. Thus

> Jaina thought agrees with the Greek atomists—Leucyppus and Democritus as to the constitution of the physical universe.... Pythogoras...preached to his followers that they should strictly abstain from meat-eating... Members belonging to the Pythogorean order were also ridiculed for their vegetarian habit. It is quite probable that Pythogoras had contact with Indian religious leaders who preached ahimsa and vegetarianism far beyond the borders of India. It is an historical fact that Jaina ascetics went to Persia, Mesopotamia, Asia (Minor) which was then called Monea...[5]

His interest did not stop at classical Greek thinkers. He indulges in comparative analysis with Descartes, Hume, Kant, Hegel and Karl Marx.

> The metaphysical idealism formulated by Hegel is a distinct monoistic theory.... But Jaina metaphysical system is distinctly pluralistic. For it, the ultimate reality consists of an infinite number of Jivas or Atmas. Though the experience of each jīva exactly corresponds to the manifestation of the Hegelian idea, the individual personality does not completely lose itself in the universal idea as suggested by Hegel. The Jaina view is that the individual personality is the most important and ultimate reality and everything else must be subordinated to the spiritual welfare of this fundamental reality.[6]

But Chakravarti's ultimate concern comes out, in the context of discussion on Marx's 'ultimate goal' of a classless society, thus:

> When we turn to Jaina thinkers, we are able to discover a possible solution of this problem of human conflict. Thousands of years ago, Jaina thinkers recognised the importance of the economic factor. They realised that peace and harmony in human society could not be secured so long as there is uncontrolled accumulation of wealth by a few persons...Thus the internal conflict will be perpetuated. In order to escape from such an evil situation, the Jaina thinkers formulated an economic principle as an ethical and religious ideal.... Agricultural produce or other requisite of economic value, should not be owned by any particular individual beyond a certain limit. Whatever is produced beyond a prescribed limit, should be considered as the property of the whole society... The modern world still suffering from internal conflict will certainly benefit itself if it accepts and adopts the ideal prescribed by the Jaina teachers for the welfare of humanity.[7]

It was necessary to have digressed and taken note of these discussions since they have a bearing on the way a text was seen and edited by an author—the way *Nīlakeci* was perceived and analysed by Chakravarti. Most of his works clearly show the working of a mind steeped in philosophical discussion and contemporary concerns of the period. It is also a mind that is rooted in the Tamil Jaina society and eager to 'bring out' into the open the literature and traditions of this community towards a 'larger aim' to 'benefit society.' This has a bearing on the way *Nīlakeci* the text is approached by him. There isn't much focus on the purely literary merits of the work.

About the 'radical' idea of taking a '*pēy*' as the heroine of the text, Chakravarti points out that

> After all, we have to remember that the author of Neelakesi, though he takes her—the Kāli of Pazhayanur—as the heroine of the story, frankly confesses that the story is merely a dream. It is an entirely imaginative creation. He wanted somebody who was revelling in cruelty and Ahimsa to be converted to the doctrine of Ahimsa and to serve as a model of harmony and non-violence. He could not think of anybody else than the Kāli of Pazhayanur.[8]

Meanwhile, moving over to another text, *Nīlakeci Viḷakkavuṟai*, was published in 1964, edited by Ponnusami Veluttevar Somasundaranar (Po.Ve.So) and reprinted in 1973. This edition focusses on the text *per se* and in his introduction, Po.Ve.So narrates the versions of Nīli story in the Śaivite tradition and gives a lucid treatise on the genre '*kēci*' such as *Kuṇṭalakeci*, *Piṅkalakeci* and so forth in Tamil literature. Po.Ve.So's work also highlights the literary merits (and flourish) inherent in *Nīlakeci*. Essentially, however, this edition is meant for scholars of Tamil literature. It must be also mentioned that even as Chakravarti points out that a few verses in the Vedavāda section (about seven of them) are missing as the corresponding manuscripts were not then available to him (with a request he makes to the readers to help locate them), Somasundaranar's book mentions the same fact as well (p. 667). Of course, Po.Ve.So's work seems to borrow heavily from Chakravarti's introduction with Nīli's stories and the Nīlakeci (Jaina) version and so forth.

So we have works of two scholars on *Nīlakeci*, both focussing on the text as a religious, philosophical contribution in Tamil, without contextualising it substantially, let's say, historically, as to why the text came about in a certain period of history of

Tamil Jaina community. Though Chakravarti does make a point or two to this effect, it is still not the primary concern.

Coming to a rather recent work on *Nīlakeci*, one finds, unfortunately, not much ground covered since the last time Po.Ve.So, or Chakravarti '*naiṉār*' (as the Tamil Jainas address him) published their volumes. In fact, this work says nothing new on the subject. This is G.V. Saroja's 'Jainism as Expounded in the Nīlakeci'.[9] The only point where Saroja differs (with the earlier scholars) is when she dates *Nīlakeci* to 10th century CE, with no particular reason for it mentioned. She assumes (based on Chakravarti's contention) that the Kāli of Paḻayanūr is the heroine of Nīlakeci—although nowhere in the Nīlakeci text itself, is there any reference to this connection. If at all, it is the goddess of the temple (Kāli) who requests Nīli-Nīlakeci of the south—to get rid of the monk. Whether or not Kāli of Paḻayanūr could be identified with Nīlakeci of the text still needs to be analysed further. Saroja follows the same sequence of argument as set forth by Chakravarti on how different this Kāli of Paḻayanūr is from the other Nīlis in different works such as Cēkkiḻār's *Periyapurāṇam*, Gñānasampantar's *Tevāram* and Sāmantabhadra's (Jaina) *Ratnākaraṇṭaka*. Then follow brief summaries of Nīlakeci's debate with different systems of thought—again, there are no new perspectives coming from these. What is amazing, however, is that there is no mention of what one would consider the most important point about caste and Pūtikaṉ calling Nīlakeci a śūdra. One wonders as to why a major point such as this would be ignored altogether. Instead, Saroja briefly summarises Nīlakeci's take on authorship of the Vedas.

It is in this context that I re-viewed *Nīlakeci*, through questions that should probably help take a closer, serious look at the significance of this work.

Alter-texting a Persona, an Idiom: A (Tamil) Jaina-'Folk'/Popular Interface?

In most studies on the history of Tamilnadu scholars have tended to focus more on the issue of brāhmiṇical hegemony, built over centuries and within the confines of this paradigm, on the socio-political and cultural hegemony, giving some excellent treatises on various aspects of the Tamil social and political history. Wherever 'non'-brāhmiṇical, non-'Hindu' traditions have been studied, the focus has again been directly or indirectly on treating these as the alternate, in contra-position, or a counter to the overarching, dominant religion-temple-land-resources-polity-brāhmiṇism (not necessarily in that sequential order), as the moving force. Most explanations for the making of this dominant/hegemonic system have rested on the notion of brāhmiṇical tradition 'incorporating' elements of the 'folk' and making an 'inclusive', as it were, religious system, closely connected to, and responsible for, certain kinds of economic, social and political relations. What is seen as 'folk'/'popular' (at times, 'Dravidian', by scholars like Zvelebil, for instance) in most of these studies, has existed at the base/substratum, to be 'picked-up' and incorporated by the brāhmiṇical ideology, thereby making for a 'dominant' force in various ways. Most of these scholarly treatises, however, fail to consider similar interactions and incorporations, perhaps, when it comes to religious systems such as Buddhism and Jainism in Tamilnadu. Both these systems seem to have had only the dominant brāhmiṇical paradigm to contest with, or challenge, each other; or to simply lose out to the other, be marginalised. What about Buddhist-'folk' or Jaina-'folk' interface? Was there one/were there a few such?

At another level, scholars (especially non-Indian scholars) have shown almost obsessive inclination towards and interest in the Tamil 'popular'/'folk' 'virgin' goddess concept. More often than not, in the process, they have focussed exclusively, extensively on the Purāṇic myths and goddesses in a larger Hindu/brāhmiṇical paradigm, speaking for a kind of syncretism or synthesis of what is essentially folk-Tamil and Purāṇic-Sanskritic-brāhmiṇical, together forming a Tamil cultural ethos, as it stands today.

In an early work, David Shulman remarked that, "A major contribution to the formation of Tamil culture was undoubtedly made by the brāhmiṇs, who became the custodians, and in some cases, the creators or the traditions of Tamil shrines..." [In the sthalapurāṇas, 'composed under significant brāhmiṇ influence'] "we glimpse the *unifying, synthesising, fertlising* force that brāhmiṇism has represented in the history of Tamilnadu. It is largely this force that allows us to speak of a single, distinctive system of *Tamil mythology* incorporated in literary texts composed over a period..."[10]

Shulman's concern was the Śaivite tradition and the above statements were made in that context. But the problem, somewhere, is the concentration and focus on this tradition to the near-exclusion of many others, on the one hand; but more important, to speak for what is termed the 'Tamil' culture as having been built by these interactive processes with brāhmiṇism as an essential ingredient therein, or the 'fertilising force'. And the problem lies exactly in the latter. Especially, when two other important religions, Jainism and Buddhism, as many other lesser known (much less studied) systems of thought, along with popular and folk traditions and systems have made this larger 'Tamil' culture. Moreover, it denies any kind of inherent conflict and tension within the process of this 'synthesising'. For instance, speaking of the idea of the two forms—the violent, virginal and the bride, mother—of the goddess, Shulman rationalised the way in which both these forms (traditions) gained an acceptable space in the bhakti tradition, with the violent elements relegated to the periphery of a shrine and the 'pure' aspect retained within. There

> 'Both realms are sacred, even if the purāṇic texts, true to the Upaniṣadic legacy and the brāhmiṇical ideal of purity, assert the superiority of the isolated, other worldly shrine. Power, or the goddess, can never be dispensed with completely, unless life itself is finally negated Tamil bhakti religion is too much in love with life... Both goals, purity and power, persist in the bhakti

> tradition; the ordering of the shrine, with the virgin goddess separate and the god with his 'tame' wife located in the centre, reflects the continuing conflict between the two vital religious ideals.'[11]

The above explanation neatly compartmentalises spaces for both these 'opposites' in the bhakti tradition; but then, where would a character/form/concept such as that of '*pēy*' Nīli's fit into this whole paradigm? Or, would it fit at all? Considering, especially, that the fear element in the *pēy* stories 'forcibly' make a demand for a shrine for these *pēy*s. And at some point, these temples have an amalgam of both brāhmiṇical rituals and animal sacrifices and are deities almost invariably, of those that come from the fringes of the social order, the lower castes and tribes. Is this a movement of 'inclusion' at one level, that the ambivalent force has been 'at least' granted the periphery? Or would it be that it just has to be 'outside of' and at the periphery (metaphorically in a perpetually '*pēy*'/ambivalent status) because it cannot be included in the prevailing norms of codified temple worship and religion? These are difficult questions to answer. And these will remain problematic issues unless there is an effort to look at possibilities of other, affirmative (or even otherwise) traditions outside of the Purāṇic/Sanskritic/brāhmiṇical paradigm that have been the focus for many years. Where is the place, in these kinds of analyses, for the story of Nīli and her transformation into Nīlakeci, a Jaina philosopher-preacher, even if she was seen as a fictitious character, and product of a dream of the author? Isn't there a need to look beyond the 'given' 'Tamil' (which is mostly read as 'folk'/'popular'/'little' tradition) meeting or merging with the Purāṇic/brāhmiṇical to create a so-called 'composite' culture of 'synthesis'? What were those elements that were never included? Or were consciously excluded? In this sense, the text *Nīlakeci* throws open numerous questions about an organised (so-called-'heterodox') religion such as Jainism's interface with the 'base'/'popular'. The larger 'Tamil' mythic corpus, or cultural paradigm needs to be seen as not necessarily, or essentially, the merger of brāhmiṇical-folk, but as one with several underlying layers of interactions with such systems as Buddhist and Jaina hitherto considered to be of 'non-sensual' orientation and therefore disenchanted by the popular rituals and traditions necessarily oriented towards the sensual and intimate god/deity/supernatural-human relationships (referring here, particularly to the bhakti concept). In the last case, one must mention an effort made in this direction in the brilliant monograph on the Pattini cult (written years ago, but still relevant) and Buddhism in Sri Lanka by Gananath Obeyesekere.[12] Here Buddhism is shown as using the popular ('folk') Pattini cult (Pattini, deified in Tamil popular tradition even before she 'moved' to Sri Lanka[13]) making her an 'eligible' candidate, so to speak, for Buddhahood. Obeyesekere's intention is to look at the institutionalisation of the cult. And significantly, the goddess Pattini is both a 'Hindu' and a 'Buddhist' deity in Sri Lanka and both have added to the mythic corpus of this cult, with a central shrine in the Sabaragamuva province at Navagamuva. The cult is supposed to have diffused into Sri Lanka and operated in a cultural context of the Sinhalas. In the Buddhist context she is an aspirant for Buddhahood. However, in the Sri Lankan context, which Obeyesekere analysed in his work, Buddhism is the overwhelming paradigm. And the Buddhist tradition takes a character like Pattini, already by then deified in popular religion, to give her a Buddhist dimension. In this sense, if we look at *Nīlakeci* (where there is certainly no ritual dimension or religious compulsion involved) the author creates a whole new character out of an infamous one, giving the character an entirely new dimension. The difference is, however, that unlike Kaṇṇaki who became Pattini (the goddess) Nīlakeci remains a character bound within a text and does not assume deified status in the Jaina religious system. The intriguing question here (which one is not inclined or qualified enough, yet, to answer/resolve) is 'why'?

What is important here, is that Buddhist and Jaina traditions, too, had been open to influences (and were also influencing) the popular, 'non' brāhmiṇical traditions prevalent in their time and it is necessary to recognise these in order to move away from the 'plot' (if one may use the term) of brāhmiṇisation altogether. For, what get referred to as 'dominant' and 'marginal' (which one also tends to use) traditions, insomuch as there are historical processes that create them, are also created and reiterated in historical writing and reconstruction, by highlighting them at a sustained level to the exclusion of others.[14]

In this context then, I have located the text, especially in the manner in which the Tamil Jaina tradition (or a representative of that tradition) seeks a culmination, a climax, to the long pathetic history of the possessing, restless, angry Nīli, the *pēy*, in/by making her a 'reformed' lay aspirant and eventually preacher-philosopher of the Jaina doctrine. Though there is almost negligible 'space' or 'distance' between her receiving an enlightened ordainment at the feet of Muṇicandiraṉ and her donning the role of a fierce, confirmed debater of Jainism thereafter. The Jaina muṇi/monk (or the creator of the text) gives her the much needed direction towards *aparigraha* (non-attachment/non-possession) both figuratively and in terms of her identity as '*pēy*' in the local Tamil tradition of the region, which was a non-possibility so long as she remained confined in the folk (and Śaivite *Tevāram*) idiom. Of course, Paḻayaṉūr Nīli, by virtue of her anger and vulnerability to destroying, does get a shrine (which again she asks for, in one of the versions of her story) to keep her appeased, or rather, controlled and confined. In this sense, of course, she gets a status of a goddess, but she would still remain a violent, possessing goddess. That part of her life story will never let go of her. In this sense, how does it help to look at her from a different mirror as the Tamil Jaina author of *Nīlakeci* did?

Nīli to Nīlakeci: The Point of 'Movement'

The genesis/origin story of *Nīlakeci* text lies, as the text's anonymous author says right at the onset, in a dream, which revealed the events as narrated in the text. The author also makes a point about not writing exactly within the 'rules' of the traditional āgamas: "*kaṇṭēn̲ kiṭantēn̲ kaṇavin̲n̲itu kaṇṭavārē*"[15] (this, I saw in a dream) and he says, "I admit to the knowledgeable ones that this text is not in accordance with our old *āgamas*."

Both these 'admissions' are important. That the events unfolding here are merely part of the author's dream, in a sense, seems to imply that the creator of the text pre-empts efforts to link what follows in the course of the text to an event or a character. In this sense, although the character is indeed based on what would be perceived—both by the Jaina laity / scholars who might read the text and the non-Jainas 'others' from other traditions—to be indeed the *pēy* Nīli. Stating that the text does not follow the rules of the *āgamas* then perhaps implies what the creator of the text feared might happen, with the introduction of a central character with a background such as that of Nīli. The author[16] even in that time was radically altering a certain form of popularising the Jaina doctrine which had the probability of being received with a certain amount of skepticism. And one believes it may not have been the 'form' as much as the 'content', especially the 'receptacle' of the content, namely, Nīlakeci or Nīli the pēy, that was likely to be questioned by the 'scholarly' audience the author is addressing. Moreover, making Nīli/ Nīlakeci merely part of an elaborate dream sequence removes the idea of the existence of such a character, or the reality of such an event. It is probable that since the text deals with a 'high-end' subject, such as comparative evaluation of Jaina philosophy against other philosophies/systems, it may have necessitated the author to clarify what were likely points of 'attack' or criticism, namely—how could a *pēy* like Nīli be capable of debating with the important teachers of the time, considering her own antecedents? Pre-empting such a critique it was simpler to set the context and link the entire manuscript to a genesis unlikely to be questioned, namely, a dream. In that sense, all the debates, too, and the characters therein, were all part of a dream. But though they were part of a dream, characters such as Kuṇṭalakeci, the Buddha, Mokkala, etc. were real characters and not fictitious, even if they were used in the text for a specific purpose. The author has picked up important names, figures of the time and woven a story around all of these, after having read what may have been a similar format in *Kuṇṭalakeci*. The author is at the same time familiar with the legend of Nīli, in order to have successfully built a theme around her. Making her a character of a dream would give the author enough freedom to mould her story in any which way that s/he wanted, without having to explain such a 'face-lift'.

Two points need to be noted here—one, that even if this was a dream, and an entirely imaginative creation, there was a reason behind it. Chakravarti himself confesses to it when he says, the author required a character "revelling in cruelty" to convert into an embodiment of ahimsā. Though he 'dreamt' it all, the author is not completely 'innocent' of the implications of such an exercise. Even if Nīli of Nīlakeci was the "Kāli of Pazhayanur."[17] In a different context (but which may not be altogether unrelated in terms of a concept) Kunal Chakrabarti points out that it may be important to seek as to "how an individual author is revealed in the text, but where the discourse comes from..."[18]

The discourse, in this case, came from a need to place a Jaina ideal in a non-Jaina context (for purposes of proselytising, perhaps) through an idiom that was familiar to the region the author unmistakably belonged to—where the 'sceptre' of Nīli (had) loomed large, in what was then Toṇṭaimaṇṭalam; in and around Tiruvalangadu, which the Śaivites made popular as the site of the dance of Śiva and defeat or submission of Kāli. A discourse was being created—by breaking the stereotype of a quintessential Tamil (?) form / idiom of the possession spirit stuck in a cycle of retribution and appeasement. The discourse in this case was not an *a priori*, but being created; it was a discourse that broke free from patterns even within Jainism. For, here was this '*pēy*' and in this sense, not part of 'this-world' on account of her unnatural death. And what's more, she avenged her murder with another act of violence, killing and drinking the blood of her husband of the previous birth. So Nīli/Nīlakeci was also someone who had killed—again, an anomaly for the ideal Jaina type for being granted the privilege of proving the superiority of its principles. In changing this form/idiom/concept a whole new "discourse" of the period was being formulated. That is how one would like to 'reveal' the position of the author of *Nīlakeci* in the Tamil Jaina tradition. Be that as it may, there is one section of the text where the likely friction, by virtue of adapting this idiom, is revealed and strangely enough, it is friction caused by the brāhmiṇcal tradition—in the *Vetavātaccarukkam.* Here, as noted, the Vedic teacher Pūtikaṉ calls Nīlakeci a 'śūdra' and makes a comment on her eligibility to critique the Vedas. This point is important since it brings out into the open—through the debate—what would be the likely points of criticism to the idea of giving Nīli the important position of examining all our philosophical traditions and religious systems. And the criticism of this kind (where caste and status become most important) happens from no other system but the Vedic (brāhmiṇical) in this text. Even though the author of *Nīlakeci* makes a confessional point about going outside the āgamic fold in writing it, one may venture to suggest that the Jaina tradition seems to have given relative freedom and space for the experiment.

This is clear also from the way the text *Cīvakacintāmaṇi* (in Tamil) styles itself. Here again, the genesis of the text is laid out clearly by the author. The context (of the composition—the way it was created) is that of ridicule by members of one of the Tamil Caṅkams: a statement that Jaina textual tradition (or authorship) could never produce a single erotic verse. The presumption (behind this ridicule) was that the Jaina tradition was more concerned with the non-sensual and the austere and not concerned with the worldly ways, especially in matters of love and erotica. Responding to this, the author Tiruṭṭakkattēvar wrote this epic which is now part of the five *peruṅkāppiyams* in

Tamil. This, of course, is the legend associated with the birth of *Cīvakacintāmaṇi*, story of the king Cīvakaṉ, his adventures and sexual affairs concluding in the final moment of becoming detached from passions. But it may well have to do with one angle of criticism that may have been in vogue in that period about Jaina textual tradition, in general, irrespective of *Cilappatikāram*. Thus, explanation for the genesis of the work, and its nature, is not uncommon: it could be criticism at the Tamil Caṅkam, or the dream, and a related explanation. There is always, it seems, a reason for the text to be, or have been.

Continuing with the question of authorship and genesis of the text (or characters in the dream who became part of the text), in the context of a discussion on authorship, it may be interesting to recount an allusion to the 4th century BC Chinese philosopher, Zhuangzi (the Master Zhuang, of Chuang Tzu), of course, in a totally different context:

> 'Once Zhuang Zhou dreamed of himself being a butterfly; he was really a butterfly fluttering around, happy...knowing not that he was Zhou. After a while, he woke up, and he was surprisingly Zhyang Zhou himself. It was not clear whether it was Zhou who had dreamt of being a butterfly or it was the butterfly who had dreamed of Zhou. Yet there must be differentiation between Zhou and the butterfly; and this is called the transformation of things.'[19]

This story persuaded me to look at some connections so far as *Nīlakeci*, the text, is concerned. Is Nīli of Paḻayaṉūr, for instance, being dreamt of, or is she 'extracting' her own text, or meta-narrative? Or, is the dream (re) constructing her? I am simply trying to posit another case for the process of 'Nīli-to-Jaina philosopher-Nīlakeci' movement, which is this one: the Paḻayanūr Nīli idiom, by itself, is a potent one, existing independent of all major organised religious systems in Tamilnadu at one point. This idiom becomes so important that it needs to be acknowledged by systems that come into contact with it (or come within its 'zone'), and hence, we have several versions of the story, with even the *Tēvāram* of the Śaivite bards making a mention of it in their own context. There, the idiom (Nīli) extracts its own place and position within a system. And in the Jaina Tamil text, Nīli-Nīlakeci is being entirely reconstructed/re-constituted. Both approaches to the Nīli idiom would seem to convey both these positions. In this sense, it may be important to consider an altogether parallel stream of thought at a conceptual level, as to whether it was imperative that Nīli be 'picked up' from her popular locale/narrative? That is to say, her character becomes the most important element to make a story, or a point out of. None of the traditions can ignore, or negate her. Thus the questions whether "creative imagination guide(s) the composition, or is the writer like the scrawl of an alien power trying out a new pen"(or) "is the author the producer of the text or its product"[20] in the case of / with Nīlakeci, becomes crucial, but difficult to answer in a simplistic manner. Especially since, at the level of methodology, this critical question of authorship of traditions, in the case of at least Tamil (Jaina or otherwise) textual tradition has not been problematised yet to an adequate degree—so as to dwell on just this one aspect.

If one agrees with Foucault when he says that the "author's name...is situated in the breach, among the discontinuities, which gives rise to new groups of discourse and their singular mode of existence"[21] then *Nīlakeci* as a text with an author (in the sense that the "author characterize[s] the existence, circulation and operation of certain discourses within a society"[22]) qualifies for an examination that goes beyond the text's immediate objective and what it claims to convey, at the face value. There are deeper layers within this text that has, on the face of it, a simplistic aim. To take just one instance, the author of *Nīlakeci* (if it is presumed it is a 'male') assumes the female voice (that of Nīlakeci) in the various debates, and in that sense the Jaina philosophy too, then, acquires the female voice, and this is important, in a context where, within the Digambara tradition, women are not eligible for attaining mokṣa (the ultimate liberation) and in a general sense, too, women are not believed to have the wherewithal to work towards this aim. At the very best, through ritualistic discipline, they may be re-born as males and attain liberation. In this sense, selecting a female character (when the author could well have composed the same text using a male voice as the one debating the other systems) seems significant. Again, the author speaks for the "śūdra" caste when Vedic teacher, Pūtikan, ridicules Nīlakeci as a śūdra and hence unqualified to critique the Vedas. In these cases, somewhere, the author 'dies' to let the characters—steeped in their own cultural contexts—speak for themselves, while the author simply records their respective points of view. A similar 'event' in the text—where the character is what the character '*is*', outside of, the textual 'situation'—occurs when Nīlakeci becomes (reverts to) *pēy*, all over again, to prove a point to the materialist Picācakaṉ. Here, perhaps, the character rebels against the author of the text, although for a brief moment, and becomes what she is/has been, historically, and culturally, a *pēy*. At this point, the text seems to have failed the character of Nīlakeci (the Jaina philosopher) herself, by allowing for that brief moment to Nīli to take shape, even if it was for the benefit of Nīlakeci. Thus, the larger context of the idiom of *pēy* of Paḻayaṉūr is its own dominant form, although subtle, yet strong and capable of overtaking other interpretations at appropriate moments. And that is the larger context the author operates in, and locates herself/himself in.

Hence, it is a person rooted in a specific context with its metaphors and motifs that would naturally appear in the work. With all the confessions made at the onset (about the dream) the basic truth is that the dream state happens to be nothing apart from the author's own immediate cultural context. In fact, the author distances from the text at this point. And if we accept what Chakravarti says about the author being a convert to Jainism[23], it serves our purpose to say that Paḻayaṉūr Nīli is a potent folk cultural idiom in an authored work of the time to fit into the enterprise.

Let us move now to another layer of discussion related to the question of authorship within *Nīlakeci*. It is interesting that Nīlakeci ridicules the claim of the Vedic teacher about the omniscience and primordiality/authorless, self-conception of the Vedas. That they are 'apouruśēya'. In her discussion on the subject, we see the Jaina ideas on textual tradition and authorship. Nīlakeci's point is that, "the Veda consists of sentences constituted by words, in their turn, by letters. Since there is no fundamental difference between the language of the Vedas and the language of the ordinary literary works, both must be considered as having been produced by some intelligent person."[24]

> *'katiyavar tampeya ri<u>nn</u>avaicuṭṭi<u>n</u>a kāṭṭali<u>n</u>u*
> *mutiyavar nāḷkaḷō ṭoppila vippo<u>l</u>u tottali<u>n</u>um*
> *vītiyatu vātali<u>n</u> vētattai yāñcolluṅ kītattaippō<u>r</u>*
> *putiyatu vēye<u>n</u>ac collutu nāmatu poruntu me<u>nr</u>āḷ'* (v. 832)[25]

Nīlakeci here uses the term "*yāñcolluṅ kītattaippō<u>r</u>*" and points out that the names associated with the Vedas are ones of a contemporary period and not from older times; and like the literary works—"gītam"—of this period, use similar language. Both editions of *Nīlakeci* I have referred to translate "*yām collum kītattaippōr*" as, "like the words of those people who composed Kumāra Sambhavam and the like."

It is clear that Nīlakeci stresses on the 'this-worldliness' of the Vedas in these arguments and as the Jaina works almost always had, and mentioned, authors of their works, the fact that Vedas could have no author, was not acceptable to the Jaina thinking on these matters. To this criticism, the Vedic teacher Pūtika<u>n</u> points out that the authors named by Nīlakeci were not authors, *per se*, but merely those 'transmitting' the content of the Vedas to the world. In this context, the brāhmiṇs were clever enough to devise a method of giving Vedas an ultimate supernatural quality. Since, perhaps as Barthes had (in a different context) pointed out (and it agrees with this idea that)

> 'To give a text an author is to impose a limit on that text, to furnish it with a final signified, to close the writing.'[26]

And in countering this effort, Nīlakeci fixes a time, period and authorial responsibility for the Vedas.

The Site of Nīli

Pal̲ayan̲ūr, the site of the legend of Nīli, needs some attention. "Pal̲ayan̲ūr in Pal̲ayan̲ūr nādu is identified with the village of the same name close to Tiruvālangādu in the Tiruttani division of the Chittoor district. The Tiruvālangādu plates of the Chola king Rajendra Chola I record the grant of this village to the Śiva temple at Tiruvālangādu. In the Tevāram hymns this latter place is called Pal̲aiyan̲ūr Ālangādu (i.e, Alangadu near Palaiyanur)."[27]

The above inscription in the 11th year of Nṛpatungadeva mentions that the assembly of Perumalai-ūr, a brahmadeya in Kākkalūr-nādu agreed to grant a certain measure of paddy and ghee as offerings to the deity at "Tiruvālangādu in Pal̲aiyan̲ūr nādu." Another offering is made to the same deity of this temple by the assembly of Pulvēḷūr in Eyir̲-kōṭṭam of "one *uri* (unit) of oil daily for burning the perpetual lamp."[28]

Again, the Tamil portion of the Tiruvālangādu plates of Rajendra I, addresses the nāṭṭār and other locality groups in Melmalai Pal̲ayan̲ūr nādu and directs that the village Pal̲aiyan̲ūr, for which place the locality was named and which was a brāhmiṇ (endowed) village (brahmadeya) was now to become a village subject to regular dues from cultivators (veḷḷān̲-vakai) and these were to be granted to the temple of Tiruvālangādu as devadāna.[29]

The site, as we can see, or its environs, where the Nīli story of revenge is played out, is that of brāhmiṇ settlements and in the above inscription, the veḷḷāḷas of the village are instructed to pay dues to the temple of Natarāja—now this being a temple to the dancing Śiva also reasserts and reconfirms the myth of Śiva defeating Kāli in a dance competition which had happened here. And in the version where this myth is narrated also mentions this as having been the site of Kāli. A Kāli shrine is said to have existed here. From the story of Paḻayaṉūr Nīli and this myth, it may not be too conjectural to infer that this place had been a stronghold of the goddess cult which later got fused into one of Śaivite worship, with the Śiva's dance myth clearly establishing the ascendance/superiority of the (male) god over others. In the *Tevāram* version, consequently, and in the *Nīli Nāṭakam* version of the Nīli story, the influence of brāhmiṇical values and mores is unmistakably felt, and the later Śaivite-brāhmiṇical hegemony over the region of this story may have a lot to do with this kind of rendering. The fact that so many versions of the Nīli story existed also reflects the significance and prevalence of an earlier local narrative of this region, deeply associated with a female cult. In fact, as noted earlier, the name of Nīli is known and in *Cilappatikāram*, the goddess of Madurai tells Kaṇṇaki she was Nīli in a previous birth. In the same epic, Nīli is one of the many names of the mother goddess. In some versions of the legend, Nīli commands that a temple be built for her, and in another, gets it done after an act of vengeance on the priest by killing his daughter, which implies that a temple to this deity existed in these parts.

There seems to have been, around 8th-9th century AD, expansion of brāhmiṇ settlements surrounding this area. Jñānasampantar, the Śaivite bard, pays his visits to these places. In fact, Jñānasampantar alludes to the myth of Śiva defeating Kāli in a dance at this place. Cēkkiḻār and Sampantar both refer to the Nīli story. Interestingly, there is yet another angle to the site—the presence of veḷḷāḷas. In the Nīli story, too, the veḷḷāḷas have an important place. The motif of 70 veḷḷāḷas jumping into a burning pyre has been mentioned. And this act of the veḷḷāḷas finds an almost central place in most Śaivite renderings of the Nīli story. It is possible that the motif of the 'word-bound' veḷḷāḷas was part of another legend, folklore that merged into the Nīli story at some point. In this connection Shanmuga Sundaram makes an interesting point. He notes that a *tīkkuḷi maṇṭapam* (a platform for fire walking/or a space for a pyre) was set up in Paḻayaṉūr in the year 1966. He remarks that Nīli worship in Paḻayaṉūr must have given way to the worship of veḷḷāḷas, and the hence this maṇṭapam. [30]

The site of Nīli story is important also in terms of how the story shapes up and how each version replays this basic story. There is yet another aspect to this story which seems to be the peculiarity of not just this, but many other stories of the 'wronged woman' who possesses, avenges, or transforms (into a *pēy* after her death by deceit). Nīli's husband (of the former birth, now a merchant in the second birth) has to pass through this tract between two places, Kancipuram and Paḻayaṉūr. It is in this no-person/no-human zone that Nīli 'possesses' him (metaphorically speaking) or accosts him (literally). In most Tamil narratives involving tales of the *pēy*/possession spirits, this is the kind of site (a mid-way) that is dreaded and most infamous. Why is this site always connected to things 'bad', 'evil', 'sinister' and dark? Who does this site belong to, in the first place? Is this kind of association of this site—with things dark, bad, at the least ambivalent—meant to keep some kinds of places (perhaps people, or even cults or cultic figures) on the fringes? In another sense, this site (where Nīli gets hold of her former-life husband) is also one of transcendence from one form to another in many such stories. For instance, Bhadda/ Bhadra transcends to the life of a *nirgrantha* (and later Buddhist nun, Kuṇṭalakeci) in one such similar site, having got rid of her husband, whom she kills. A similar case is that of the (chaste) wife turning into Ambicā, the Jaina yakṣi.[31] Kāraikkāl ammaiyār, too, 'throws' her worldly associations (both literally and symbolically by shedding her clothes and adornments) in one such site, to become a complete Śiva devotee from having been a dutiful wife.

This site is one on the periphery of land-ownership-resources-temple-bhakti paradigm of the brāhmiṇical system, as well. The need to control the *pēy* or folk goddess monopolising this region is signified in the version of Nīli's story where thorns are placed on her head to control her prowess, by the temple priest. This control also extends to control and suppression, and fixing, of a wandering tale and a wandering spirit outside of the accepted brāhmiṇical norms and practices and ritual context. Again, it also controls and hegemonises the site/sphere of the tale and the people to whom the metaphor/idiom of Nīli (or such goddesses) belonged, as also the (lower) caste story teller who keeps this idiom/story alive.

The temple to Nīli in one of the versions and the making of space for rootedness of the shrine (deity) through a brāhmiṇical control mechanism also begins with this control of the *pēy* and the folk idiom. Śiva's dance and defeating Kāli of Pal̠ayan̠ūr (or may be Nīli, as she may have been known earlier) has as its sub-text this control of the folk idiom. A comparison of the *villuppāṭṭu* version of Nīli story and the Tevāram (and other narratives influenced by it) and Jaina versions of the Nīli tale all do suppress the wandering/possession woman in their own ways (besides inferiorising the folk base of the story). Only, in the Jaina text, Nīli is given an affirmative voice through her character while the *Tevāram* works show her ultimately controlled by a priestly, temple based context. And yet, she remains an ambivalent figure, 'sanitised', yet not eligible for a status akin to the goddesses in the Purāṇic fold.

On Motifs in the Nīli Stories, Yakṣis, Kāraikkāl Ammaiyār, et.al.

In this context what is this Jaina-folk interface that one refers to? How and when does it operate and what does it do to the Nīli legend? Before taking up this issue, it would do well to draw attention to a few other 'non-Nīli' tales that had been in circulation in Tamilnadu over a period of time. This is just to look at ways in which traditions (Śaivite or Buddhist or Jaina) incorporated these layers of folklore, many of them with common motifs. That is to say that they were operating in a common context and the ways they used these themes depended on the message they wished to convey and the audience they wished to convey them to. Let me take up for discussion four tales—Nīlakeci/Nīli of the Jaina text Ratnākaraṇṭaka Śrāvakācāra (different from the Nīli of *Nīlakeci*) and Māriammaṉ; and that of Ambicā, the yakṣi of the tīrthankara Nemināthа and the Śaiva saint Kāraikkāl Ammaiyār. The stories of Māriammaṉ and Nīlakeci/Nīli have parallels as do those of Ambicā and Kāraikkāl Ammaiyār.

Nīli is the beautiful daughter of a Jaina merchant of Brgukacchā. One day another merchant's son named Sāgaradatta (a Buddhist) chanced to see her and fell in love with her. He desired to be married to her, but since he was a Buddhist, Nīli's father wouldn't give his consent. Sāgaradatta's father, to keep his son's heart, claimed that they followed the Jaina faith and thus got them married. Once Nīli was married, she realised, gradually, that she and her father had been cheated, and that her husband was a Buddhist. Despite this, she continued to remain a dutiful wife, though she herself followed the Jaina faith most scrupulously. One day, her father-in-law commanded her to cook for the Buddhist bhikkus he had invited home, including meat, which bhikkus were used to eating. Nīli couldn't disobey. But she cleverly took hold of the bhikkus' leather sandals and cooked a meal for them. The guests loved every morsel of it. When they got up to leave, they found the sandals missing. In the meantime, Nīli instructed some children in the neighbourhood to tease the bhikkus saying they had eaten their own slippers and were looking for them. When the children did as told, it enraged Sāgaradatta and his father threw Nīli out of the house, calling her an unchaste woman. Now in the same city was a gate that was shut and would not open. The king was told that only the truly chaste woman of the place would be able to open the gate.

Sure enough, the gate opened the moment Nīli touched it. Her husband and father-in-law, 'chastised', were ashamed to have unjustly charged her the way they did.

According to A.K. Ramanujan

> 'The excess of rage, the power of an ordinary woman to explode into a goddess when she is given a sufficient charge of anger, seems...the underlying pattern. It is as much a theory of emotion as a theology; together they make a special recognisable genre, the folk myth of the village goddess.'[32]

Now comes the story of Māriammaṉ, based on Kannada folklore (but also prevalent in parts of Tamilnadu, Kerala and Andhra Pradesh, with probably minor regional variants): once a brāhmin girl was abandoned by her father for she menstruated before her father could get her married. A Lingayat man, out of pity for her, took her home and looked after her. One day, a Madiga (considered among the lowest in the Hindu caste system), man saw her and fell in love with her. He desired to marry her. His mother instructed him learn the brāhmin ways if he wanted to marry her. Claiming to be a brāhmin, he asked her hand in marriage. The Lingayat, believing him, married her off to him. She had two sons by the Madiga man. One day, her sons found their father sewing sandals for people. They got back home and enacted what they saw, playfully. Their mother, horrified, dissuaded them from doing so, to which they responded that this is what their father did all day long. She was so disgusted and angry (realising that she, a brāhmin, was after all married to a Madiga cobbler) that she assumed the dreadful form of Māri and went after her husband and her children. The children took refuge in goats and buffaloes; she killed them and drank their blood. In yet another (Tamil) version, we have the woman feeding her mother-in-law and her husband cooked slippers; the mother-in-law and husband are enraged, call her unchaste, and in anger she assumes the form of Māri-ammaṉ.

If we look closely at both these tales, there are common motifs. Both the women are married to people from another social category—a Jaina to a Buddhist, a brāhmin to a Madiga—on the sly. There is the idea of pollution and the wife getting her revenge for that. The motif of cooking leather slippers is common to both stories. This would be seen as the ultimate insult (as an act of vengeance) that the women, as housewives, are able to throw at those who 'polluted' them—the husband and father-in-law, the husband and mother-in-law. In both cases (in the case of Māri, at least in the Tamil version), the women are charged as unchaste. But while the Jaina versions removes the violent 'second half' of the story and makes do with a relatively subdued resolution to the whole case, with (the Jaina) Nīli getting to prove her chastity by opening the gates of kingdom, the Māri story has the ordinary housewife turn into a dreaded demon goddess, killing whatever came in her way, including her own children, in the bargain.[33] No doubt that the Jaina author of Ratnākaraṇṭaka Srāvakācāra was picking up the tale from a folk layer for the story of Nili and her marriage to the Buddhist on the sly. The name Nīli that he gave his heroine was also part of the same folk base, and surely, a popular enough name for him to name the protagonist of his tale Nīli. We must also note that even in the Nīli stories Kancipuram is mentioned, showing it fell within the circulatory space of the story.

Coming to the story of the Jaina yakṣi Ambicā and her antecedents. Her story appears in the *Śrīpurāṇam*. Incidentally, her story almost lives on the lips of the Tamil Jaina women. After *Cīvakacintāmaṇi*, this is the most popular Jaina story among Tamil Jaina women. Ambicā was the wife of a brāhmin named Somasarma from north Girinagara, who had two sons and a woman who helped about in the house.[34] One day, during a death ceremony (śrāddham) he went with his relatives for a bath in the river. In the meantime, a Jaina monk passed by his house and Ambicā gave him some food. When Somasarma returned and learnt of this he was furious and called her unchaste.

Extremely dejected at this she left the house and sought refuge with the Jaina mendicant in the forest, with her two children. Meanwhile, Somasarma, repentant of his action, went looking for her. When she saw him approaching them in the forest (in some versions, with a torch flame, since it was dark), afraid that he might harm her, she killed herself, leaving her children there (in some versions, he takes the children back home) and thus became a yakṣi. When the children saw her in this form they were frightened. She granted them a boon that she would assume the human form when she visited them. One day, when she was visiting her children thus, Somasarma asked her to show him her yakṣi form. When she did, though, he was so terrified that he killed himself (or, simply, died). He was reborn as the lion that became Ambicā's vehicle. She went on to become the protective deity of Nemināthа tīrthankara. Incidentally, she has a shrine dedicated to her in the Jaina temple at Jinakāñci (Tiruparuttikunram, near Kancipuram) and the local Tamil Jainas believe this image was originally part of the Kāmākṣi temple complex at Kancipuram which they believe was originally a Jaina temple. Ambicā is portrayed as one holding a mango leaf, a child and a staff. She is supposed to be a powerful deity in her own right and a giver of boons.

Incidentally, most of the shrines dedicated to Nīli, show her with a child at her waist.

Kāraikkāl Ammaiyār, the Śaiva (woman) saint (whose time is between that of Appar and Jñānasampantar) has an almost similar tale. Her story is narrated in Cēkkiḻar's *Periyapurāṇam*[35] in Tiruniṉṟaccarukkam. She belonged to a merchant family and was called Punitavati. She was married to Paramadattan, son of a judge in Nagapattinam. His friends once gave him two mangoes, which he sent across to her. Meanwhile, a Śaiva saint passed by their house and Punitavati gave him one of the mangoes. Paramadattan came home for dinner and ate the remaining mango that was left. Finding it sweet, he asked her for the other one. But she had given it to the saint. She was scared. But Śiva saved her by producing another mango. Paramadattan found this even more delicious than the first one. He asked for another and she produced the mango by the same means. Now he was terrified as he thought she possessed supernatural/divine powers. Hence he abandoned her and married another woman. Punitavati, dejected, yearned to become a *pēy*, went to Kailāśa and Śiva gave her the name Ammaiyār.

According to Vedachalam, Ambicā's form and her story is the older of the above two in Tamilnadu.[36]

Karen Pechilis notes that

> 'Cēkkil̲ār's patriarchal narrative [of Kāraikkāl Ammaiyār's story]...contributes to a feminist consciousness by raising a woman to the level of exemplar of a religious path, and dramatizing the nature of her struggles therein... The thesis of bhakti (participation, devotion and sharing) religious perspective is a theology of embodiment, that embodiment is a necessary and desirable state for a relationship with god... Cēkkil̲ār advanced this thesis by providing previously unexpressed details on the specific conditions of embodiment of each saint, framed by their achievement of spiritual liberation. That he included women as primary exemplars of the Tamil Siva bhakti path is significant for the development of feminist consciousness...'[37]

However, the Śaiva (or even Vaiṣṇava) hagiographies were not the initiators of these kinds of narratives. The Pāli canon's *Therigāthā;* the Tamil *Kuṇṭalakeci* of the Buddhist woman and; the Tamil Jaina *Nīlakeci* were among the earliest narratives exemplifying the idea of 'raising a woman to an exemplar of a religious path'... The Śaivite tradition only borrowed from a schemata already available to it from these contexts since these texts pre-date the hagiographies of Śaiva and Vaiṣṇava women poets.

Again, Karen states that

> 'Through the categories of place, body and identity, the story of Kāraikkāl Ammaiyār foregrounds her social context as

> it portrays her transformation from a social to a socially constituted antisocial being. While the story explicitly portrays her trajectory from wife to saint, it offers an implied critique of a social world that cannot accept her as a religious exemplar...'[38]

But in the case of Nīlakeci, the movement is from an obviously 'antisocial' (even non-human, embodied in *pēy* form) being to a socially exalted status of philosopher (and she is not given the status of a saint). Her being a philosopher is not considered so unusual as to confine her within forced 'ghoul-ising' of her body. Her *pēy* body is in fact redeemed as a woman's body with attributes of an intelligent debator, just as Kuṇṭalakeci is not made a ghoul simply because she cannot fit into the patriarchal norms (she is not made super human or non-human), but is a person within this world, very much within the social constructions of self and society, debating with different schools of thought and establishing the Buddhist order. In the case of Nīlakeci and Kuṇṭalakeci, there is an affirmation of this same kind of positive trajectory. The critique of the social world comes from affirming the bodily presence of these women within the social worlds, not making them non-human, anti-'body', *pēys*.

Nīlakeci did not get the chance to become popular—perhaps on account of the religious strife that emerged due to the bhakti movement's popularisation at both political and popular levels. But the *pēy* Nīli was perhaps coming back in the form of Kāraikkāl Ammaiyār, at least in terms of the movement of a popular story within the Śaiva tradition. The Śaiva tradition perhaps took from both the Nīli story and *Nīlakeci* (and prior to that, *Kuṇṭalakeci*) in order to create a tradition of Kāraikkāl Ammaiyār becoming near-*pēy* and singing praises to Śiva. The transformation element within both the Jaina and Buddhist tradition (especially in the context of transformative possibilities for women within these traditions—as nuns, or as the voice of the tradition) and the popularity of the concept of a *pēy*, perhaps together helped construct the image of Kāraikkāl Ammaiyār. But there was a yakṣi concept already in the Jaina and Buddhist traditions. Usually, the Śaiva tradition is interpreted as a unique and first-of-its-kind process when it comes to ideas of 'liberating' the 'low castes' and women, through bhakti. Perhaps there is need to see it differently.

Now in the two stories narrated here, both the housewives turn into supernatural beings—a yakṣi, and a *pēy*;[39] in both cases, the women treat/feed a person from (another) social/religious order—Punitavati, probably a Jaina (?) to a Śaiva saint, and Ambicā, a Brāhmin, to a Jaina monk. In both cases, there is this association with divinity at some level (in case of Ambicā, a divine power forces the gates shut and visits the king in the dream to say that only a chaste woman can open them); in case of Kāraikkāl Ammaiyār, Śiva helps produce a mango and blesses her too. In the case of Punitavati going to Kailāsa, the concept (of going to Kailāśa) is common in the *villuppāṭṭu* genre, especially in what Blackburn called, "death stories" (usually pathos filled and violent) wherein the woman after death usually "goes to Kailāśa, receives boons from Śiva, returns to earth as a deified figure..."[40]

In all these stories (*Kuṇṭalakeci* included) the women marry/get married to men who are not 'their kind'—being from different social orders, religious order, caste, etc. In Kuṇṭalakeci's case, it is a thief she consciously marries. In almost all cases, the husbands accuse them of being unchaste or they 'fear' them or are awed by them in one way or the other. In the case of Kāraikkāl Ammaiyār, Ambicā and Māri (and our Nīli, too, though in different circumstances), the husbands show fear of the women's supernatural powers. In one case, the husband even leaves the woman to marry another, seeing her divine prowess (Kāraikkāl Ammaiyār). While Kāraikkāl Ammaiyār, Ambicā, and Māri become saint, protective deity, goddess, respectively, Kuṇṭalakeci and Nīlakeci take a different course, as preachers. Only in the case of Nīli of the Jaina story, wife of Sāgaradatta, there is no apparent shift in her status as dutiful wife, more in keeping with the main aim of the text in which she figures, meant as everyday rules for the laity, śrāvakācāra; so this last character is 'fixed' within a this-worldly paradigm.

Women wronged, in some way, in their domestic lives (in all these tales, at least) assuming a form above normal, almost nearing godhood, or to a state of higher existence seems to be the common larger narrative of the period. Organised religions were taking from these wandering/prevalent tales of women, as central to all these. The Śaivite tradition gave a bhakti twist to the Punitavati story; Nīlakeci would be ordained into the proselytising mission of the Jainas; Ambicā becomes the protecting deity of Nemi tīrthankara, and so on.

If there is something unresolved, however, in all these stories, it is the question, perhaps of sexuality. Which could be translated as the 'fear' element that comes along with the single-ness of these women, 'abandoned' as they are by (or they abandon) their husbands. They are thus confined to a de-sexed image, curbed and 'imprisoned', as it were, to an image of a philosopher (Nīlakeci; Kuṇṭalakeci), saint (Kāraikkāl Ammaiyār), yakṣi (Ambica) or a goddess (Māri). In case of such women characters as Nīli, they would remain wanderers in a sense, and their dominion would be the stretch, both literally and metaphorically, between spaces: between two villages or a village a town (*paṭṭiṉam*).

The striking similarities in the motifs that operate in the story of Nīli the Jaina wife in Ratnākaraṇṭaka and that of Māri; or Ambica and Punitavati suggest borrowings from common narratives.

The villuppāṭṭu begins not with invocation to any other deity but with the villukkārar (the bow songster) seeking 'permission' (probably of Nīli herself) to narrate the story of Nīli, story that has been narrated with fear by this storyteller.

It is important that Nīli is identified with the goddess Cāmuṇṭi and also called Caṇṭāla, as also icakki (yakṣi). The association comes in a period when yakṣi worship was prevalent in the Tamil country. Nīli had already been deified by this time. Incidentally, yakṣi worship, according to some scholars, is a contribution of

Jainism to Tamilnadu—more so because of the concept of the yakṣi as protecting deity of a tīrthankara. However, it can also be seen as an incorporation of the local goddess cults into Jaina cosmogony. Of course, debate as to which happened earlier is not one's aim here. The worship of yakṣi Ambicā-Dharumadevi is supposed to be the older of the other yakṣis propitiated in the Jaina temples in Tamilnadu. Interestingly, this *villuppāṭṭu* is also performed in the summer months in the Icakkiyammaṉ koil at Muppandal which is, incidentally, a village in what was, centuries ago, a Jaina stronghold. Speaking of Paḻayaṉūr Nīli's story, perhaps the only early attempt to analyse it as a folk tale was made in the 1960s by Hameed,[41] as mentioned earlier. In the first place, his choice of two folk tales—quite distanced from each other in terms of themes and treatment—is problematic. Secondly, he uses a single version of Nīli story (when there were others) where Nīli is the brāhmin wife of a brāhmin man who kills her. Had Hameed used a similar hypothesis for the many versions of Nīli story, or even stories of Ambicā, Kāraikkāl Ammaiyār and Māri-ammaṉ, there would be a more fruitful delineation of the structural pattern in these narratives; more connected and similar as they are to each other than Nīli and Kaṇṇaki are to each other, the only similarity being, the husbands were having an affair with another woman. Even within the Nīli stories, not in all versions is the man married. For instance, in one of the *villuppāṭṭu* versions, there is no mention of a wife in the first place. This being so, transposing Propp's hypothesis (on Russian folklore) on to a Tamil milieu without as much as contextualising the subject did not work, in Hameed's case. But his article now has vintage value, considering the advances in the discipline since Propp's times. The underlying historical, social reasons for the prevalence and circulation of similar streams of narratives are missing in Hameed's paper. Yet, that remains about the only work which at least tries to analyse the Nīli folklore within the question of structure of Tamil folklore, though 'Tamil' as an undifferentiated category, and 'folklore' as a universal category is no longer tenable. And I do not engage with the term 'folklore', for the present moment. The interesting web of cross-cutting narratives of women 'doing the rounds' in Tamil history by themselves make (or ask) for a wealth of studies in popular Tamil religion and culture; many of these wanting to be explored.

One of the versions discussed earlier, is the anonymous[42] *Nīli Nāṭakam (NN)*. Now this version begins with what is called *tuti* (invocation) to various deities and sages, as mentioned in the earlier parts of this book. As mentioned before, this dance drama is performed at the Ekambaranatha temple at Kanchipuram (as it states) and is fairly more elaborate than the villuppāṭṭu version. The invocation section ends with '*maṅkaḷam*' to "*kēcava madhusūdana*" and "*tirukacci ekambaranāthan̲*" and to the "*vedi*" (brāhmins) besides Nīli (*anta pal̲ayan̲ūril vantu pal̲i vānkuñ cuntarikkum*):

> *"maṅkaḷaṅkēcava matusūtan̲ukkum*
> *maṅkaḷam avarmārpil vāl̲pavarkkum*
> *maṅkaḷantirukacci yekamparanātarukkum*
> *maṅkalam...*
> *vētaṅkaḷaināḷum ōtiyuṇarntiṭum*
> *nītamikavur̲u vētiyarkkum...*
> *muntiyapir̲appin̲il nintaiyāykoḷaiceyta*
> *antaṇan̲ceykaiyai cintaikoṇṭē*
> *pintiyapir̲appin̲il antapal̲ayan̲ūril*
> *vantupal̲ivāṅkuñ cuntarikkum maṅkaḷam..."*[43]

This sets an auspicious mood for the play/performance to begin, with all the deities invoked, including Pal̲ayan̲ūr Nīli: "to that beautiful woman, who avenged in her next birth, at Pal̲ayan̲ūr, her unfortunate death at the hands of the brāhmiṇ in her previous birth."

Each scene in the *nāṭakam* is set to a specific *rāga* and *tālam* (melody and beat, some of which I have mentioned earlier) and in all probability this version came into existence after the time of codification of Carnatic music in Tamilnadu and was performed in the manner of a traditional '*pārāyaṇam*' or '*katā-kālakṣēpam*' (elaborate story recitation, mostly mythology), mostly in temples and in the context of reciting stories from the Purāṇas, and the epics. Rāgas such as Kalyāṇi, Pantuvarāḷi, Sankarābharaṇam, Etukulakāmbodi, Puṉṉākavarāḷi, and tālams such as ādi, aṭatālam, and a few others are used.

Then follow prayers on the stage/performative space to Vināyaka, the elephant-headed deity. The *nāṭakam*, interestingly, does not begin with invocation to Vināyaka (as is usually the case), but to Subrahmaṇya. Vināyaka worship happens later; after the *maṅkaḷam*. In the first few verses of the invocation at the beginning of this work, different aspects of Nīli and her story are invoked (recounted) as well. For instance,

> *"eḻupatiṉmar eri muḻkiyirakkacceyta ā ā*
> *paḻayaṉūr nīli katai pārmītiṉāṉpāṭa*
> *aḻakumayilēṟivarum aṟumukavaṉ tuṇaiye jeya jeyā"* [44]

'Salutation and seeking the benign guidance (blessings) of the six-headed one, who rides on the beautiful peacock vehicle, (so that) I (may) sing of Paḻayaṉūr Nīli, who caused the seventy to be consumed by flames.'

The entry of each character of the story is 'announced' as it were by the panegyrist with, interestingly, a '*pōṟṟi*' (salutations). This *pōṟṟi* is sung to each character—even the 'villain' of the piece. The stage/performative space for this is a sacred space, and each actor playing a character, of whatever bent, is by extension sacred. When the temple priest comes into picture, his (wrongful) association with the courtesan is mentioned and at the same time he is credited with due '*pōṟṟi*':

> *"ayyaṉē pōṟṟi...tuyyamāmaṉaiyāḷ taṉṉait tuyarpaṭavīṭṭilviṭṭē*
> *paiyaravalkulinta parattaiyiṉmayaliṉvīḻum*
> *vaiyakampukaḻumuntaṉ malaraṭipōṟṟipōṟṟi"* [45]

> 'Salutations to the Brāhmiṇ, who, leaving his wife at home (abandoning) fell in the snare of the courtesan (*parattai*) and lost his wealth, name...'

The brāhmiṇ in this version, the priest of the temple, is thus shown as a married man who fell for the prostitute (the term *parattai* is used only in this version; in others it is *dāsi*) and left his wife. The wife here is killed by the brāhmiṇ (as opposed to the *dāsi* being killed by him in the *villuppāṭṭu* version) and she becomes Nīli in the next birth. And in this version she is pregnant with his child when she is murdered by him. The play gives significant 'hints'—in the nature of a great tragedy—as to what is to follow in each character's life and there is an exaggeration in sketching of each character. For instance, the importance (to the story) of the brāhmiṇ and Nīli in the second birth is stressed on the basis of the long time they take to be born. In both cases, Nīli and Nīlaṉ—the brother sister duo—and the priest, are born in the tenth month after their mothers go through phenomenal labour pains. They seem larger than life figures, unlike in the *villuppāṭṭu*, which is a simple story sans embellishments and literary flourish. The larger Sanskrit mythic corpus is included in this version of Nīli story—which is not the case in the *villuppāṭṭu*. The temple priest (in this version) is, in fact employed by the Ekambaranatha temple, unlike in the *villuppāṭṭu* where he is the priest of a temple at Ponnur.

NN obviously has a more brāhmiṇical slant to it, in terms of the ritualistic traditions mentioned. The 70 veḷḷāḷas motif comes out in this version as well. That the Śaivite (or influenced by Śaivite tradition) versions give great importance to this story is interesting and intriguing as well. In the *villuppāṭṭu* version it is mentioned but not played out too much. One has already noted that perhaps the veḷḷāḷas' motif got interpolated into the simple Nīli story of 'wrong doing' and revenge at some point. It needs to be studied in greater detail. It may not be highly conjectural to draw certain linkages though: the Śaivite bard Jñānasampantar belonged to the veḷḷāḷa (social) group. The 70 veḷḷāḷas' sacrifice could be, what in another context Ramanujan refers to as

> '...[A] solemn, gory and cleansing ritual for an entire community, which feels the purgation, the terror of the victim, the raging power of the numinous goddess...'[46]

Let us get back to *Nīlakeci*. The significance of this text lies in the altering of Nīli from an unfulfilled possessing spirit, a dreaded female form on the fringes moving to the centre of a text/narrative. This is the movement of a wandering tale towards a structured text/a philosophical treatise. Nīli's antecedents set the context for the creation of the text, but are not important to the text's 'existence'. They are used to highlight the idea of 'becoming'. Once Nīli has 'become' Nīlakeci, of her own volition (as the text states, giving her agency) after hearing the discourse of the Jaina mendicant at the Kāli temple, her antecedents are no longer central to the flow of the text. The text's 'being', and Nīli's 'becoming', then, are no longer mutually exclusive categories. In Nīli's becoming is the essence of *Nīlakeci*, the text, the treatise, the kāvya. Nīli and her being were most crucial to the creation of this beautiful literary work. Without her there was no Nīlakeci.

There is also, in the text, a movement of a *pēy* to a woman of this world—a Jaina nun. If one looks at stories such as that of Kāraikkāl Ammaiyār (even here transformation from housewife to saint-poet) she is still referred to as *pēy* of Kāraikkāl. Being a woman and a housewife, she cannot be a poet in her 'everyday' bearings. It was easier to give her that '*pēy-ness*' to construct those eulogies to Śiva. A saint-poet, she would still be referred to as *pēy*. A woman deft with words cannot but have been defined in terms of an extraordinary, or extra-normal concept. Thus also Auvvaiyyār (or, one of the auvvaiyārs) becomes an aged woman in her very prime by a miracle.[47] Similarly, Kāraikkāl Ammaiyār, and her associations—hair let down, shedding clothes, walking on her head, etc—is also given some kind of fearful image. These women, then, who sang, or wrote, or had extraordinary qualities, are not perceived as being with the 'normal' course of affairs. They had to be 'elevated' / condemned to extra-human qualities and associations in any which way.

But the Jaina story subverts this tendency, differently. In terms of 'redemption' to a subject that had long suffered, Nīli-Nīlakeci becomes a Jaina teacher, deft with words and theory. Barring a momentary 'lapse' into *pēy-ness* (with Picācakaṉ), or in event of flying across from one place of debate to another, within her debate, she remains rooted in this world, especially in case of debate with the Vedic teacher, where she is shown her (this-worldly) social identity of a 'low-caste woman', and responds by lampooning both caste, and hierarchy.

If one has to look at the question as to why the author chose Nīli for the story perhaps the explanation should lie in the larger sphere that Nīli wandered about in. Chakravarti writes

> 'All the Thevaram singers when they refer to Alangādu or Pazhayanur, they refer to the Amman there—Goddess as Vandārkuzhali. This seems to be an exact Tamil equivalent to the Sanskrit Neelakesi. This probably refers to the conquest of Kāli who was probably accepted by Siva as his own consort in the form of Vandārkuzhali... At one time the Kāli temple of Pazhayanur must have been a very well-known place where animal sacrifices were offered to Kāli. Probably as a result of Jaina influence this Kāli temple was converted into a place of worship according to the Jaina doctrine of Ahimsa. The story of Neelakesi evidently suggests some such reform.'[48]

Chakravarti suggests that the Jaina influence was in place "a few centuries till the period of Saivite revival"[49] [when] "this Neeli temple of Pazhayanur which was reformed by the Jaina teachers brought under the sway of Ahimsā dharma was taken over by the Saivite reformers and the goddess of the place elevated to the status of Siva's consort, still retaining the old name Neelakesi translated into...the Dravidian...Vandārkuzhali... [Since the] place Pazhayanur is situated in Tondaimandalam.

Tondaimandalam in the early centuries of the Christian era was entirely under the influence of the Jainas..."[50] Chakravarti also notes that in the sthalamāhātmya of Tiruvalangadu, Kāli (the goddess of the shrine there) is called Neeli.[51]

The author of *Nīlakeci* brings Nīli right into this world's debates/contestations. The question arises, where do we place this character, Nīli-Nīlakeci in the maze of mother goddesses (or "breast" and "tooth-goddesses"[52]) in Tamilnadu or in historiography that has emerged around these in Tamil history? The genesis of *Nīlakeci* the text and the protagonist must be seen in the context of the centrality of the goddess in popular Tamil culture—where even goddesses ambivalent in nature, such as the *pēy*, 'seek', and get, shrines for themselves—the 'parallel' to which is the centrality of Nīlakeci to the text of deep cerebral indulgence, her own site and space. She is the protagonist, the philosopher, teacher, who is important to the text and its objective.

If at all there is something not quite so parallel, it is what happens to Nīlakeci, the character, outside the text. For, Nīlakeci—though she may be the central figure in the text holding her own does not extend beyond the text itself. She does not become a popular figure among the Jaina laity (especially the female laity with an intense bond with some of the yakṣis). Nīlakeci 'breathes' within the text alone. The text, and its status as a literary creation, overpowers or overwhelms Nīlakeci / Nīli the character / heroine. Unlike Kaṇṇaki, who assumed a cultic status outside *Cilappatikāram*, the text, though there is the debate about the precedence of a Pattini cult prior to the creation of the textual Kaṇṇaki. One of the reasons for Nīlakeci not assuming a role / status of her own outside the text also lies in the fact that there is no 'space' for such a possibility in the already codified Jaina schemata with its components of yakṣis, tīrthankaras and minor devatas. Nīli-Nīlakeci is created by the author for a purpose. Nīli is the muse, who inspires a re-inventing of her popular form to suit the doctrine.

At the social level, the *villuppāṭṭu* continues to 'celebrate' this pathos-filled story. In the alter-texting that *Nīlakeci* does, of this story, there is no automatic movement into a possible alter-texting of the course of Nīli worship by remembering and *singing her pain* in performance, almost annually. Reasons for the same are well worth analysing. However, it could be said that one of the reasons for this may also lie within the Jaina community which was not interested in deifying this character in her transformed Nīlakeci self, for whatever reason.

Moving out of the subject of radicalising Nīli, there are a few other interesting angles to *Nīlakeci* in a certain social context. The Jaina comment on the brāhmiṇical social construct based on their sacred texts is visible in the debate with the Vedic teacher Pūtikaṉ as seen earlier. For the first time in the text, a real social conflict is mirrored. If one were to extend the concept of alter-texting of Nīli to this section, the comment on the caste question becomes all the more important—with Nīlakeci, once a pēy and on the fringes, given the agency to question the idea of high and low birth. This section is also important for its longest debate on authorship of tradition, a concept which distinguishes the Jaina Tamil (or Tamil Jaina) textual tradition which almost always has an author and an authorial context. Nothing is left to the sphere of ambivalence and myth-making. The genesis of the work, or the author, or the commentator with an authorial presence, is always mentioned. However, there is a kind of supremacy of the text over the author, as well, in cases where the text highlights the fundamentals of the Jaina doctrine. The author there becomes merely the instrument for achieving this larger purpose. In this sense, the Sanskritic brāhmiṇical tradition, too, gives an overwhelming position to the text / treatise over the author. But in the case of the Vedas, the primordial-ness of the Vedas is the quintessence. That such a text could have had a 'this-world' author would have diminished the idea that became the basis for building a system of upholders and receptacles of the tradition, namely, the brāhmiṇs, who alone could render the primordial text meaningful to ordinary men and women of this world, through an entire paraphernalia of rituals and practices.

In transforming the popular legend of Nīli, whose circulatory space was, broadly, the northern part of the Tamil country, the author of *Nīlakeci* also removed Nīli from her interactive aspect with people who feared, and hence, worshipped her. The author, thus, both liberated, and bound her, at the same time, to a life of austerity and metaphysical contemplation, elevating, as also desexualising (while not deifying) her.

Yet, *perhaps*, Nīli-Nīlakeci herself, too, desired a new narrative and a new construct, just as the deity in the dream of the author of *Nīlakeci*, perhaps, asked that her story be committed to writing, preempting its affirmative tone. For the moment, and within *this* book, let me allow for Nīli her last word as Nīlakeci, towards that ultimate liberation. There is a reason for that: if one were to locate this text in today's times, a woman forced to stay on the margins of some 'great tradition'—however 'sensual' it may seem, with songs and dances that make it seem that way, and located within the context of everyday people—must get her own text and her own point of view across. But what if her point of view is a view of yet another tradition? Not a problem, so long as she has risen in her intellect and surely the text of this tradition would not exist if it was not for her, as the central character. She is the philosopher in this story. And by chance, or strategy, the 'author is not known'; Nīlakeci, then, *is* the text, the character and the author of these philosophical discourses. For a woman whose caste status was thrown at her face by the tradition that created it, this is the space—an intellectual who can 'play around' with, and construct, words to lampoon that tradition—she should justifiably occupy, at all times, but in today's times, specifically so. It should be remembered that this space happened in a non-theistic tradition, of that time, in the Tamil country, and in a Tamil text of the time, and I leave it at that.

So I end where her journey had begun in the text, Nīlakeci, until, perhaps, someday she might seek another radical history for herself and seek someone out, all over again, from some more 'open-access', liberal space. Perhaps a space that will break free from the *text* itself?

Let us go, then, to that point in *tarumavuṟaiccarukkam,* before she commenced her travels

> '*...pēyēṉ ceyta piḻaiyellām*
> *peruma poṟuveṉ ṟiṟaiñciṉāḷ*' (v. 134)[53]
>
> [She prayed to the wise one (mendicant), saying she has had enough of the misfortune / mistakes in her life as a *pēy*.]

She tells the monk that if she (a *pēy*) could give up her path of violence and vengeance through this (Jaina) doctrine, she must then help others, too, do the same. She wants to put an end to her bad karmas accumulated over the years. Importantly, it is her decision (in the text). She then receives blessings to propagate the message that he has shared with her, among others.

> '*uytal vāyurait tāyataṉ mēlu*
> *muyiruḷḷiṭ ṭapala vuḷporuḷ coṉṉāy*
> *naitalil lātteḷi vōṭunaṉ ñāna*
> *nāṉuṅkoṇ ṭēṉuṉ naṟkuṇa mellām*
> *peytutan tāypiḻait tēṟkiṉi tāvōr*
> *pirāyaccit tamperi yōyaru ḷeṉṉac*
> *ceyta tīmai keṭakkaṭa nāṭṭir*
> *ciṉava raṉṉeṟi yēteruṭ ṭeṉṟāṉ*' (v. 148)[54]
>
> [Hearing that, (Nīli) sought blessings, saying, 'Great one, like showers of rain, your good qualities fell upon me and I am enlightened by right faith and right knowledge. Having entered your realm I attained a life desirable, forgetting my (past) nature and I seek your blessings to expiate for the bad deeds (misfortunes) of my past as *pēy*. Hearing which, the monk told her, 'May you go and spread in the world the true/right knowledge of the Jina to dispel the mire of bad deeds.']

Notes

1. A. Chakravarti (English), pp. 336-337.
2. Ibid, pp. 20-21.
3. Ibid, pp. 21-22.
4. A. Chakravarti, 1957.
5. Ibid, pp. 229-230.
6. Ibid, p. 251.
7. Ibid, p. 253-254.
8. A. Chakravarti, 1984 (English), p. 18.
9. In N.N.Bhattacharya, 1994, pp. 185-197.
10. David Shulman, 1980, p. 8. Emphasis mine.
11. Ibid, pp. 222-223.
12. Gananath Obeyesekere, *The Cult of Goddess Pattini*, University of Chicago Press, Chicago, 1984.
13. Ibid, p. 363: post-5th, pre-6th century CE.
14. This point is meant as a general observation of the larger trend in most (not all) writing on religion and religious processes. There is no denying the fact that this larger trend has in its own ways sharpened the points of debate and discourse on brāhmiṇical and purāṇic religious processes. Though one would wish there were (and there is not) a relative intensity of debate and discourse (at least in English language scholarship) on Buddhist and Jaina religious processes in Tamil Nadu.
15. Verse 3. Chakravarti (Tamil), p. 15; Po.Ve.So, p. 1.
16. A point that I will not discuss here but is important nevertheless: when no one knows who exactly the author of Nīlakeci was (and only knows of the commentator), interestingly, nobody wishes to give the author the female gender identity. It may not be impossible to conjecture that the author of *Nīlakeci* could have been female, considering the number of Jaina nuns and women preceptors mentioned in historical records in the ancient Tamil country.
17. Other versions of Nīli story seem to say that Nīli was one of the ambivalent deities identified with Kāli at some later point, perhaps. In *Nīlakeci*, the text, there is no indication that she is Kāli of Pa<u>l</u>ayan<u>ū</u>r.
18. Kunal Chakrabarti, 2001, p. 28.
19. Sean Burke, 1995, p. xv.

20. Ibid, p. xv.
21. Michel Foucault, 1995, p. 235.
22. Ibid, p. 235.
23. In the 5th stanza of *Nīlakeci* (Po.Ve.So), there is reference to a *Tēvar* from whom the author learnt the doctrine of the Jina; in this connection, Chakravarti says, "if the reference in the fifth stanza is accepted to be a reference to the author of Kural, then it may be inferred that the author of Neelakesi was a direct student of the author of the Kural...[and] a convert to Jainism..." (Chakravarti, 1984 (English), p. 10).
24. Chakravarti, 1984 (English), p. 309.
25. A. Chakravarti (Tamil), p. 345; Po.Ve.So, p. 684.
26. Roland Barthes, 1995, p. 128-129.
27. *South Indian Inscriptions (SII)*, no. 64 (*AR* 460 of 1905); pp. 26-27; on east wall of Nataraja shrine in Vataranyesvara temple.
28. Ibid, No. 66 (AR 461 of 1905), p. 27.
29. *SII*, vol. V, No. 3; p. 427.
30. Shanmuga Sundaram, 1978, p. 27.
31. The story of Ambicā is narrated here, in the context of common motifs in folklore (and tales of transformation, transcendence). Kāraikkāl ammaiyār's story also closely follows that of Ambicā.
32. A. K. Ramanujan, 1986, p. 64.
33. A. K. Ramanujan points to a Kannada proverb which says, "*nāri munidare māri*"—'a woman, when furious, is Māri'. Ramanujan, 1986, p. 56.
34. Ve. Vedachalam, 1989, p. 89; also from narratives of Tamil Jaina women in Tamilnadu. I owe the intensive reading sessions of Vedachalam's entire book to my mother (Ramani Rajamani).
35. Ibid, p. 93.
36. Ibid, p. 97.
37. Karen Pechilis, 2008, p. 18.
38. Ibid, p. 22.
39. Kāraikkāl Ammaiyār refers to herself as Karaikkal pēy—Aruputta Tiruvantāti—"*pērirava tīmaperuṅkāṭṭiṟ pēyōṭum āralalvāy nīyatu maṅku*" (the intelligent woman who dances in the forest like a fearsome pēy)—see Pechilis, 2008, p. 92.
40. Mentioned in George Hart, "The Manikkuravan Story: from Ritual to Entertainment", 1985, p. 249.
41. K.P.S. Hameed, 1968. He takes Nīli and Kaṇṇaki.

42. The library copy (of RMRL) did not have the first two pages, or the name of author, date of the version, date of publication, etc. It was retrieved with some effort and was never accessioned before. I was informed by the library staff then that this may be one of the few copies of this *nāṭakam* available.
43. *Nīli Nāṭakam (NN)*, p. 4 "*maṅkalam*".
44. NN: "*Subrahmaṇya tuti*"—verses 1-4; p.1. Translation help from my mother.
45. Ibid, p. 7.
46. A. K. Ramanujan, 1986, pp. 71-72. Ramanujan discusses here the underlying pattern in village goddess tales, especially ones involving the concept of 'caste pollution'—as in the case of Māri leading to a "communal conflagration involving the whole village..."
47. This is what one of the legends says about Auvvaiyār, who, not wanting to get married, sought blessings of Ganeśa and transformed into an old woman while still a young woman. Few scholars in Tamil have seen this as necessarily de-sexing a creative woman, making her a saint, an old woman. A Tamil play on Auvvaiyār, *Auvvai*, written by playwright Inquilab, directed by Mangai (V. Padma), which showed Auvvai as a young, free-spirited woman with independent thoughts, was apparently severely criticised for this presentation. Mangai who had played the central character, always recounted this (when we were colleagues for a short while at Stella Maris College, Chennai) as an interesting experience, defining the *closing-in* of women characters within patriarchy, in her life as a theatre person.
48. A. Chakravarti, 1984 (English), pp. 18-19. Chakravarti points out, elsewhere in the same section that, "In spite of the onslaught inflicted by the Hindu revivalistic movement, the Jains have survived to carry on the banner of Ahimsa up to the present time... For, it certainly requires much greater courage and strength to undergo suffering oneself than to inflict suffering on others. This is also the fundamental message of all religions and also of Christianity— a message beautifully illustrated in the person of the founder of that religion..." [pp. 35-36].
49. Ibid, p. 19.
50. Ibid, p. 19.
51. Ibid, p. 13.

52. After one of A. K. Ramanujan's on southern Indian myths and folklore; on the nature of mother goddesses as benign and violent, or married, or virginal, and so forth.
53. A. Chakravarti, (Tamil), p. 53; Po Ve So, p. 102.
54. Ibid, (Tamil), p. 56; Ibid, p. 111.

BIBLIOGRAPHY

Principal Sources: Tamil and English

Chakravarti, A. *Nīlakeci: The Original Text and the Commentary of Samaya-Divakara-Vamani-Muni*, Tamil Palkalakkalakam, Thanjavur, 9th Edition, 1984. Originally published in Kumbakonam, 1936.

Aiyer, Swaminatha, U. Ve. *Cilappatikāra Mūlamum Arumpatavuraiyum Aṭiyārkkunallāruraiyum*, Dr. U. V. Swaminatha Aiyer Library, Chennai, 2013. Originally published in Chennai, 1892.

Nīli Nāṭakam, author unknown, date unknown. Folk theatre version. Title page missing. From collection of Roja Muthaiah of Kottaiyur, Ramnad district, Sourced at RMRL Library, Chennai.

Shanmugasundaram, Su. ed, *Pal̲ayan̲ūr Nīli Nāṭṭuppāṭal* (Villuppāṭṭu), Kodumudi Shanmuga Bragadam, Tenolai (Tinnevelly), 15th edition, 1978.

Somasundaranar, Po. Ve. *Nīlakeci: Viḷakkavurai* (Tamil, text and commentary), South India Saiva Siddhanta Works Publishing Society, Tirunelveli, repr. 1973. First published, 1964.

Srichandiran, J. *Maṇimēkalai, Valaiyāpati, Kuṇṭalakeci: Mūlamum, Telivur̲aiyum,*Vardhamana Patippakam, Chennai, 1996.

Therigatha: Poems of the First Buddhist Women, Translated by Charles Hallisey, Murthy Classical Library of India – 3, Harvard University Press, Cambridge, Massachusetts, London, England, 2015.

Vedachalam, Ve. *Iyakki Val̲ipāḍu* (Tamil), Agaram Printers, Madurai, 1989.

Others

Ayyangar, Ramaswami, M.S. *Studies in South Indian Jainism*, Satguru Publications, Delhi, reprint, 1982. First published in Madras, 1922.

Bahm, A. J. *Philosophy of the Buddha*, Harper and Brothers, New York, 1958.

Barthes, Roland. 'The Death of an Author', (pp. 125-130), Sean Burke, ed, *Authorship: from Plato to the Post modern: A Reader*, Edinburgh University Press, 1995.

Bhattacharya, Hari Satya. *Reals in the Jaina Metaphysics*, The Seth Santi Das Khetsy Charitable Trust, Bombay, 1966.

Bhattacharya, N. N. ed, *Jainism and Prakrit in Ancient and Medieval India*, Manohar, Delhi, 1994.

Bhattacharya, Narendranath. *Jain Philosophy: Historical Outline*, Munshiram Manoharlal, Delhi, 1976.

Blackburn, Stuart H. 'Death and Deification: Folk Cults in Hinduism', *History of Religions*, Vol. 24, No. 3 (Feb., 1985), pp. 255-274. Stable URL: http://www.jstor.org/stable/1062256. Accessed: 28-12-2015 11:12 UTC.

Blackburn, Stuart H. 'Oral Performance: Narrative and Ritual in a Tamil Tradition', *The Journal of American Folklore*, Vol. 94, No. 372 (Apr. - Jun., 1981), pp. 207-227. Stable URL: http://www.jstor.org/stable/540125. Accessed: 28-12-2015 11:12 UTC.

Burke, Sean. ed, *Authorship: from Plato to the Post modern: A Reader*, Edinburgh University Press, 1995.

Caldwell, R. *A Comparative Grammar of the Dravidian or South-Indian Family of Languages*, 3rd edition, revised by J. L. Wyatt and T. Ramakrishna Pillai (eds), New Delhi: Oriental Books Reprint Corporation, 1974 [1913].

Chakrabarti, Kunal. *Religious Process: the Purāṇas and the Making of a Regional Tradition*, Oxford University Press, Delhi, 2001.

Chakravarti, A. *Jaina Literature in Tamil*, Bharatiya Jnanpith Publications, New Delhi, 1974. Originally published in 1941 by Jaina Siddhanta Bhavan, Arrah.

Chakravarti, A. *Religion of Ahimsa: The Essence of Jaina Philosophy and Ethics*, Ratanchand Hirachand, Bombay, 1957.

Chakravarti, Uma. *On the Social Philosophy of Buddhism: Four Essays*, IIAS, Shimla, 2015.

Coomaraswamy, Doña Luisa. 'The Perilous Bridge of Welfare', *Harvard Journal of Asiatic Studies*, Vol. 8, No. 2 (Aug., 1944), pp. 196-213. Stable URL: http://www.jstor.org/stable/2717956. Accessed: 03-02-2016 09:05 UTC.

Cort, John, E. 'Svetambara Murtipujak Jaina: Scripture in a Performative

Context', Jeffrey Timm, *Texts in Context: Traditional Hermeneutics in South Asia*, SUNY, New York, 1992.

Dundas, Paul. 'The Digambara Jain Warrior', Michael Carrithers, Caroline Humphrey, eds, *The Assembly of Listeners: Jains in Society*, Cambridge University Press, Cambridge, 1991.

Fausböll, V. ed, *Buddhist Birth Stories or Jataka Tales: The Oldest Collection of Folk-lore Extant, Being the Jatakatthavannana*. Translated by T. W. Rhys Davids, Vol. I, Trubner and Co, London, 1880. Digitised by the Internet Archive in 2010 with funding from University of Toronto, https://archive.org/details/buddhistbirth00daviuoft (Open Library).

Foucault, Michel. 'What is an Author', (pp. 233-246), Sean Burke, ed, *Authorship: from Plato to the Post modern: A Reader*, Edinburgh University Press, 1995.

Ganeri, Jonardon. *Mind, Language and the World: The Collected Essays of Bimal Krishna Matilal*, Oxford University Press, New Delhi, 2002.

Graham, William. *Beyond the Written Word: Oral Aspects of Scripture in the History of Religion*, Cambridge University Press, 1987.

Granoff, Phyllis. 'Being in the Minority: Medieval Jain Reactions to Other Religious Groups', in N. N. Bhattacharya, ed, *Jainism and Prakrit in Ancient and Medieval India*, Manohar, Delhi, 1994.

Hameed, K.P.S. 'The Structural Pattern of Two Traditional Narratives in Tamil', in R. E. Asher, ed, *Proceeds of the Second International Conference Seminar of Tamil Studies*, (pp. 196-204), Vol 2, International Association of Tamil Research, Chennai, 1968.

Hart, George, L. 'The Manikkuravan Story: from Ritual to Entertainment', in Stuart Blackburn and A. K. Ramanujan, eds, *Another Harmony: New Essays in Folklore of India*, OUP, Delhi, 1985.

Jaini, Padmanabh, S. *Collected Papers on Buddhist Studies*, Motilal Banarsidass, Delhi, 2001.

Jaini, Padmanabh, S. *The Jaina Path of Purification*, Motilal Banarsidass, Delhi, 1998.

Matilal, B. K. 'Nyaya Critique of the Buddhist Doctrine of non-Soul', Jonardon Ganeri, ed, *Mind, Language and World: The Collected Essays of Bimal Krishna Matilal*, Oxford University Press, New Delhi, 2002.

Monier-Williams, M. *Buddhism*, The Chowkhamba Sanskrit Series, Varanasi, 1964. (2nd edition).

Murton, Brian J. 'Geography and the study of south India', in Burton Stein, ed, *Essays on South India*, Honolulu, 1975.

Obeyesekere, Gananath. *The Cult of Goddess Pattini*, University of Chicago Press, Chicago, 1984.

Ohnuma, Reiko. 'The Gift of the Body and the Gift of Dharma', *History of Religions*, Vol. 37, No. 4 (May, 1998), pp. 323-359, Stable URL: http://www.jstor.org/stable/3176401 Accessed: 03-02-2016 07:28 UTC.

Parthasarathy, R. Transl., *The Cilappatikaram of Ilanko Atikal: An Epic of South India*, Columbia University Press, New York, 1993.

Pechilis, Karen. 'Chosen Moments: Meditation and Direct Experience in the Life of the Classical Tamil Saint Karaikkal Ammaiyar', *Journal of Feminist Studies in Religion*, Vol. 24, No. 1 (Spring 2008), pp. 11-31, Indiana University Press. Stable URL:http://www.jstor.org/stable/20487910. Accessed 15/1/15. 04:56.

Pechilis, Karen. 'Introduction: Bodily Transformations across Indian Religions', *Hindu Studies* (2006), 10: pp. 167-170. Published online: 2 March 2007.

Pechilis, Karen. 'The Story of the Classical Tamil Woman Saint, Kāraikkāl Ammaiyār: A Translation of Her Story from Cēkkiḻār's Periyapurāṇam', *Hindu Studies* (2006) 10, pp. 171-184.

Ramanujan, A. K. 'Two Realms of Kannada Folklore', Stuart Blackburn and A.K. Ramanujan, eds, *Another Harmony: New Essays in Folklore of India*, Oxford University Press, Delhi, 1985.

Ramaswamy, Vijaya. 'Chaste Widows, Cunning Wives, and Amazonian Warriors: Imaging of Women in Tamil Oral Traditions', *Asian Ethnology*, Vol. 69, No. 1, pp. 129-157, 2010.

Ramaswamy, Vijaya. 'The Metamorphosis of Alli and Neeli: Folktales and Mythic Images of Tamil Women', in Vijaya Ramaswamy, ed, *Re-searching Indian Women*, Manohar, Delhi, 2003.

Ramaswamy, Vijaya. 'Tragic Widows or Cunning Witches? Reflections on Representations of Women in Tamil Myths and Legends', *Economic and Political Weekly*, Vol. 44, No. 12 (Mar. 21 - 27, 2009), pp. 57-67.

Shulman, David. 'The Murderous Bride: Tamil Versions of the Myth of Devi and the Buffalo-Demon', *History of Religions*, Vol. 16, No. 2 (Nov. 1976), pp. 120-146, University of Chicago Press. Stable URL: http://www.jstor.org/stable/1062239. Accessed on 26.6.15. 12:25 UTC.

Shulman, David. *Tamil Temple Myths: Sacrifice and Divine Marriage in the South Indian Śaiva Tradition*, Princeton University Press, 1980.

Sutton, Florin Giripescu. *Existence and Enlightenment in the Lankavatara-sutra: A Study in the Ontology and Epistemology of the Yogacara School of Mahayana Buddhism*, Sri Satguru Publications, New Delhi, 1992. Originally published by SUNY, New York, 1991.

Thallam, Sarada. 'Cekkilar's Periyapuranam and the Story of Karaikkal Ammai', *Journal of South Asian Studies*, 01 (01), 2013, pp. 83-90.

Todeschini, Alberto. 'The Maiden who Fell in Love with a Thief: Considerations on the Story of the Nun Bhadda Kundalakesa', *Dharma Drum Journal of Buddhist Studies*, No. 13, pp. 153-188, New Taipei City, Dharma Drum Buddhist College, 2013.

Umamaheshwari, R. 'Dislocations, Marginalizations, Past and Present: Pain-Experiences of Two Marginalized Communities', (pp. 227-247), in Siby K. George, P.G. Jung, eds., *Cultural Ontology of the Self in Pain*, Springer, New Delhi, Heidelberg, New York, Dordrecht, London, 2016.

Umamaheshwari, R. *Reading History with the Tamil Jainas: A Study on Identity, Memory and Marginalisation*, (Sophia Studies in Cross-cultural Philosophy of Traditions and Cultures, No. 22), Springer (India), New Delhi, 2017.

Vanamamalai, N. 'Materialist Thought in Early Tamil Literature', *Social Scientist*, Vol. 2, No. 4 (November 1997), pp. 25-41. Stable URL–http:www.jstor.org/stable/3516360. Accessed: 03-11-2015 13:34 UTC.

Vijayalakshmy, R. *A Study of Cīvakacintāmaṇi: Particularly from the Point of View of Interaction of Sanskrit Language and Literature with Tamil*, L. D. Institute of Indology, Ahmedabad, 1981.

Warder, A. K. 'On the Relationship between Early Buddhist and Other Contemporary Systems', *Bulletin of the School of Oriental and African Studies*, University of London, Vol. 18 (No. 1), pp. 43-63, 1956, Cambridge University Press. Stable URL: http://www.jstor.org/stable/610128. Accessed on 27.6.15. 11:06 UTC.

Winternitz, M. *The Jainas in the History of Indian Literature*, in Jain Vijaya Muni, edited series of the Jaina Sahitya Samshodhak Sangh, (no. 2), Ahmedabad, 1946.

Zvelebil, Kamil, V. 'Some Tamil Folklore Texts: Muttuppattan Katai, Kāttavarāyan̲ Kataippāṭal, Pal̲aiyan̲ūr Nīli', *Journal of the Royal Asiatic Society of Great Britain and Ireland*, No. 1 (1989), pp. 290-303. Stable URL: http://www.jstor.org/stable / 25212489. Accessed – 15/1/2015. 04:56.

Zvelebil, Kamil, V. *Tirumurugan*, International Institute of Tamil Studies, Chennai, 1981.